QUEEN
UNSEEN

MY LIFE WITH THE
GREATEST ROCK BAND
OF THE 20TH CENTURY

QUEEN
UNSEEN

PETER HINCE

MUSIC
PRESS

Published by Music Press,
an imprint of John Blake Publishing Ltd,
3 Bramber Court, 2 Bramber Road,
London W14 9PB, England

www.johnblakepublishing.co.uk

www.facebook.com/johnblakebooks 🅵
twitter.com/jblakebooks 🅴

First published in hardback in 2011
This edition published in 2015

ISBN: 978 1 78418 771 2

British Library Cataloguing-in-Publication Data:

A catalogue record for this book is available from the British Library.

Design by www.envydesign.co.uk

Printed in Great Britain by CPI Group (UK) Ltd

1 3 5 7 9 10 8 6 4 2

SOME OF
THE PRAISE FOR
QUEEN UNSEEN

'This is a book that will satisfy the curiosity of anyone who has ever wanted to know what it was *really* like to work with a famous rock band.' *Mojo*

'I could not put the book down. Extremely accurate, well-written and entertaining. I know – I was there. Read it.' *Mack, Queen record producer and co-producer of Freddie Mercury's* Mr Bad Guy *album.*

'Peter captures a magical and unique time in the life of Queen and Freddie. His photography displays the energy of a historic period in classic rock. Nice one Peter. Freddie would be proud' *Alfie Boe – award-winning classical singer, actor and performer. Presenter and narrator of* Freddie Mercury Saved My Life *TV documentary.*

'A rare glimpse behind the scenes from a man who occupied a front row seat on tour and in the studio with Queen for more than 10 years. Fascinating.' *Carl Johnston, BBC producer, and director of* The Story of Bohemian Rhapsody, *BBC3.*

'A must for all admirers of Queen. An honest, accurate and humorous insight into one of the greatest showmen of all time – Freddie Mercury.' *Mike Moran, musician, co-producer, arranger, keyboards performer and co-author of 'Barcelona' with Freddie Mercury.*

'Whether a Queen fan or not, this is a fascinating look at life on the road with the biggest band in the world. Funny, entertaining and full of glorious pictures. Loved it!' *Rhys Thomas, BAFTA nominated, Emmy and Rose D'Or winning director, producer, actor and writer.* Queen: Days Of Our Lives *and* Freddie Mercury: The Great Pretender *documentaries.*

'An informative, humorous and insightful rock 'n' roll narrative. Ground zero for Queen fans.' *Billy Squier, musician.*

'I'm not really interested in books on Freddie and the band, but actually, probably the best is by one of our old roadies – Peter Hince. Of course it's written from his perspective and has compromises, but it's the closest to reality – and quite amusing' *Roger Taylor – Queen. interview with* This Is Rock *magazine. Spain.*

'*Queen Unseen* stands out as the best book on the band. Written from the heart, it is a testament to the bonds formed between people on that rocky touring road. A true behind-the-scenes account that deals with the real personalities that formed Queen. You will read it over again.' *Fred Mandel, musician – toured America and Japan with Queen and played keyboards on* The Works *and Freddie Mercury's* Mr Bad Guy *album.*

'If you want an inside track on Queen and Freddie – you must get this book.' *Mike Sweeney, Real XS Rock Radio, UK*

'This really is a rollicking good read. Anyone who ever wished they had sampled life in rock's fast lane should read this book.' Fireworks *magazine.*

'A witty and revealing insight into one of the world's greatest bands. Peter Hince takes you as close to Queen as you can possibly get without being in the band.' *Mark Blake, music journalist, author of* Is This The Real Life? The Untold Story Of Queen, *and books on Pink Floyd, The Who and the sixties.*

'A thorough, well-balanced work with the added bonus of some jaw-dropping and hilarious true stories.' *Morgan Fisher, keyboard player with Mott the Hoople and backing musician for Queen on their 1982 European tour.*

'A beautiful, simple, real document, that attests an era. Peter Hince is able to share a little bit of Queen and Freddie with all of us.' *Giulia Salvi, Virgin Radio Europe.*

'It was like being there with them.' *Ferdinando Frega, queenmuseum.com.*

'A humble and interesting view about Queen's life on the road. Honest and respectful – a must-read for any Queen fan' *Laurent Rieppi , Classic 21/RTBF – National Radio Belgium.*

'World tours, outrageous partying and hidden turmoil. With *Queen Unseen*, Peter Hince provides a unique human insight into the life of a band that has reached immortality in public imagination.' *Mitchell Toy* – Herald Sun*, Melbourne.*

'Such a different take on the rock 'n' roll story – a unique perspective on working in the industry at that point in time. Hince's approach is amazingly refreshing.' *Gail Worley, Rock Critic-at-Large, New York, worleygig.com*

'Sex, drugs and rock 'n' roll – what a cliché, yet it's what this book is all about. An absolute must-read for all Queen fans!' *Martin Skála, queenconcerts.com.*

'Unmissable. No gossip, no sensationalism. Peter Hince was there and thanks to him we travelled back and lived the real thing.' *Alessandro Cannarozzo and Luca Cuoghi, queenItalia.it.*

'A book you just cannot put down. A glorious insight into the backstage activities of the most famous band in the world, compiled by someone who couldn't have been any closer to the facts.' *Tony Keys, Central FM, Spain.*

ACKNOWLEDGEMENTS

My sincere thanks go to the following people who, since my time with Queen, have made this book happen and encouraged me to 'go for it': John Blake, Michelle Signore, Louisa Somerville, John & Nadia Cameron-Blakey, Vernon Reeves, Julianna Mitchell, Stefano Pesenti, Ian Craig, Alastair Campbell and David Martin.

I have been fortunate to travel widely and meet people of all nationalities and from various walks of life. Apart from all of Queen and the obvious friends and family, I would like to thank the following people from the thousands I met and worked with over my many years with Queen, and who were supportive, generous and appreciative, and respected and believed in me. Also included are those who got me out of various forms of trouble, kept me company at the bar or simply escorted me safely back to my hotel room. If you aren't there, and think you should be – I apologise. There is always another reprint to put things right…

In no particular order: Gerry & Sylvia Stickells, Reinhold Mack, Jimmy Barnett, Billy Squier, Joe Trovato, Mike Moran, Jim Devenney, Trip Khalaf, John Collins, Chris Taylor, Brian Zellis, John Harris, Geoff Workman, Mike Stone, Roy Thomas Baker, Fred Mandel, Morgan Fisher, Richie Anderson, Phil John, Michael Hince, Robin Mayhew, Pete Brown, Mary Austin, Veronica Deacon, Chrissy May, Dominique Taylor, Joe Fanelli, Peter Lubin, Mike Wilderink, Edwin Shirley, Chris Wright, Ian Haynes, David Bernstein, Neal Preston, Barry Levine, Tony Williams, Robert Usher, Pete Cornish, David Morris, Dick Ollet, Doug Taub and Vicky Everett.

CONTENTS

INTRODUCTION

Q*ueen Unseen* is about a rock 'n' roll band and the rock 'n'roll lifestyle, as told through my experience of working for Queen during the '70s and '80s. My story is for anybody who has ever wondered what it was really like spending your youth travelling the world and living with one of rock music's biggest ever bands.

I was lucky that I got to live that life – and survive. Some sadly didn't, including one notable genius who was a huge influence on me and my life.

My journey comprises of many stories, anecdotes, observations and memories. It is not a definitive or chronological history of Queen; I write only about my unique first-hand experiences, which I hope convey a sense of being with the band, whether on stage or backstage, in the studio, at a video shoot – or in the bar. For all the Queen 'experts' out there – please note: the Queen live show I take you through incorporates elements and incidents from various tours we did through the years. It is not meant as a representation of a specific show, but to try and convey and relive the experience of being there – on stage with Queen, as it happened. Live.

I have written this book for various reasons. Perhaps it has been an exercise in catharsis. Most importantly, it has been written as a tribute – not just to dear departed Freddie and many others featured in this book no longer with us, but as a salute to the wonderful times and our shared experience. They were truly magical days when we were young; feeling we could take on the world and win. Invariably we did.

A warm recollection of that era, when our hairlines were thicker and our waistlines thinner.

If you want tabloid dirt and revelations – buy a dirty tabloid. If you would like to join me on a journey, and enjoy some laughs and surprises along the way, please be my guest – an access-all-areas guest.

Mine may have been reflected glory – but what glorious light to bathe in.

So, to recollect a phrase that Freddie often used, 'Come on – get on with it!'

CHAPTER ONE

THE SHOW
MUST GO ON

(THE CREW ARE READY – WHERE'S FRED?)

'I can't do it! I simply can't go on! It's no good – the show will just *have* to be cancelled!'

Freddie Mercury, the singer with rock band Queen, often expressed to his beloved live audiences that he'd like to have sexual relations – with all of them. Well, looking at him right now, it appears that last night he did, plus a few of their friends. And shared drinks with them all too.

Queen are at the peak of their successes – and excesses. A pale and fragile-looking Fred is sheltering backstage in the comfort of the dressing room. Outside there is a packed arena containing nigh on 20,000 baying rock fans and it's less than an hour until show time. Mr Mercury is in one of his *moods* and nobody present dares to say anything in response. They just ignore him and hope it will go away. It doesn't.

Fred stands, waves his arms theatrically and loudly states

his feelings again: 'I'm telling you – I *can't* do this show – my voice is fucked. *I'm* fucked!'

Well, what do you expect – screaming and ranting like that?

Brian May and Roger Taylor start to mutter support and try to win him round, while bassist John Deacon stretches out on a couch, a Walkman plugged into his ears – nodding and smiling. Grinning actually. Meanwhile, 'management' stop picking at the copious plates of food laid out like a banquet, and begin to get twitchy as they search their address books for lawyers' and insurance companies' telephone numbers. The promoter's face has turned white.

Fred is precisely where he wants to be – at the centre of everyone's attention, and is playing the drama queen role to perfection. Silly old tart! This scenario has happened before, but this time it looks like he might be serious.

One of the band assistants thumbs through his *Spartacus* guide and gleefully tells Fred that there is a gay telephone box, pedestrian crossing or even a late-night hardware shop in the area that they could go to after the show. Fred isn't impressed.

A drink, perhaps – to raise the spirits? Champagne – your favourite – Moët? No. Vodka, a large one? No. This is going to be hard work.

'Give me a ciggie!' Fred demands of one of his 'valets'.

He snatches a low-tar king size and takes a perfunctory draw.

That'll *really* help the voice Fred...

Gerry Stickells, Queen's wily tour manager, who has been hovering and observing in the background, approaches, and candidly reminds Mr Mercury that a hell of a lot of people – a sold-out crowd in fact – have waited a long time and paid good money to see him perform tonight, and that it wouldn't be very nice to let them down, and Fred was never somebody to let his people down. Was he?

Me? Peter Hince (aka Ratty), Fred's and John's roadie and head of Queen's crew. I'm ignoring all this melodrama and ambling around the dressing room, being one of the few people allowed in during this pre-show period. Fred calms down a little as he ponders the tour manager's words, passes the cigarette to somebody to extinguish, takes a drink of hot honey and lemon and, with a frown, huffily settles into a comfy chair. He says nothing, as the rest of Queen leave him to it and excitably begin asking the perennial questions of their tour manager, assistant or roadie:

'What's the sound like out front now the crowd is in? The show is *completely* sold out tonight – *isn't it*? How are ticket sales for the rest of the tour going, are they sold out too? Is the new single number one yet? What time are we on? What time will we be off? Is it hot/cold out there? Has that nasty buzzing sound in the monitors gone? Is it *really* true Van Halen have more lights in their show than us? And what about the tour merchandise – how are the Queen toasted sandwich makers selling...?'

Queen's dressing room varied in size and style, depending on the venue. Theatres had dedicated dressing rooms, but sports-arena and convention-centre-style venues had functional facilities that had to be 'dressed' before they could be deemed a dressing room worthy of Queen's visit. Carpet and rugs were laid down on the cold concrete floors, bare walls draped with material or pictures, and furniture, lamps, flowers and '*objets*' were introduced to make it more comfortable and relaxing for the visiting artistes. There were adjoining showers, make-up mirrors, areas for Queen's wardrobe cases and a central space for relaxing, with tables of food and bins of iced drinks against the walls.

Meanwhile, beyond the comfort of the dressing room, the distant drone of the support band can be heard bashing away on stage. On occasion, when some of Queen were feeling tense or irritable, they would insist that the opening act turn down the volume so they could prepare in peace...

'So then, Fred?' I venture jovially, to one of the world's greatest showmen.

'Yes, dear, what is it?' he replies with a little more verve.

He seems a bit better now.

'Songs for this evening? Your choices?'

'Ah. Yes, right.'

The silly old tart, for whom I held the utmost respect, admiration – and exasperation – has decided he will perform after all. I never really doubted he would let down the audience, the rest of the band or the crew – who have spent the last 12 hours or more sweating blood to put all this together, just so he can prance around in a few silly costumes for a while. As usual he would get through on his formidable willpower, self-belief and determination. In other words – professionalism.

Few people could approach Fred as he prepared for a show, but I would saunter over to him, while he was surrounded by 'beautiful and important' people, and ask, 'Oi! What do you fancy playing tonight then, Fred?'

'I don't know – why don't you guess?'

'Guess?'

'Yes, Ratty – guess!' he would giggle, playing to his immediate audience, who would laugh rather superficially with him.

'That's not exactly helpful, is it?'

'I'm not telling you then!' he would state with camp authority – again playing to the gallery of his invited coterie.

'Oh all right then,' I would shrug, knowing this was just a game he wanted to play.

'I'll arm wrestle you for it!' he said, pumping himself up and flexing his muscles.

'What?'

'Come on – I'll take you on!'

Those not used to our rapport would be amazed that this dishevelled and irreverent roadie could hold the attention of one of the world's biggest rock stars. Fred would then usually reply with a laugh, twirl his hands in the air and say dramatically, 'OK then – *you* choose!'

This was quite flattering but not very constructive, so I would suggest a couple of Led Zeppelin songs, a Stones classic and 'maybe you could even play some of your own songs, Fred?'

'C***!'

Playfully whacking me with a towel or whatever was to hand, he would chase me out of the dressing room, screaming: 'Same as the last fucking show!'

The voice certainly seems somewhat better now, Fred?

The set list was now set. The content of this sheet of paper was the burning question on the lips of the entourage as show time approached; the final selection of songs always being down to Fred and how he and his voice felt. Sometimes he just wanted to mix things up a bit – to keep everybody on their toes. He occasionally referred to the Queen set as 'our repertoire'. Well, after all, Freddie Mercury was a very well-spoken man and highly literate.

'Scaramouche, and doing the fandango?'

He was extremely intelligent and well educated.

'Thunderbolts and lightning, appeared to be very frightening!'

An eloquent man, who wrote songs of depth and intricacy – and full of meaning.

'He wanted to ride his bicycle…'

Having been told to get on my bike by Fred, I now had to convey the set list to the relevant crew so they could adjust and make notes on their personal set lists, on which the song titles were always abbreviated: 'Bohemian Rhapsody' became 'Bo Rhap' and 'We Are The Champions' was simply 'Champions', for example. Annotations were made in black felt-tip pen as songs were dropped or added.

Cues for Queen and the crew were noted adjacent to song titles in code. Fat D, for example, was a reference for John to tune the low E string on his bass guitar down to D, prior to playing 'Fat Bottomed Girls'. (Fag B was merely a cigarette break for John and me, as Fred would be off stage at that point and I didn't have to constantly watch him.) The irreverent crew cheekily renamed the songs on set lists: 'We Will Rock You' – 'We Will ROB You', 'Now I'm Here' – 'Now I'm Queer', 'I Want To Break Free' – 'I Want To Break Wind', 'Flash!' – 'Trash!' And so on…

The set list taped to the top of Fred's piano was the first piece of 'inside information' given to outsiders during the show set-up. His black nine-foot Steinway D concert grand was the first piece of band equipment to take the stage and, as it was lowered from its enormous flight case to await the graft of its third leg, the local crew would already be studying and making comments on Queen's proposed show selection. Meanwhile, yours truly would be lying underneath one ton of wood, metal and imitation ivory, screaming at them to 'lift the bloody thing' so I could hammer the last leg in place.

With show time approaching, towels and drinks for the band's refreshment on stage would now be strategically placed: water and beer for Fred, beer for Brian and Roger and the Backstage Bar for John, comprising water, beer, soft drinks, wine and whatever spirit or cocktail he fancied at the time: Southern Comfort, vodka or tequila. Added to John's cocktail lounge were mixed nuts and chocolate M&M's. All of this was located discreetly to the side of his electronics control rack, where he could simultaneously knock the volume up and a drink down. A copy of the set list was taped here for John, and others to refer to – along with opening hours.

Fred had champagne glasses on top of his grand piano to sip from. I kept these wrapped in an old towel in the bottom of a flight case, and before the show I would give them a wipe with the bottom of my T-shirt and fill them with local tap water.

It was never champagne. I did try using Perrier water in places where the water was a very dodgy colour as it came out of a backstage tap, but Fred cursed me – the bubbly water made him burp! After an incident where one of the champagne glasses caused a member of the audience to be injured, I was told I had to replace them with plastic champagne glasses. Fred was horrified when he saw these tacky items from a party shop and we switched to plain plastic cups and Evian or still mineral water, as our backstage catering became more sophisticated.

With show time very close, Brian would be escorted to the backstage tuning room to tune his guitars and warm his fingers up. He would invariably be in conversation with somebody as he did this, get carried away and forget which guitars had been tuned, which not – and have to start all over again.

Show time is imminent and Brian is fruitlessly trying to plug a ukulele into an electronic strobe tuner.

'Brian, it's an acoustic instrument!'

He grins and tunes it by ear.

All of John's and Fred's guitars would be tuned by me on stage, prior to the show, being closest to the temperature and environment in which they would actually be used. In the early Queen silk and satin days I had to hang a triangle on John's mic stand, so he could take and strike it once during 'Killer Queen', then hand it back to me. Triangles? Not seen those since the days of my primary school band. Fortunately, I didn't have to tune it. A local piano tuner would be hired by the promoter to tune Fred's Steinway before sound check, and touch up again in the early evening. The strobe tuners for all the guitars would take their calibration from the piano setting. Over the years I got to know many of the tuners personally; one excellent tuner and lovely man, who always did the shows in Boston, was Sal Corea – uncle of legendary jazz musician Chick Corea. Sal wasn't blind, but several piano tuners were, and I once made the embarrassing mistake of offering a blind tuner 'tickets to see the show?'

After the first few shows of a tour, Fred and John very rarely did any kind of sound check. They trusted all of their crew. It also meant they could sleep in much later.

Queen were confident individuals, but sometimes at huge outdoor shows or vast arenas in major or new cities, nerves could start to creep in. That was the time that irreverent crew banter would help to relax them and keep their spirits up. Queen could usually laugh at themselves and see the funny side of some of the pompous things they did, and it also helped keep their feet on the ground, as there were plenty of sycophants ready to assure them everything they did was wonderful and beyond reproach.

'The audience is all in now, Fred.'

'Good – how do they look?'

(How do they look? Keen? Smart? Angry?)

'Well, they seem like a very nice couple to me.'

'You bastard!'

'Oh, by the way, the new album has just gone…'

'Gold? Platinum? *Double* platinum?' one of Queen would snappily interject.

'No – vinyl.'

'Fuck off!'

'I've heard a woman in Slough bought a copy…'

'Fuck off and die! Now let's get on with it! When are we on?'

With Queen itching to get on stage, the buzz increased, and you could feel the hyped nervous energy in the corridors backstage. With Access All Areas passes slung around their necks, crew members would wander the stage to check the equipment and check out any female 'leisure potential' in the front rows.

Meanwhile, Queen's dressing room had been cleared of non-essential personnel as the band donned costume and regalia; preparing themselves for the daunting, yet exciting, ordeal to come. In order to exorcise nervous tension and warm up their voices, Fred and Roger would screech loudly at each other in high-pitched squeals, like a couple of late-night tom cats. Roger would have a pair of drumsticks in hand, repeatedly tapping and hitting things – including his assistant and former roadie, Chris Taylor (aka Crystal – and no relation)

Queen were sometimes late appearing on stage but once, at a show in Spain, it was not their fault. Joe Trovato, Queen's lighting designer at the time, had been partaking of the cheap and plentiful local wine, causing him to spend several sessions in a backstage lavatory. Forlornly sitting there, he lost track of time until there was a polite little knock on the door and a concerned, recognisable voice asked, 'Are you all right in there?' Joe opened the door to see Fred peering in, along with the rest of Queen – all ready to take the stage. With a grimace and an apology, he adjusted his attire and took off to the lighting console.

Now it's show time – what today has been all about. The next couple of hours are all that matter. Shortly Queen will be on stage in your town playing for you – *just for you*, you privileged ticket holders. The four famous faces will be up there on stage – attached to their instruments, in moving, living person – and colour. They have travelled over land and sea and overcome obstacles and hangovers to give you this special personal experience. So be sure and enjoy it!

The stage is ready; everything taped down, the carpet vacuumed, all equipment powered and humming, everybody on standby at their assigned station. The crew are standing to attention – but not in uniform, despite attempts to get us to wear things to camouflage ourselves on stage. Influenced by their first visit to Japan, Queen gave the crew black 'Happy Coats': short kimonos, with Queen printed in red Japanese letters on the back. Very stylish, but not very practical loading-out attire and it would be hard to gain the respect of a six-foot-plus, 300-pound union teamster or truck loader while wearing a boudoir garment. All onstage spotlight operators wore fitted black overalls, but I found them restrictive, as I was constantly scuttling under, over and about during the show; so jeans and a T-shirt – preferably a Queen freebie, to show some mark of loyalty – were what I wore.

The final check of instruments was done in conjunction with a line check. Not *that* kind of line, but a check that all the instruments were placed back into the correct channels after use by the support act. That's why you often hear chords crashing on guitars, drums banging and pianos tinkling before a band takes the stage. There is a distinct art and calculated procedure to these exercises; knowing too much is dangerous, but so is knowing too little. Don't play a recognisable riff (poseur) and, if it's a Queen riff, you run the risk of getting a cheer from the audience, your 15 seconds of fame and enraging the band. It would also brand you as a total wanker to the rest of the crew. The middle path of single notes or chords was preferable. However, there was still an enormous temptation to crank the volume up and let rip with a couple of power chords...

It *is* very important to check instruments immediately prior to the show as things do change after the sound check. The positioning of speakers has to be exact and the acoustics can alter dramatically. The classic sound engineer's excuse is 'Don't worry – it will sound fine when the audience are in.' All types of radio transmitters can suddenly become operational, which affect the 'wireless' systems for guitars and mikes. Temperature and humidity cause tuning problems, and with drums an awful booming feedback. The local cab company or radio station could now be broadcasting through Brian's Vox AC30's, or the building's freight lifts could be on the same phase of electrical power as the sound system, and now transmitting a spluttering 'motor boat' noise. It's guaranteed that all manner of unexplained electronic gremlins only come out of the darkest depths of Mordor to plague you two minutes before show time.

'ONE – ONE – TWO – TWO.' A familiar call shouted by onstage sound monitor engineer Jim Devenney, into Fred's trademark silver Shure 565 SD microphone, as he wandered the stage with the famous 'wand': a custom-made chrome-plated tube, like a section of microphone stand, which Fred used together with the mic as his stage prop. It could be a sword, guitar, machine gun, golf club, baseball bat or whatever Fred wanted to convey with it. Most commonly it was 'My cock, darling'.

The stage manager, having checked that all was *definitely* ready, would call the dressing room by crackling walkie-talkie to bring the band up.

Having emptied their bladders, Queen, flanked by minders, wardrobe 'mistress' and assistants, were now bouncing on the balls of their feet in their hidden position and itching to get up on stage. A message was conveyed by headset to the house electrician to 'kill the house lights', and as the venue plunged into darkness, it created a huge adrenaline rush for both crew and audience. Queen would be swept by a combination of this energy and torch light on to the stage and into the Dolls House: a free-standing frame covered in black drapes, located in the back corner of stage right. This was where the band would rest, or hide from view when not active on stage.

Not even Access All Areas gained access into here.

The intro tape pumped through the PA and monitors, battling for level with the audience noise – as smoke machines hissed out an atmosphere for the lights to cut through as they came pulsing to life. No going back now. The hundreds of lamps in the rig flashed and flickered but remained tethered, not yet releasing their full power until the dormant metal monster slowly began to rise in the air, spitting light beams of multi-coloured fire. Awesome, but also quite scary…

Queen would take up their positions: Roger crouched low down on a drum stool, behind his gleaming kit; Brian, with his homemade 'red special' guitar plugged into its extended umbilical curly cord, concealed behind a large black monitor on stage left. I would put John's Fender bass on him and he would pace nervously up and down behind his stacks of speaker cabinets like an expectant father in the corridor of a maternity ward – waiting for news of a new arrival.

On cue with the intro tape, the trio would crash perfectly into the opening song as Brian and John bound on stage. Fractionally after the opening bars, Fred would glide out of the Dolls House like a cat, and swoop his wand mic from my hand as he effortlessly strode on stage. The initial roar for the band was pushed to another level as Fred took his place upfront, and when the overhead rig manoeuvred into its final position, blazing and scorching with light as the pyrotechnics exploded, the energy created was truly tremendous. Queen's mantra of 'Blind 'em and deafen 'em!' worked every time.

Queen are here to entertain you! BIG show, BIG hits and right now – the BIGGEST band in the world! Queen may have played the venue before but, like secretly agreeing to meet an ex-lover, there is a certain expectation from both sides – how far will it go? The air is charged with energy and sexual tension – who will make the first move?

Fred. He would tease and cajole his audience like an experienced lover, using strength, stealth and power to take control. Drawing his conquests in closer, he would slow the pace to show his own vulnerability, before taking them back to the heights of excitement and final consummation.

Hence his announcement: 'I'd like to fuck you all!'

A promise he did his best to keep. Having adjusted my eyes to the dimness of the blackout, my photoreceptors are now in overdrive. Here we go again – another day at the office. Most nights Queen were very good, and on occasion absolutely magnificent – or not quite so good. However, they were undoubtedly a great live band that were exciting to watch. The secret to this was simple: they could play. Musicians who had mastered and applied their instruments, firmly believing in quality in all they did. When Queen took to the road after a new album was released, they always strived to give their best to the paying public as these four guys unashamedly wanted to be The Biggest Band in the World.

The first song was naturally a little tense; was everything working OK? It was audible to me, but could the band hear themselves well enough? This was the point when you would catch each other's eyes. The system of nods, winks and gestures between us would indicate their level of satisfaction. The discomfort of the smoke and showers of dust hailing down from the pyrotechnic explosions and building ceilings were brushed aside as concentration intensified. The first song seemed to speed by like lightning, and often lead directly into a second hi-tempo number without break or introduction. After the final chord crash of that song, Queen would bow and acknowledge the audience, Fred offering a shrill 'Thank – YOU!' before enquiring:

'Are you ready to rock?'

YES!

'Are you ready to roll?'

YES!

'OK – let's (fucking) do it.'

Another fast-paced rock 'n' roll number would sometimes sustain the crowd's excitement, followed by the first piano song, which gave Fred and the audience a brief rest, and him the chance to give me any relevant message.

'Tell him he's out of tune – how can I pitch my voice??!!'

'Who would that be, Fred?'

'You know! And that C*** can't even pick the beat up! What's wrong with him?'

I would simply nod in agreement.

'Never mind – never mind, how do I say *Good Evening* in Belgian?' he would pant.

'It's written in pen on the back of your hand, Fred.'

'I can't see that in the fucking dark, can I!?'

(Roadie: mind reader, whipping boy and infrared linguist?)

'No – and it's now rubbed off – all that sweating you do.'

'What then?'

'Uuuuh – *Guten Soir, senoras*?' I'd shrug.

'Oh fuck 'em!' Fred would splutter, then take the safe option – and use English.

The hand-over exchange I made with Fred was his microphone on a stick for a freshly made drink of hot honey and lemon. A sip was taken to ease the throat and he would sit down, shuffling himself to adjust to life at the piano. A major testing time – was Fred happy with how things were going? Was all well in his Mercurial world? As he gently tinkled the keys, got comfortable and threw morsels of comment to his hungry public, I would be crouching at the end or in the curve of the black Steinway grand, focusing on him intently and trying to avoid the multi-coloured glare and hypnotic reflections from the highly polished piano lid.

The rest of the band would take this opportunity to catch their breath, have a drink and give their instructions about the onstage sound. John's instructions were minimal and usually about the snare drum and hi-hat in his floor monitor.

Fred's first piano song was a crucial part of the show and, when I got *the look*, which was a series of nods, hand waves and expressions. I could tell if Fred wanted his vocal louder, the piano sound was too hard, if he was tired from the previous night's escapades or even how he felt the rest of the c***s were playing... all from his facial contortions, finger twirls and head inclinations. One particular Mercurial twirl meant he was hot, and I would turn on a fan under the piano to cool him down. When Fred gave me an unscripted nod, wink or smile, it was like an older brother showing confidence and support. I admit, it gave me a glow, made me feel good, appreciated and special. So what did I do in return? I took the piss by staging a glove puppet show at the end of the piano with Crystal or wearing a baseball cap given by a fan in Japan that had a giant pair of large clapping hands protruding from the front. I would pop up from the end of the piano, pull the string to operate the hands and applaud Fred along with the audience. He laughed. Fred laughed a lot. Then he chased me into the wings to administer a playful slap or punch. When Fred whacked me it was seen as part of the job and him releasing some fired-up energy, and the strikes were just playful and didn't hurt. And of course I was dead hard myself in those days!

The onstage crew could clearly see the audience as they were illuminated by the glow from the stage lights, but for the band, however, this was difficult as they were constantly being tracked by powerful spotlights focused directly into their eyes. A dozen or more could be on Fred alone, so he would gauge the crowd by audible response and feel, as he could rarely see further than the first few rows.

But that was enough.

Post-show, provincial US town, Mr Mercury comments: 'Did you see those people at the front! Did you? They were all ugly! I will *not* have that at a Queen show!!'

So, are audiences to be vetted at a casting session before premium Queen concert tickets get released? Check with the promoter on that, will you...

It was always tempting to glance into the audience to see the reaction of the 'ugly people' or check out the 'talent', but, if Fred caught me straying, the glare I received across the stage or piano would freeze me. I was expected to watch him like a hawk and be prepared to scuttle urgently on stage, half crouching, to release him and his mic cable from any onstage obstacle, while attempting to avoid detection by the audience – like a Wimbledon tennis ball boy scampering on at speed to retrieve the ball, then returning to a kneeling sentry position. I bent over so much I looked like I had a permanent lumbar condition, so, between me and the front row 'uglies', we could have made the perfect Quasimodo.

Nevertheless, Fred was very sharp and aware on stage, and could keep himself out of potentially embarrassing situations despite being caught up in his expressive creativity. Brian, however, would go charging back and forth across stage, oblivious to the surroundings and totally into his playing, a black curly umbilical cord thrashing in his black curly-haired wake. Fred would deftly side-step so their cables didn't cross, get tangled and inhibit each other's movements. As Brian returned across stage, still on Planet May, Fred would even pass his 'wand' under Brian's cord to avoid being locked together. When tangles did unavoidably happen, Fred would drop the mic, give me the eyebrows raised signal and take his spare mic set-up. Sometimes he'd sit on top of me and laugh while I was on my hands and knees unravelling the mess in the middle of the stage, then bounce up and down and chuckle. Fred, enough of that – people are beginning to talk...

John was not involved in any tangled-cable fracas and usually kept upstage or on the steps of the drum riser; he didn't use a cable for later Queen tours and utilised Nady radio transmitter packs on his bass guitars. John had an electronics degree – no fooling him if technical things went wrong!

However, an early experiment in the late 1970s using a radio pack on John's bass was not quite successful. I was trying the then state-of-the-art Schaeffer system at sound check, and after trying different notes on the bass called over the PA system to Trip Khalaf, Queen's sound engineer.

'What's it sound like – is there much compression?'

'It's like an alligator farting' was the less-than-enthusiastic reply.

Back to the cable for now then...

Fred loved a microphone cable, using it as another prop on stage by gripping and twisting it with levels of intensity, cracking it like a whip or flicking it like a lasso. Only on the final *Magic* tour with its vast outdoor stages and walkways did he switch to using a wireless microphone:

'Mmmmm – it's very modern' he exclaimed when shown the latest piece of expensive technology during rehearsals: 'And quite horny as well!'

The phallic-shaped Sony mic was different to his classic

Shure one; longer, fatter and matte black. It would not have looked out of place in a Soho sex shop.

Queen's show continued with the medley – sections of old and new hits generally based around piano-oriented songs, which helped Fred pace himself. After an intense bout of rushing around stage, a spotlight picks him out, collapsed over the top of the piano. 'I'M FUCKED!' he would scream, and get a roar of approval from the crowd. This would inspire him to rise and thrust himself at the piano as if shagging it.

More audience appreciation followed.

Fred did not address the audience from the piano, just the occasional acknowledgement, thank you or reference; he liked to do it centre stage, on the extended catwalk with all the spotlights focused on him. This is where he would use his formidable presence to communicate. He was never predictable and surprised occasionally by asking the front rows: 'Any requests?'

Somebody once asked for an old Queen song that was never included in the live show: 'Play that? Hah! Yooooooou'll be lucky!' he replied in a shrill, camp, rising voice as he threw his head back and walked away. 'Yooooooou'll be lucky!' became a Queen catchphrase that traversed many tours. And beyond.

Back at the piano, I'd hand Fred another soothing hot drink that he'd asked for.

'How are we going down – how is it?'

'Good, it's going great, Fred.'

'Good, that's good – and so it fucking should be!'

However, occasionally the audience response would not be

as expected, so in response Fred would force himself to work even harder to get the crowd on his side – as he had to for Queen's first ever show in Madrid in 1979. One expects a Latin audience to be hot-blooded and excitable. No. The initial crowd response and light applause faded rapidly. This enraged Fred, so he strode to the edge of the catwalk and toasted the paying public with his champagne glass and a few limited local phrases. The response didn't improve, so he threw the water over the front rows and snapped: 'Take that! That's for being Spanish!' He then gestured to the sound engineer, and screamed: 'TURN IT UP!'

The volume increased considerably, and Fred worked with fervour to get the Spanish going, and it inspired the rest of Queen too. It worked and from then on the show and crowd response was as Mr Mercury thought it should be. Fred always led by example. Returning to the piano in the blackout having won them over, and amid the screaming and calling that followed the applause, he banged his fist hard on the piano lid to emit a low hollow resonance through the speakers and pronounce loudly off mic: 'That's the way to (fucking) do it'. Self-reassurance of the magnificent talent and unwavering belief that he held.

'Is everything all right now, Fred?'

'Yes – yes, but tell Brian to turn it down, I can't hear myself fucking sing!'

And just *how* do you get a rock guitarist to play softer or slower?

Give him some sheet music. In the spoof rock band movie *This Is Spinal Tap*, the heavy metal guitarist is proud to show that his amplifiers don't go to the standard volume of 10, they go to 11. Just that bit extra – for when you need it. Brian May had his volume go to 12 – and a half. And he always needed more...

The answer? Everybody else turned up.

QUEEN WERE DEAFENING ON STAGE.

Sorry, I said, 'Queen were deafening on stage.' My ears are testament to that. During a hearing test some years ago, I was asked if I had ever worked in a noisy environment.

I'll probably have to put my few bits of Queen memorabilia into auction in order to buy a decent hearing aid for my old age.

When Queen were playing well live and really 'cooking', there was a huge buzz and energy felt on stage, so that even a crew member could vicariously feel part of the band. On stage, the sound you heard varied according to where you were positioned. You didn't hear the balanced mix of 'out front', but whatever was coming from the closest monitor would dominate. The sides of the stage were good as most things in the mix could be heard, but standing behind the drum kit gave a strange perspective. You heard the real sound of the acoustic kit being hammered plus the amplified sound of it in the monitors, and then a boom and echo off the back wall or roof of the venue.

Behind the 'back line' of band gear you could close your eyes and – even with the loss of vision – still feel the energy and sensory bombardment. The odour of gels burning in hundreds of lights, a warm electronic whiff of humming amplifiers and the taste of smoke and dust biting in your throat. You felt the vibrations of speaker cabinets, and a kick in your chest as the bass drum was pumped. You could reach out and touch it all: the rough edges of flight cases, the tough weave of the stage carpet, the chill of iced water in the drinks bins, the smooth and sensual contour of guitar bodies, and the burn of Fred's rubber-coated mic cable as I pulled and coiled it tight. It was best to avoid being behind the drum area when Roger threw his head back – as he would then usually spit high in the air, purging his lungs from the exertion of drumming and Marlboro cigarettes. His poor roadie was tasked with mopping up the cymbals the next day...

The show moved on with various hits and new songs, until around halfway through the set there would be the solo spots, where Fred would chant and scream vocal scales at the audience, for them to respond back louder. This was when he showed his true stagecraft of taking thousands of people in the palm of his hand with just his voice and charisma. Usually the show included some form of (fortunately) short drum solo, where Roger turned into Animal from *The Muppet Show*, and the extended guitar solo that worked... some of the time. (I was a young man when Brian started his solos...)

Time to take a break: Roger would come down off his riser and into the Dolls House for a rest, a drink and maybe a hit of oxygen. Fred would be relaxing in there too, removing his shirt, towelling down, changing outfit, taking refreshment and then having a suck on a Strepsil antiseptic throat lozenge. John would stroll off, take the cigarette I had lit for him and go behind his speakers for a quick puff, pausing only to throw peanuts at Brian, who would be lost somewhere in his extended solo.

Next up, the acoustic interlude: time to sit on bar stools at the front of stage, and when Roger would sometimes come forward to play tambourine, bass drum and sing. This was the only opportunity the fans got to see RMT (Roger Meddows Taylor) clearly, apart from his bow of appreciation at the end of the show. Unfortunately, he couldn't see them, as he had weak eyesight and needed to wear corrective lenses. Blind Melon Taylor he had been nicknamed in Montreux, when rehearsing a New Orleans 'bluesy' number. Roger had many nicknames, the most popular being Rainbow Man. The most fashion conscious in Queen, Rog was always buying clothes, the majority in bright, bold colours and worn in the most unlikely combinations. (He could have auditioned for the lead part in *Joseph and the Technicolor Dream Coat*.)

Some of the other members of Queens' nicknames were:

Freddie: Kermit – after Muppet character Kermit the Frog. During Fred's 'ballet' period in 1977, he took to wearing white leotards on stage and when exposed under green lights, his lithe body in the skin-tight costume made him look like the Muppet character – especially when he sat on the steps of the stage set. 'Halfway up the stair?' (Nobody dared to call him Kermit personally, I hasten to add.) After interviewing Fred during this period, the *NME* music paper ran the headline: IS THIS MAN A PRAT? As you can imagine, he was not happy – and a long taut relationship with the press followed.

Usually, he was referred to by the crew simply as Fred, but, if he was being difficult, he could become The Goofy Toothed Rascal or, if he was being *very* difficult, all manner of uncomplimentary names – including 'Horsey'. Nothing to do with Fred's teeth, but his appreciation of Russian-born ballet dancer Vaslav Nijinsky.

'Who?' the crew asked. Didn't he win a few horse races?

Fred used this cited dancer of the early 20th century and his costumes, particularly the black and white patterned leotards, for inspiration in Queen's live shows. Mary Austin, Fred's girlfriend of many years, was still living with him in 1977, and had presented Freddie (she never called him Fred) with a glossy coffee-table book on Nijinsky as a gift. She had inscribed it to Freddie and added: 'To the true artist that you are'.

And typically, like Fred, Nijinsky the racehorse was a thoroughbred and multi-award-winning champion.

Brian: Percy – after Percy Thrower, the original British TV gardener. Brian was very keen on nature and gardening, and in 1976, when I was delivering some equipment at night to his London house, he answered the door in ragged clothes, a torch in hand, with his mane of hair interwoven with twigs and leaves. He had been out in the dark attending to his beloved plants and trees. He immediately got an update to The Infrared Gardener, due to his academic degree in infrared astronomy.

John: Birdman or Deaky (self-explanatory). John had all his hair cropped off military-style at the start of the '78 USA tour and looked like The Bird Man of Alcatraz. He received it in good spirits and wore the convict's outfit adorned with black arrows the crew bought him for the show encore.

The gay contingent had their own unique way of giving nicknames by assigning girls' names to all male members of the entourage and any other 'friends'. They would then refer to everybody as 'she'.

Queen's secondary nicknames:
Freddie Mercury: Melina (Melina Mercouri – Greek film star)
Brian May: Maggie (Maggie May – Rod Stewart song)
Roger Taylor: Elizabeth (actress Elizabeth Taylor)
John Deacon: Belisha (Belisha Beacon?)
I was called Helen. Don't ask.

The culmination of the acoustic interlude was Fred and Brian performing a simplified version of 'Love of my Life'. Time for audience participation and sing-along. It's easy to become very cynical on the road and blasé towards the paying public, as the siege mentality sets in. However, to see and hear over 130,000 people in a stadium singing perfectly in a language not their own was really something special. It may sound like an old cliché but music does transcend all barriers.

By now, the show was steamrollering into the home stretch with big hits such as 'I Want To Break Free', bang-your-head rockers like 'Hammer To Fall' and more audience participation 'clap-your-hands' with 'Radio Ga Ga'. While rehearsing 'Ga Ga' for the live show, Fred had substituted the word *radio* with the rhyming word *fellatio*. This caused the band to break down in fits of laughter. Fred liked to surprise and provoke, but above all he loved to perform and to perform well.

There was only one occasion where I was really disappointed with Fred's live performance, as to me he was the consummate professional. It was at the only show the band ever played in New Zealand, an outdoor venue at Mount Smart Stadium in Auckland. New Zealand: beautiful country, but hardly a rock tour paradise with its severe lack of clubs, drugs and loose women; which inspired us to suggest that the authorities put a sign up at immigration stating: Check your genitals in here – you will not be requiring them during your visit. Unless you like sheep…?

When Fred came on stage, he was late and clearly drunk. Boredom or bad influences? Both. He was late, due to Tony Williams our wardrobe 'mistress', having dressed him with his trousers back to front, which had gone undetected until Fred began his long walk to the outdoor stage. Tony was invariably drunk himself and often had the shakes, asking: 'Dear boy, could you help me thread this needle?' Lovely man, who became Mr Hyde when he drank. At those times, just being his friend became a full-time job.

As the show started, Fred was giggling and forgetting words to songs, his timing was off and he even asked me what songs he had to play – and how did they go! The show was not a disaster, but Fred sporadically lost his grip and the rest of Queen suffered as a result. The encore was the classic Elvis Presley song 'Jailhouse Rock' and invited on stage to join in was Tony – not drunken 'wardrobe' Tony thinking he could have a sing-along, but Tony Hadley, singer and front man of Spandau Ballet. Tony, who was on a break from his own tour, is a great, unpretentious guy – but he didn't know the words! A rock singer who doesn't know the words to Elvis Presley's 'Jailhouse Rock'?

While crouched at the end of Fred's piano watching him singing his heart out, I occasionally looked out at the audience and pondered on life, death and where I was going on my own personal journey. What would I do? What was this life all about? Why was I doing it? By my mid-twenties I had become a sub-Steinway Sage. 'Is this the real life? Is this just Battersea?' The penultimate line in Bohemian Rhapsody: 'Nothing really matters...' became poignant to me as I often reflected on the futility of all this 'rock stuff' and how easily jaded we could become on the road. However, as the song ended and all the lights came up, illuminating the thousands of people in raptures over 'Bo Rhap', then I guess it did really matter to some people and was an important part of their lives at that time.

Queen would then rip into the next rocking song and my introspection evaporated. Back to business... The final song of Queen's set often climaxed with me setting off a chain of pyro explosions across the front of the stage – and singeing a few photographers and security guards in the process. Fair sport. Brian was the only other member of Queen to address the audience directly, and usually only once or twice. In the mid-1970s, before the final song of Queen's set, Brian would announce: 'We would like to leave you as we always leave you – In The Lap Of The Gods.' (Crew version: 'We'd like to leave you as we always leave you – bored and screaming for your money back!')

Queen would exit the stage to tremendous applause, leaving us in the twilight zone before encores. All around were thousands of lit matches and lighters held aloft, sparkling in the air, thick with smoke, pyrotechnic dust, humidity and an energy-charged atmosphere. This became a common sight, but the first time I saw it in America I just wanted to stop, stare, absorb it all and see how long the lights could be sustained. Would you like one more? An encore?

CHAPTER TWO

ANOTHER ONE PLEASE – AN ENCORE

(MAKE MINE A DOUBLE)

The rock show encore – you know it's coming, a spontaneous second coming. Or three. In the mid-1970s, a Queen encore featured Fred throwing stems of red roses into the audience. The roses had to be de-thorned by an assistant; a laborious task, and Fred complained that there were never enough blooms. Inevitably, some small prickles would remain on the stems and Fred's delicate hands were punctured. To improve Fred's flower distribution, keep to budget and avoid any further spillage of blood, the choice of flower was later changed to carnations, which I kept secreted in buckets of water under the piano.

On cue, I would rush on with an armful for Fred, and, while he tossed stems to the sea of outstretched grasping hands, I'd take his microphone to the side of the stage and prepare the next bunch. When the carnations were all finished, he would sprint urgently towards the piano and, as planned, I would rush to meet him halfway on stage with his mic. If he was in a particularly frisky mood, Fred would take the plastic buckets as well as the flowers, and throw them and the water over the audience, himself – or me!

Early Queen tour encores included the Shirley Bassey camp cabaret song 'Big Spender' ('The minute you rolled up the joint…'). Fred would slink on stage in an embroidered Japanese kimono, which he would peel off like a stripper, revealing red and white candy-stripe shorts with matching braces. He would yank dramatically at the belt of the kimono, at which point it was supposed to fall free. Not always.

In front of a packed house at Hammersmith Odeon as I frantically tried to free him, I inadvertently pulled his shorts halfway down, before nervously cutting him free with a razor-sharp Stanley knife. After that, a more manageable and safer pair of scissors was always to hand; Fred's voice was high enough without any impromptu surgery from his roadie.

Freddie Mercury kept everybody on a Queen tour on their toes – everybody, including himself. He would be spontaneous when you least expected it and change the pattern of his moves, rapport and even the lyrics. Whenever 'Jailhouse Rock' was used as an encore, we awaited new words to be added to the English language. Fred would half-talk and half-sing as he muttered phrases in time with the band, who played an ad-lib boogie. The ones I took to heart were 'Shaboonga', 'Shehbbahhh' and 'Mmmmmuma muma muma muma muma muma muma muma muma muma muma – Yaatch!' Mmmm? Ancient Persian? Local Zanzibar dialect?

When questioned as to the meaning and origin of these words, Fred would reply defensively: 'I don't really sing that – *do I* ?' He did, and it was confirmed by playing him a recorded tape of the show. It was also pointed out to Brian that when he started his guitar solo it sounded like the theme tune to the TV western show *Bonanza*, and finally it was pointed out to Roger and John that they were the rhythm section. The ones responsible for keeping time.

The fixed Queen encore soon settled into place: Brian's 'We Will Rock You', followed by Fred's 'We Are The Champions'. When Fred strode into Shepperton Film Studios for recording rehearsals prior to the *News Of The World* album in summer 1977 and announced he had this football fan song, it was received with caution and an element of disbelief – what was he doing now? From rock to opera, to the terraces and hooligans? It worked. Fred may have been a private and often quiet and reserved man, but not when it came to stating Queen's achievements: 'We are the champions – of the world!'

I'm sure he had already seen the potential of his sporting anthemic idea and knew it could carry successfully into live shows. However, I seriously doubt if Fred had ever played football or stood on the terraces (Zanzibar Rovers?), but what he did have was an understanding of the unity involved in football matches, the passion and the fervour. Despite his somewhat privileged upbringing, Fred could communicate with and relate well to the common man – the fans. He did watch football on TV and loved major sporting events. His favourite football team, after England, was Brazil and the wonderful silky skills they had, the smiles they always wore and their dedicated carnival army of enthusiastic fans. Fred did occasionally play 'footie' on stage when a ball had been thrown up from the crowd, and he would dispatch it back with power and some style. I fancy he could have made a powerful and exciting attacking central midfielder – playing in the hole behind the big man upfront. The only outdoor sport I recall seeing Fred play was tennis, which Roger played too, whenever an opportunity arose.

Sport occasionally crept into Queen live shows and for the first ever performance of 'Champions' at Madison Square Garden in New York in December 1977, Fred came on stage wearing a blue and white NY Yankees jacket and baseball cap. The New York Yankees had just won the World Series and the crowd of 20,000 people made the 5th floor venue tremble with their enthusiastic response. An unsettling, but powerful experience. Fred was adept at stage baseball, getting good practice as a batter when various objects came hurtling towards the stage, whereupon he would deflect them with his inverted mic stand. The Japanese are passionate about baseball so it delighted them when Fred hit home runs with the coloured plastic balls they liked to throw on to the stage. Then he'd throw full bottles of Heineken beer back in reply...

On the *Magic* tour, a potentially magical scenario unfolded during the second show in Munich. It was the day of the World Cup final between West Germany and Argentina that was being staged in Mexico City. All the German crew and staff backstage at the Olympiahalle were glued to a small TV. The game was drawn and went into extra time as Queen went on stage, and the final result not yet known. Fred's master plan, if Germany were victorious, was to come out for 'Champions' dressed in the German football kit and kick a ball or two into the surely ecstatic crowd. However, Argentina eventually won, and a fitting climax to Fred's last performance in a city he loved was denied him.

Football is the game of the people and, despite their university degrees, and somewhat arrogant stance at times, Queen were a people's band. They always gave good value and their best show and certainly put their money where their mouth was, continually defying all the critics. It became unfashionable to like Queen and their music, presumably because they were very successful. Now, we can't possibly have that in England – people who are popular *and* talented! There have been plenty of 'one-hit-wonders', but to sustain a career in the music business you have to have, above all, quality and talent; determination, belief and endurance are also required in order to achieve at a consistently high level. Queen had it. Fred in abundance.

He also had an abundance of crap piled on him from some areas of the press and tabloids, who were only interested in his weaknesses, lifestyle and sexuality. Despite being a very strong-minded man, it did hurt him sometimes. When the fans are getting on to a top football player because he's out of form or not scoring, he answers them in the best way – by getting the winning goal or, better still, a hat trick. Fred answered the media by writing another hit single, and Queen by producing another platinum album and getting rave reviews for the record-breaking live show to prove they truly were 'the champions'.

The end of the 'Champions' encore was the end of Queen's show, when the lighting rig, with every light full on, moved and tilted towards the audience as smoke and/or dry ice covered the stage, engulfing the band. After taking their bows, Queen would bounce off stage right, to the sound of audience appreciation and the 'God Save The Queen' tape. Towelling robes were thrown around their hot, sweaty bodies by assistants as they were ushered back to the dressing room, where they would either celebrate, argue or sit in stony, stunned silence.

How had they played tonight? How did they go down? On the nights when Queen played really well, they were truly something special and magical. When they did not, we knew and they knew, but the audience seemingly never complained. However, certain cities and venues certainly brought out the best in Queen and their audiences: The LA Forum, Madison Square Garden, the Montreal Forum, the Fest Halle in Frankfurt, the Budokan in Tokyo and shows in Holland or London immediately come to mind, and were where the band found something extra. The band excelled at the huge outdoor venues on the final *Magic* tour in 1986, and the 1981 South American outdoor shows were magnificent – the third Buenos Aires show at the Velez Sarsfield stadium was, in my opinion, the best outdoor show Queen ever played.

Nobody except the closest personnel would be allowed into the dressing room after a show until the mood was deemed right. At times, the room would be cleared completely while just the four members of Queen discussed the evening. If things had gone wrong during the show then the respective heads of department would be summoned to explain why. Gerry Stickells, Queen's tour manager, would get most of the initial wrath for missed cues, equipment problems, poor sound, a woman in row 23 leaving during a solo, or simply the pattern of the dressing-room carpet.

Once Queen had left the stage, the show was over. Except *we* still had our show to do, and the activity immediately began in earnest, the moment the band left the stage – even before the tape finished and house lights came back up. The stage had to be cleared ASAP, as until that happened none of the sound or lighting in the 'air' could be lowered down for dismantling. Firstly though, a quick check of the stage was done to see what goodies or interesting items had been thrown up. These varied depending on which country we were in and included cards and letters addressed to the band (binned), coins, grass joints, key rings (kept), soft toys (kept, then blown up with pyrotechnic powder), cassettes (usually kept – to record over), sketches of the band and heart-felt poems (binned), cigarettes, T-shirts (sometimes kept) and female underwear (kept – and filed...).

On the 1980 US tour, a few disposable razors were thrown on stage by fans, in protest at Fred having grown a moustache – he predictably told them to 'Fuck Off!' Then, as he chatted to the audience between songs, a moustached and check-shirted 'clone' placed a small shiny metal circle at Fred's feet at the front of the catwalk. Fred picked it up.

'What have we here? It's a cock ring!' he screeched, holding it up. 'Thank you, my dear.'

He came over to stage right and handed it to me. I thought it looked like a designer napkin ring. I was putting it away into BLU 8, my road tool-case, which held many surprises, when Paul Prenter, the band's voraciously gay assistant, bounded over and barked in my ear: 'Give it to me – I want it!' No problem – it would have ended up in the toolbox hardware drawer with the other screws, bolts, nuts, etc. Paul obviously had other plans for it, which no doubt included screws, nuts and bolting...

Having stashed any decent booty, the 'tear down' began in fraught but well-organised order. Anything taped down was un-taped and the heavy-duty gaffer tape rolled and moulded into hard balls, which were thrown at whoever was in line at the time. The local stagehands immediately cleared the stage of all liquids: drinks in cups, open cans, etc., into large plastic bins that were placed at the back of the stage. As John always had a good selection of drinks laid out for him, some of these would be consumed first as a bonus. Soundman Tony 'Lips' Rossi would be first in. The economic Rossi, also nicknamed The Love Criminal, over a period of three shows took the remnants of different bottles of John's red wine to make up a full one. When quizzed as to why he had this re-corked and by now dubious winter 1980 vintage, he explained he was planning to woo the upper-class manageress of support act Straight Eight, a formidable fiery redhead. Fully armed with the wine and a tiny amount of toot he had squirreled away, Rossi slipped over to The Park Hotel in Bremen to undertake the grand seduction. It worked. They even got married! But not for long.

Rossi would do anything for an extra buck – or actually for $100. He once dove off a chartered pleasure boat into Sydney harbour – only to be picked up by very displeased harbour police. He also licked clean a one square foot area of the front of a truck, covered in grime and splattered insects. All for the wager of a $100 bill.

Once the stage was almost clear and all my gear was safely away, I would dash out to the truck, which was already in position with the ramp attached, to start packing. I would run into the empty trailer with the driver, and together with a team of loaders stack and place the cases like a jigsaw. In some places in America the house unions would only allow the crew to point and direct loading but not physically touch the equipment, which slowed things up considerably.

While loading out, one of the obstacles incurred was that of liggers: tenuously connected persons who attend rock shows – and are somehow always in the way! The cast of 'has-beens who never were' included all manner of poseurs, only interested in being seen backstage (in the company of the band or celebrity visitors), enjoying free food and drink, invites to after-show parties and exclusive passes or souvenir handouts. Anything that made them look or feel important.

Liggers adopted the attitude that the whole show has been put on solely for their amusement. Dirty roadie types? Uuugh! These self-important 'luvvies' and friends of friends never attended in Wurzburg, Wolverhampton or Omaha, Nebraska.

At least they were never allowed on stage during a show. That was strictly for crew, and occasionally very close associates and wives or girlfriends were allowed to watch from the wings.

'Ratty, there's a special guest here tonight. We've said he can watch the show from your side of the stage.'

'No way! These people just get in my way. They don't

understand how much I have to do during the show, and you know what Fred's like? No way!'

'Sorry Ratty – we've already told him yes.'

'And I've told you! No! That side of the stage has to be kept clear for me to work.'

'Ratty…'

'No, absolutely no way – do you hear me?'

'It's Mick Jagger…'

'Oh, all right then. What would he like to drink…?'

An Englishman's home is his castle and an English roadie's castle is the stage – his fortress and safe haven, secured during show time by Queen's minders, a mixed bunch of wall-to-wall muscled Americans and likely lads from London's East End: Big Paul, Big Doug, Tunbridge, Big Wally, Terry, Wally Gore, Big Black Vic. All the US-born minders were very BIG lads indeed. At one time in 1981, all three minders on tour were called Wally – the three Wallies! Minder Mad Jack, a scary martial arts expert, once saw a seedy-looking figure lurking beneath Fred's piano and pounced to drag him out. That shadowy character was me. Jack didn't last the tour.

Another short-lived minder was a muscle-bound chap whose revealing photos were discovered in a gay magazine – and handed around the crew of course.

The band party also included, at Fred's request, a physiotherapist from Munich who had looked after Fred when he was recuperating from a knee-ligament injury, inflicted in 1984 during his tour of duty in the city's bars and clubs. Fred was understandably nervous that his knee might not stand all the punishment he gave it on stage. Freddie

Mercury was many things, primarily a musician who sang and performed on stage with the stamina of a professional athlete. Did he train? Did he work hard to get in shape prior to gruelling tours? Did he have a disciplined exercise and diet regime? No. A few stretches occasionally and an enormous self-belief.

And a few vodkas.

Dieter Breit, the physiotherapist, was known as The Fizz and deemed a luxury in some quarters, but rescued Fred and several shows when the Mercurial knee went during a performance in Hanover later in '84. He also sorted out Roger's badly sprained ankle after a fall in Sun City weeks later. Touring is hard on the body and The Fizz regularly worked on my back when it 'went'. Usually after being thrown across the lobby of a hotel by one of my large drunken American crew mates!

So, load out took varying times depending on the state of my back, the liggers, access for the truck, the local crew and whether we were staying in town and had the incentive of a good club or bar to go to. Load out could take hours, but in Tempe, Arizona, where the truck backed directly up to the stage, and we had a very efficient local crew, it took around 45 minutes from Queen leaving the stage to the band gear truck doors being closed. A 45-foot trailer. A foot a minute; a personal record.

Fred would have been proud, he wanted everything connected to Queen to be the best – including the truck drivers. The truck access at the Forest National venue in Brussels was tricky – reverse down a ramp and then negotiate the curve of the building between concrete pillars, until physics declared you could scrape the trailer no further towards the stage area. There were scribbled markers in place to mark which driver from which trucking company, on which tour, had manoeuvred the furthest. When Fred heard about this competitive event, he sent word that all Queen's truck drivers should practice until one of them held the record.

Packing trucks is a grubby and unpleasant procedure, punctuated by banged shins, scuffs, splinters, bruises and trapped fingers. As I packed the truck, I always made sure I had cigarettes and drinks at the back of the truck to smooth the way with the locals. Truck packing was never fun, just a task that had to be done in high spirits in order to get it done, but when we endured sub-zero temperatures, it was a miserable experience. Old communist Yugoslavia in 1979, midwinter: Fred presents me with a gift to keep warm while packing the truck – a brightly coloured matching set of woollen hat and gloves. I was touched. Woven by local craftsmen and bought from some Eastern European artisan co-operative shop? No: the local branch of C&A, Zagreb.

It was while loading a truck as a teenager that I acquired the origins of my nickname. Called on to do all the dirty jobs, including crawling in the gap between the top of the stacked gear and the truck roof, to slot some small item into the puzzle, the truck driver on this particular Mott The Hoople tour in 1974 said that with my long, lank greasy hair and skinny body I looked like a rat scurrying about. 'The Rat', as I was called, became 'Ratty', courtesy of Brian May at my first Queen rehearsals a year later – and it stuck. On the first day of rehearsals Fred was told his new roadie was one of the guys who had worked for Mott, and called the Rat; with a twirl and flick of the Mercury wrist, adorned with a silver snake bracelet, he replied pompously: 'Oh no! – I shall call him Peter.' Didn't last long.

Fred, being Fred, put his own embroidery on my nickname, and with a French slant, I became '*Ratoise*'. Or occasionally he would shout in a mockney accent: ''Ere – Rats!'

Once the truck doors were shut and padlocked, it was time to try to come down off the adrenaline rush from the intensity of marshalling the equipment after an energy-packed show. Now we were free – until the next show. And I wouldn't have to fret about Fred until then. The crew effectively led two lives – one with the band, where we had to deal with their foibles and sometimes capricious behaviour, the other with the people we worked and effectively lived with; the rest of the crew. Both were equally enjoyable and annoying.

After load-out, what happened was subject to where we were or where we were going. If we were travelling overnight by bus, then there was time to wind down on board until the sound crew, with whom we travelled, were finished packing their truck. If staying in town, we either headed to the hotel to clean up and splash on a bit of Brut aftershave – or, if time did not permit, we'd go in our working clothes straight to the club, bar or party. Some women like the smell of a working man – so I'm told.

Pheromones or something.

Queen often played multiple shows at venues, which gave us opportunity for a night out – after a night's work. Once the gear was shut down and everything secured and locked away, we would go to the band's dressing room, as they would usually be there, still winding down. Apart from getting some free booze, and a post-show snack, maybe, it was also an opportunity to chat directly about any aspects of the show.

Sometimes there would be invited guests in the dressing room after the show, but never many. My mum and dad would attend shows on UK tours, usually in the Midlands or west of England areas. At the NEC Arena in Birmingham, I took my parents into the dressing room, where Fred was still lounging in his dressing gown. He immediately made a huge fuss of my mum, and sat her on his knee, asking all about her and what she had been doing. Despite not having a large family, Fred was very family orientated, and involved himself with other people's relatives with genuine enthusiasm. My dad sat outside the dressing room on some steps with John Deacon, chatting like two regular blokes – cans of beer in hand. Brian and Roger also warmly welcomed my parents, always recognising and remembering them.

Mum would often embarrass me by bringing food to shows for me.

'Mum – they do feed us, you know.'

'You look very pale – and so thin'

'Well, it's hard work – and I'm not thin – I'm lean – fit.'

A popular homemade item were Mum's jars of pickled onions, which Trip Khalaf, Queen's American sound engineer, in particular loved and would scoff at leisure. However, their effect on Trip was not appreciated in the close confines of the tour bus later that night.

He always greeted her by saying, 'Hello, Mrs Hince.' Then

he'd point at me and add, shaking his head, 'What's it like to be the most embarrassed woman in England?'

She took it in good spirits.

When Queen had vacated the dressing room, we would make that our first stop to see what scraps of food could be plundered, but on early tours in the mid-'70s before we had our own caterers travelling with us, there was very little. The economic promoter had got his aide to clear the remaining food once the band had left – and it could be recycled the following day, no doubt the promoter charging full whack for it. The same aide had been critical of Queen's crew, so we decided he needed to be taught a lesson. He had bought himself a smart white sports shirt and left it in the dressing room for safekeeping. It was hijacked, placed on the pavement outside Newcastle City Hall and set on fire with lighter fuel.

When he asked if anybody had seen his prized new purchase, he was handed a set of Polaroids showing the shirt ablaze and final charred remains.

He left us some cheese and biscuits every night after that.

In Europe, we could always raid the catering area, where 'trough time', the evening meal, was served by our tour caterers: Toad In The Hole of Barry Wales. Barry Wales? Not a person, but the small seaside town of Barry Island in South Wales where the caterers lived. They put Barry on the map way before TV comedy Gavin & Stacey! Now I realise that St David is the patron saint of Wales, but are *all* the male inhabitants named after him? The company owner was Dave Keeble and his regular cooks were Dave Thomas and Dave Lewis. These three were collectively and affectionately known as 'Dave, Dave and Dave'. As Queen tours got larger, they took an extra cook out with them called Steve, and they became: 'Dave, Dave, Dave and not Dave!'

This Welsh quartet – also known as The Taffia, Stomach Saboteurs and Culinary Criminals – prepared generally hearty fare to sustain a hard-working crew: steaks, shepherds pie, spaghetti bolognese, chilli con carne etc. They did, however, cater for the growing band of vegetarians – omelettes! They also catered Queen's dressing-room requirements, and Dave x 3 + 1 attempted to vary their basic menu by using local products from the regions of Europe we visited. The American contingent of the crew nagged them to get turkey to celebrate their traditional Thanksgiving dinner, though the stage manager tried in vain to convince them that in Boston the traditional holiday food was the finest fresh lobster. He had to settle for Thousand on a Raft – known in haute cuisine circles as beans on toast. Local produce was supplemented by all the vital garnishes transported from England: Marmite, HP sauce, Worcester sauce, marmalade and English mustard.

Replete on dressing-room leftovers, we would amble around the venue as the show was dismantled and the building rearranged for its next engagement. Walking into an empty arena at this point was a prosaic experience. A vast space, that only an hour or two earlier had transfixed a gathering of thousands with a glittering spectacle, was now a cacophony of folded metal chairs being stacked, industrial cleaning machines humming, rattling forklift trucks manoeuvring, lighting trusses and chains striking abrasive contact and a multitude of voices straining to shout and bark

instructions and insults above the din. Smoke and
pyrotechnic dust still hung in the air and mixed with pungent
cleaning fluids, fuel vapour and squashed, abandoned
popcorn – it all left a sickly, sweet rasp in the throat.
Tomorrow was another day and the concrete cocoon would
house the hopes and dreams of another section of the
community and their particular passions. Meanwhile,
tonight, the victorious gladiators had left the coliseum and
the magical genie was safely back in the bottle – ready to be
unleashed again tomorrow.

The uniformed Hispanic and Asian immigrant cleaners
who mopped the floors and cleaned toilets in the US arenas,
with their fluorescent yellow buckets on wheels, didn't care
who Freddie Mercury or any rock act was as they tried to
keep America sanitary. They just wanted to be at home with
their families and the better life America and her dream had
given them. The good life.

Hang on a moment – what was I doing with my *own* life?
True, it was a *good life*: travelling the world with lashings of
sex, drugs and rock 'n' roll thrown in, but I could have been
doing something worthwhile: working for charity in the
third world, medical research, campaigning about global
warming and pollution. These are things I have thought
about since – but certainly not at the time – I was having too
much fun. And just how did I get here? Where did it all start?
In a supermarket in Fulham, south west London. Not
stacking shelves, but amps and speaker cabinets.

An old cinema had previously stood on the site of the
supermarket and, after it closed in the early 1970s, 'super
group' Emerson Lake and Palmer commandeered the building

for their vast cache of equipment, renaming it Manticore. Apart from housing ELP's equipment and offices, it was hired out to the major bands of the time for office, recording and rehearsal purposes. The cinema seats had been ripped out, and a threadbare slope led to the proscenium stage, which was big enough to handle large touring rock shows of that era. Despite being insulated by swathes of parachute silk hung from the balcony over the old stalls area, Manticore was a cold, dank miserable place in early November '73. I was working for Mott The Hoople, who had just returned from a successful tour in America, and was impressed by the US paraphernalia that Richie and Phil, Mott's full-time roadies, had accumulated. That was all I really ever wanted to do – go to America. To go with a rock band would be a dream come true – with bells on. Liberty Bells.

Mott were big at this point, probably at the peak of their career and ready to embark on an intense UK tour.

Huge jet heaters, powered by Dalek-sized gas cylinders, did little to warm the rehearsal space, so band and crew all wore heavy jackets, coats and even scarves. After a few days in Manticore, Queen, the support act for the tour, showed up at the rehearsals. It seemed strange that Queen, who were signed to EMI records, should tour with a band on the CBS label, as support acts were usually from the same management or record company stable. However, these four guys, with what was perceived as a silly collective name, were very keen and being pushed – hard. We may have all been shivering with cold that November in Manticore, but Queen rehearsed wearing their full stage costumes of lightweight silk, lace and flowing satin. Even John Harris, Queen's sound engineer, wore a black velvet suit and fancy gloves to do the mixing! And just *who* was the strutting poseur in make-up, prancing about the stage with a chopped-off microphone stand and sporting a single chainmail glove?

Queen only had a short rehearsal time and, to be honest, I took little notice of them, as I was busy making the tea, painting things black, running errands and doing all the tasks that a young 'rookie' of 18 years old was expected to do. Brian May was the first to be congenial to Mott's crew, and he let me try out his weird homemade guitar. I was surprised he didn't have a *proper* guitar: a Gibson, a Fender or even a Guild, like the guys in Mott The Hoople played. Brian also played using old sixpenny pieces rather than plectrums, so I put it down to the fact that, as Queen were a new struggling band, he probably couldn't afford good equipment. Even his battered old Vox AC 30 amplifier stood on a rickety chair. It appeared he'd sacrificed his equipment for the Zandra Rhodes 'dress' that Queen were into wearing at the time. However, I soon stopped feeling sorry for him when I heard him play! I had never heard sounds from a guitar quite like the high-pitched and rich-toned material Brian produced. He rocked! Queen were definitely a heavy rock band, with some of the feel of Led Zeppelin – but different, their harmonies more melodic maybe?

I don't remember speaking to Freddie Mercury then. Daft name for a rock singer I thought. 'Freds' were farmers, builders or the bloke playing darts in the pub. Little did I know the profound effect he would have on my life in the future. During that '73 tour the Mott crew got on nodding terms with Queen, speaking to them occasionally, but not really mixing. Roger showed some offers of acknowledgement; John was John, quiet and kept to himself. And Fred was simply Fred: even in those early days he was quite unique. He always acted like a star. A big star.

Support acts on major tours were expected to stay rightfully in their place, but, despite not having had any success, Queen were aloof, arrogant even, and demanded a lot on that tour, upsetting people along the way. That didn't change, incidentally.

It was generally thought among the crew that Queen were a bunch of poseurs, and, though I personally liked a few of their songs, their super-confident, strutting singer irritated me. The consensus was Queen would *never* make it! However, I was impressed by Queen's girlfriends: four attractive, cool-looking and funkily dressed ladies who came to some of the shows. However, it was the band who wore the more expensive and impressive dresses and blouses.

The following year, Queen supported Mott for a short time in America, but I was spared the prancing one-gloved poseur as I was back working for David Bowie guitarist Mick Ronson on his solo UK tour. I had still not made it to America. A year later, there was a fleeting offer to work for Queen as Brian May's roadie. His man at the time had walked out – and a replacement was urgently needed for a US tour. Brian's man decided to come back, so I was offered another job with Queen doing drums and piano. Drums: like putting together big Meccano sets. Pianos: fiddly pick-ups to fit – and an awful lot of strings to tune. I didn't fancy it – didn't take it. Yet again: no America.

Subsequently, after the various guises of Mott The

Hoople had been exhausted, Richie, Phil and I took the offer to work for Queen, who were now starting work on their fourth album: a collection of songs entitled *A Night at the Opera*. Queen had said to Richie and Phil when they were supporting Mott that they were going to be *huge*, and wanted Richie and Phil to come and work for them. The prophecy was coming true, Queen were now big and wanted a crew with big experience – and a skinny 20-year-old who knew the difference between a Les Paul and Les Dawson to do bass and piano. (Bechstein? Wasn't that a German beer?)

'He's young, he's keen – let him look after Fred.' Thanks, guys. This was the mid-'70s: flares, plenty of hair with feather cuts, stack heels and platforms, satin, velvet, tight attire, stars and glitter – and *that* video for *that* song. Bohemian Rhapsody! Made on Stage 5 at Elstree Film Studios in early November 1975 during a couple of hours' break during tour rehearsals, it was an unwelcome diversion. We were working around the clock to get Queen's new show together and this was an inconvenience, as we had to shift things around, stay out of camera vision, keep quiet and wait. However, it came out quite well, I thought, and did Queen a bit of good too, that piece of film. There were possibly other bands I would have preferred working for, but this was a defining moment in my life and career; Queen were scheduled to do a world tour, so after the drudge of touring the UK I would finally be going to America, followed by Japan and Australia.

My ambition as a young lad was to go around the world with a rock band, meet lots of girls and have a good time.

Money was secondary – a bonus. Queen's ambition was to be the biggest and best band in the world. We both succeeded.

I was a working-class kid (*He's just a poor boy from a poor family – spare him his life from this monstrosity*) who got lucky, and, by working hard and being loyal, stayed reasonably lucky. I had found a way out of life in the factory and got to achieve a lot of my ambitions – and the biggest ambition of all had been to go to America.

CHAPTER THREE

AMERICA

(PLEASE BE GENTLE WITH ME)

It's big that America – very big. You can fit the U.K into the state of Wyoming – and get change. The United States brashly hosts and boasts the best (and sometimes worst) of many things, and, whatever they are, they're sure to be the BIGGEST! America was and still is *the* market to crack for any aspiring rock band, and, if you don't make it in America, you haven't *really* made it.

New York City might be the Big Apple but, in the 1970s and 80s, all of America was a big ripe peach just waiting to be plucked. Among British rock bands there evolved a form of colonial ethos that it was somehow our historical right to plunder the new world, then sail home with the treasure like polite pirates – without upsetting anybody too much.

America gave us Rock 'n' Roll, but we bounced back over the water with the Beatles, as British harmony bands with either 'cute' or dangerous appeal continued to take America by storm.

Fred boldly wanted to be 'Queen of America'. And in order to conquer the vast, segmented and uncrowned territory, Queen tours needed to cover all markets: the rock 'n' roll heartlands of the Mid-West, the raucous South, the major cosmopolitan cities, east and west coastlines, and countless other towns with a horse and an arena. Due to the enormous size of the USA, tours could be several months long and particularly gruelling in winter. Tour dates were usually set up by a portly American booking agent with an unpatriotic fat Cuban cigar and a percentage.

Sitting in his 'Bel Air'-conditioned office he would seemingly plan the tour with a Rand McNally map of the continent, a blindfold and a set of darts. To Queen he gave expensive gifts and bought them fancy meals. To the crew – who had to make it all work – zilch. He wasn't too popular. But Queen were. Very. They became a big act in America almost immediately, just as they had in Britain. Brian's 1974 song 'Now I'm Here' contained poignant words about becoming America's new bride.

Well, I had no intention of getting married, but the honeymoon had already started.

For a roadie, going on tour in America was the icing on the cake; a reward for slogging around all the stale-beer-carpeted clubs and bleak halls of Britain in a tatty old van, with no food, no sleep, no help and if you were lucky – very lucky – some dodgy bird with a face like a robber's dog – and bad teeth.

However, getting to America was not always on merit; it

was being with the right band at the right time. As is often said in rock 'n' roll: 'It's who you know and blow.'

One of the great things about America is its continual sense of optimism; nothing seems impossible. If you want to do something – then just go do it, it's all out there – if you want it. And it certainly attracted me.

The US was a young country, with boundless energy, and didn't carry the baggage, class system and stifling tradition of 'good old England' – and American women did not disappoint either. They were very forward and open to making new and brief friendships with people in the music industry. Yes! However, the type of band you worked for was very important to the girls they attracted, and luckily Queen were not only hugely popular but also held the type of allure and mystique that girls wanted to be around. I am eternally grateful I didn't end up working for Cliff Richard (no disrespect, your holiness) or a folk group.

Big girls with *big* hair, mouths, arses and appetites. This I had been assured by a roadie or two who had toured the US and tasted from the top table. They were right. And even the ugly ones had good teeth.

If you had long hair, a *cute* English accent and were with an English rock band, you had it made. Great!

Since I was a child I had always wanted to go to America, nowhere else attracted me, just America. I had absorbed American culture by avidly watching all the American TV shows screened in Britain and thumbed through the imported DC Super Hero comics. I enjoyed the stories of Batman and Superman but what I really liked were the little ads for one-man submarines, X-ray specs, your own ant colony and other novel things unheard of in Britain. Did they really exist? These comics held many opportunities for lucky American kids: sell 24 boxes of greeting cards and you could claim a Liverpool Drum Set as a prize. I truly imagined you could get anything in America as the lifestyle appeared to be so rich and glamorous; even the breakfast cereals looked far more exciting. Touring certainly was.

There was a youth culture in the United States – and I could watch *Happy Days* every single day on a fuzzy 525 line television set with a shifting green/magenta cast. One thing that was inferior to Britain was the picture quality of TV, our 625 line system far sharper – like our wit. However, who wouldn't want to be 'The Fonz' with his cool wit and style.

In early 1976, America indulged us with decent hotels, tour buses with beds, union crews to load and unload trucks, catering at shows, endless drinks in bins piled with ice that never melted, promoters' T-shirts for Queen shows and per diems of $30 a day as extra living expenses. All this gave me a feeling of wealth and wellbeing. I liked it! I longed to open the door of one of those huge walk-in refrigerators that are mandatory in American kitchens and step inside to consume all the goodies bathed in the comforting yellow glow.

TALKING IN TONGUES, EATING AND DRINKING WITH GUSTO

The US had comprehensive communication facilities with thousands of TV and radio stations, yet the majority of America remained frighteningly parochial. This would become evident as Queen toured provincial places, where the corn-fed waitress in the bar of a ubiquitous Holiday Inn, Howard Johnson's or other chain motel would, upon hearing us talk, squeak: 'Oh gee! Are you guys English? That's great. Now, tell me – how's your royal family?'

'Fine – thank you.'

'So you're all from London, then you must know Mrs Jones – and is it still foggy?'

Foggy?! The provincial American's view of London was usually derived from daytime TV and repeats of old Sherlock Holmes movies.

'Yes, madam, we are still engulfed by a pea-souper of a fog, it's all in black and white and they still haven't caught Jack the Ripper, you know.'

'Really…? But I just love yer accent – it's so neat! Would you say something for me – in British?'

I'm not Rex Harrison, love!

'OK, here's something in my best British accent – how about getting the beer I ordered, I'm dying of thirst!'

Inquisitive locals approached with the same gambit: 'Are you guys a band?'

As the crew, we got tired of the constant implications that we might be 'arty' musicians, so would reply, 'No, we're welders from Cincinnati.'

'Oh really, that's great – are you in town for some kind of convention?'

'Yeah, something like that.'

'No… you're kidding me? You guys *are* English, right?'

'Correct.'

'You MUST be a band – the Beatles were English, you know?'

'Really? That is fascinating. Actually, yes – we are a band.'

'See, I told you I could tell. What are you guys all called?'

'We are Harry Stomper and the Snot Gobbling Fuck Pigs From Wigan.'

'Harry Stomper? Huh – would I know anything you've done?'

'No I doubt it, we're an underground band.'

'Oh... well have a nice day now, won't you.'

The penny drops...

'Hey, you guys, you've been kidding me – you're all Queen – right?'

(The Queen T-shirts, jackets, stage passes and headbands – a bit of a clue.)

'No – we *work* for Queen.'

'Great band! I just *love* that "Stairway To Heaven" of theirs – didn't know they were English though. OK – tell me, that singer, Mercury? He's a fag – right?'

'No, no – it's all an act,' we whisper back. 'He just has a keen interest in motorcycles. And their gangs.'

'Yeah – figured so, he's such a cute-looking guy in that black leather – great butt too – can I git yah another beer?'

'Sure – and would you like to see the show tomorrow night?'

'Wow – you bet! And I get off in an hour, and... if you're not busy at all.'

'No – I think I may have some spare time on my hands...'

It is quite remarkable how many people never knew Fred was gay – or didn't want to believe it. Some never will. And of course what did it matter if he was?

Somebody famous – Oscar Wilde? (He was) Or maybe Mark Twain? (Don't know) It could have been George Bernard Shaw? (Good mates with Lawrence of Arabia...) Who knows, but it was definitely one of them – once said that America and England were countries divided by a common language.

'Fags' being a classic example. To us in the UK they are cigarettes – to Americans it means gay men. Many is the time I have asked if I could 'have a fag' – or requested 'what kind of fags do you have?'

And received some very odd looks in return.

As virtually the entire crew smoked, we had to find an alternative to our normal brand of smokes when the 200 duty-free Benson and Hedges King Size ran out. Winston or Marlboro were the preferred choices, and occasionally Kool menthols. But don't ask for 20 Winston in the USA – you'll get a weird look back.

'20 Winston – you sure?'

'Actually I'll have 40.'

'You got the money?' he asked suspiciously.

'Of course?' It was only a couple of dollars.

In the USA you ask for a 'pack' of cigarettes, not the number inside.

After an early-morning ciggie it was time for breakfast.

Having Breakfast in America (credit to Supertramp) was a sharp introduction to the stateside lifestyle. Many restaurants and coffee shops enjoyed a new-world maître d' system where you had to 'Wait To Be Seated' before being called to your table by a female voice that could cut steel plate at 10 yards.

You were never 'table for two or four' – you were always a 'party'.

'Hince – party of one – this way please.'

After being seated by 'Hi – I'm Sherri – your hostess today' with her far-too-cheery attitude for this time of the morning, you were then engulfed in the shadow of large hair and sucked into the void of the gaping smile of: 'Hi I'm Bobbi! I'll be your waitress this morning – how you guys all doin'?'

In case you forgot Bobbi's overwhelming introduction, the huge plastic name badge on her starched uniform reminded you – from up to 50 feet. She would already have the mandatory pint glasses of iced water in hand and, as we perused the laminated menus, she would rattle off the breakfast specials, through teeth braced with a scaffold of dental metal.

Amid the confusion of choice, the waitress remained, bouncing round the table like an oversized Barbie doll on speed.

'OK, OK – *what can I get you guys?*'

'I'll have eggs please.'

'How d'ya wan 'em – boiled, poached, scrambled, over easy, sunny-side-up or an omelette?'

'Bloody hell! What a choice!'

Protracted discussions follow about whether I want my sausages as 'patties or links' with nine varieties of potato – and grits? Orange juice came in small, regular, medium, large or jumbo size? Then we get to the hot beverage...

'*Great – and kin I git coffee fir yuh all?*'

'No, I'd like some tea.'

'*No problem, iced or hot?*'

'Well, hot of course!'

'Cream or lemon with that?'

'No, milk – cold milk!'

'You mean half and half?'

'No – milk – the white liquid that comes from cows!'

'OK, sir, I'll see what I can do… and will that be separate checks?'

'No – we'll pay cash!'

'You got it! Hey, you guys are a riot – you're all a band – right?'

'Yeah – right!'

'And be sure you have a nice day now.'

Why would I want to have a nice day? In the Land of the Free do I not have the right to be melancholy?

Despite the differences, and a cup of American tea is a poor substitute for our national drink, food in America was very appealing for a young visitor with a not-yet-discerning palate, but industrial-strength digestive system. This was the 1970s, when a sophisticated night out back home was steak and chips at the Berni Inn. Not Texas steaks, that fell off the side of your plate like a cowboy's saddle, and if you ate all of the first one the second came free.

Back home our experience of hamburgers was the Wimpy Bar, and in comparison to a US burger they were very wimpy! I had never seen or tasted hamburgers so good – or big! They needed both hands to hold and came with fries, salad and familiar garnishes, plus some suspiciously long, pungent, green warty things on the side. Better leave them there!

When the US promoters offered Fred a hamburger as the band meal, he replied with his usual aplomb: 'A hamburger? You *will* bring me a steak!'

They did.

On to dessert...

Jello is the substance in the US that we Brits call 'jelly', normally seen at children's parties – and on one occasion in the tub of a Holiday Inn hotel guest bathroom. One balmy summer's evening in 1980 in Charleston, West Virginia, a local lass, upon being invited to a crew member's room for a nightcap, confided that her fantasy was to be put naked in a bathtub of liquid cherry-flavour jello and to allow it to set around her. She also wanted sprayed whipped cream included in the 'dessert'.

Not wishing to disappoint the young lady, a local cab company was rapidly called, and the driver dispatched to the local 7-Eleven store with a fistful of dollars and instructions to get a receipt...

While our cabbie was grocery shopping, the game young girl asked to be tied to a chair with some velcro straps normally used for securing cables.

We then called the local FM rock radio station and got directly to the DJ on air, where a conversation about our activities was conducted – live. Being a decent bloke, he broadcast that, if any like-minded young ladies were up for some fun with the Queen crew, they should get over to the Holiday Inn.

After dispatching our perplexed cabbie with a tip and a pass for the next day's show, we ran a hot bath to dissolve the jello. Once this act of physics was accomplished, the young lady jumped in, lay down and relaxed, as we waited for it to solidify.

Not a story my mum would be very proud of, and I'm sure she would not have been at all impressed with me on my 21st birthday, which was celebrated on US soil. On 23 January 1976, at the Holiday Inn in Waterbury Connecticut, I received 'the key of the door' and a whole lot more. We were in the midst of a hard east coast winter and deep, drifting snow surrounded the hotel and Palace Theatre where rehearsals for the forthcoming US tour were taking place. Everybody, including Queen, was staying at the Holiday Inn – the best hotel Waterbury had to offer. I'm not sure what Fred thought of it as he skipped in and out of the venue and hotel in his short fur jacket and skin-tight satin trousers. The crew wore thermals. Brian, as always in those days, wore his clogs and I saw him slipping and sliding around in them as he walked around a sporty two-seater Volvo P1800S – just like Simon Templar drove in the TV series *The Saint*. Brian had a car just like it back in London – albeit in a different colour. This car belonged to Chuck, one of the American lighting crew, and he and Brian chatted in the cold about their mutual love of this model of car.

As the baby of the crew, I was used to being the brunt of practical jokes and for my 21st I feared the worst. In the end, I played all the jokes on myself.

In the hotel bar, I was treated to many large brandy and ginger ales. I rarely drank in those days and was soon well away, heckling the solo guitarist playing country cover songs in the corner: 'OI, MATE! How about playing "Close To The Edge" by Yes! Come on! D'ya know it?'

The smirking crew fed more fuel to my fire and it was not long before my face met the carpet and I was escorted to bed by Crystal, my room mate.

Having passed out in an alcoholic haze, I woke a few hours later to be horribly sick over the side of the bed. I then spent an awful torrid night, tossing, turning and nursing a splitting headache, sprawled all over the regulation Holiday Inn king-size bed, the bed clothes pulled out and strewn everywhere.

The high nylon content of carpets in American hotels was notorious for creating static electricity and, when you were connected to metal, by either putting your key in the door lock or pressing the button for the elevator – whack! You got a nasty snap of raw electricity that you could distinctly see as a blue or white spark.

I had been rolling around in anguish, with one foot out of the bed, dragging on the shag pile. As I turned over yet again, my foot came up and hit the metal bed frame – BANG! A huge bolt of static launched me out of bed right into the area where I had been sick. All rather unpleasant.

I crawled into the shower to clean myself up. There is no doubt this was the worst I had ever felt in my life. Despite clearing some of the mess up, the guilt of having to face the maids who cleaned the room compounded how dreadful I felt. I tentatively made my way down to the coffee shop to be met by my grinning peers.

'So what's it like to be 21, eh, Ratty?'

'Fucking awful,' was all I could muster.

'Come on, have a glass of milk. It'll settle your stomach.'

The waitress came over and asked at maximum decibels: 'What can I get yoooh, huuhnneeee?'

'Just a glass of milk – NOT half and half – and my youth back please,' I groaned.

Seeing my urgent need, she brought the milk straight over.

I sipped it gingerly as the others continued to give me sanctimonious glances. I could feel the milk sliding down and a biological reaction of indeterminate result building. Then, without warning, someone's breakfast thudded down next to me: bacon and eggs, sausage, fried potatoes, pancakes, waffles, syrup, toast and jam – all on the same plate.

The sight and smells hit a sensitive nerve and I vacated the table immediately. Picking up my check for the milk, I managed to reach the cashier's desk but was sick over both the check and the cash register. As I handed over the soggy bill and some soggier cash, I feebly suggested to the astonished cashier that she kept the change. I hobbled back to bed, where I swore I would never drink again. I did...

LOOSE CHANGE

During my first trip in America I was initiated into the habit of tipping. I had occasionally given tips in England but just to round off a bill or a bit of loose change, besides I rarely had the money to pay the bill – let alone tip. Now I was being asked for 15 per cent – and more!

Sky Caps, the official airport porters, *always* expected a tip. If you didn't give a dollar per piece of luggage for the leg-sapping 20 yards or so to the airline check-in, strange things might happen to your luggage as a result. I once lost all my luggage on returning from a break in Bermuda during the lengthy 1980 *Game* tour. I was feeling very relaxed as I had discovered the joys of scuba diving, and checked in my two bags – expecting to be reunited with them at Chicago's O'Hare airport.

After changes of aircraft and long delays, the plane finally touched down in Chicago several hours late. Jim Barnett, Queen's lighting designer with whom I had travelled, collected his luggage and together we waited for mine – and waited and waited until that sickening moment when the carousel stops and the sole unclaimed case is taken off and put to one side. An eerie silence falls, and the realisation hits – your bags are lost. It was now late in the evening and this had already been a very long day, with the two-hour drive to Milwaukee yet to come. After filling in a form at the airline's office, I was presented with a complimentary airline emergency kit comprising of a mini toothbrush and paste, a plastic razor, a minute tube of something that promised to metamorphose into enough cream for a couple of shaves, a comb (less than useful in my case, as I groomed my hair with my pillow) and a single tissue. The tissue was presumably provided because by now I might be crying.

The 'misdirected' baggage office – *'not lost sir, just temporarily misdirected'* – assured me that my bags would be delivered to my hotel in Milwaukee the next morning. After picking up the rental car from a vast grid of cloned, bland automobiles, we drove north towards Wisconsin. On the Interstate, the car developed problems, and, as we pulled into a gas station as a precaution, the car died.

Jimmy Barnett was furious, but I was by now so numb from the rigours of the day, I just chuckled in disbelief and lit another cigarette. As we waited for a replacement car to be delivered, Jimmy got more enraged, and in true Basil Fawlty style got out and proceeded to kick the car all over – punishing it for failing us.

He then got back into the driver's seat and punished it from the inside, just to make sure it had learned its lesson.

Next day, after a couple of hours' sleep, I kept calling from the gig to the hotel to check if my bags had been delivered. They had not. My bags then proceeded to follow me around for a week playing catch-up. As I left each town, they would arrive, so I survived on tour T-shirts, hotel gift-shop items, personal hygiene tolerance and acts of clemency from others my size. I turned down Fred's kind offer of his old leotards and codpieces. And Brian's clogs.

I did take the offer of a drink in the bar of our hotel from Frank Sinatra (junior). Chatting to Frank at a table in an unremarkable setting, the singer and musician, who was on tour himself, said he really liked Queen but would have already left town when Queen were due to perform. Nice man – and the large, dark-suited gentlemen who hovered close by to Frank at all times gave me a reassuring nod of approval when I smiled nervously at them.

THE BEAUTIFUL SOUTH

Tour after tour, America continued to excite me, as I saw for real the things that I had previously only witnessed on TV. The electric excitement of New York, where the neon glow of Piccadilly Circus was like a roadside diner in comparison. The hum of the city, steam rising from street grills and the distant screech of sirens – they really sounded like they did on TV and so did the phone ringing. It was just like an episode of *Kojak*!

Touring was one great adventure and I looked forward to

everything on the itinerary ahead. All the big cities: LA, Chicago, San Francisco, Dallas, Boston, Detroit, and even the ones I had never heard of with intriguing names like Fort Wayne, Indiana, or Des Moines, Iowa. Everything excited me: checking into a hotel, eating at an interstate truck stop, days off, show days, travel days – every day, as I enjoyed chalking up all the many states we travelled to.

In the Deep South, I met a thick-set, crimson-necked man at a truck stop, who told me his job was to scrape the 'dead critters' from the freeway – 'including armadillos', he proudly stated with bulging eyes. We didn't exchange telephone numbers.

Texas: the biggest state in the union, home to armadillos and a wild untamed place, where, in 1977, I met the most beautiful girl in the world. Elizabeth Macy was from Houston, tall and dark, with an exotic hint of Indian (Native American) blood, a stunning figure and the most gorgeous dark eyes you could drown in.

She was escorted by the Ugly Buddy, who often accompanied attractive girls to make them look even better. The Buddy was blond, round and not unattractive – in a chunky sort of way. She was the type I often ended up with, but not that night.

We had just endured one of the coldest US winters on record, where walking across the street from the hotel to the bus was enough to make your hair freeze. So the warmth of Texas, followed by the guaranteed heat of Phoenix, Arizona, and a few days off was something to really look forward to. So was Elizabeth. I walked on air for days – life was perfect. I don't think I saw her again...

During rehearsals in Dallas for the '78 *Jazz* tour, I was enjoying an evening with the band in one of their suites in the Hilton, when I got abducted by a gal with an accent that sounded like treacle being poured over gravel. She was so wasted I could barely understand anything she said. Not that it mattered. Her intoxication made little difference to her capabilities, so we left the hotel in her pick-up truck, complete with mandatory Texas gun racks. She drove back to her apartment with one hand over her eye in order to 'focus better on the road'.

Upon waking, I found I was alone in bed with only a thin white cotton sheet covering me. The morning sun streamed through the window and all was well with my world. I looked around and noticed on a wooden trunk at the bottom of the bed, a tall entity with a domed top, draped by a cloth. I shouted to the kitchen if I could use the phone and she croaked back: 'Yip and can I git ya sum cawfee?'

I called a music store, where I had tracked down a vintage 1955 Fender bass guitar that John Deacon wanted, and was just confirming the pick-up of the guitar when the bed sheet was pulled back and my new 'potential future ex-wife' kissed me good morning... I finished on the phone to see my southern belle at the end of the bed, where she had uncovered the shrouded shape. It was a bird cage, which was now open – and its occupants, a toucan, a cockatoo and some parakeets, were hopping up the bed. My ecstasy quickly turned to agony and I froze, telling her urgently of my concerns as I lay there stark naked. My relaxed muscles had all tightened hard and my hard muscle had relaxed completely. Had these peckers been fed yet? And what were they used to pecking on? For a moment I thought I was in some B-movie horror, where young men's members are fed to exotic birds by a crazed harpie.

'Yow downe nade tuh wurry they shure wone bite y'all,' she assured me.

Back at rehearsals at the Convention Centre, we had finished shooting a quick video with the new 'Pizza Oven' lighting rig for 'Fat Bottomed Girls', when I told my story of this slim and firm-bottomed girl to Fred. He thought it was wonderful, and was in hysterics. I had never seen him laugh so hard – he was almost in pain. Sexual conquest teamed with misadventure is a compelling combination. He then told me of his own previous evening's antics. I believe he had just encountered the entire Dallas Cowboys (or some other group of muscular men in ten gallon hats). There is nothing like the feeling after you have pulled, it's gone well and you didn't disgrace yourself. As another Queen member once remarked: 'It puts a spring in your step and a smile on your face.'

In the 1970s, America had night-time establishments that certainly put a smile on your face – table dancing clubs, or 'titty bars' as they were known. Long before lap or pole dancing, these were bars where young ladies danced at and on your table. And being America, one was expected to tip the performers. I'm fine with that. The girls were generally topless – depending on state law. Some states allowed girls to be topless but their nipples had to be covered with flesh-coloured sticking plasters/Band-Aids. These bars were very popular with the band and crew and, being with an English rock band, we were immediately interesting and attracted a lot of attention from the girls at places such as The

Harem Club, Patio Show Bar and The Kit-Kat in Boston's Combat Zone.

A 'cute' English accent magically opened up many doors in America.

'You God-damn Limeys and yer fancy accents! Stealing all our women!' some of the jealous and unsuccessful American crew would rant.

I saw it as retaliation for the flash US GIs who steamrolled through British towns and villages during World War II with teasing offers of nylons and chocolate to the fair maidens of England.

Being a guitar player, which is what I longed to be in my early teens as I strummed in the bedroom on my red Vox Stroller, was a guaranteed 'fanny magnet'.

Sadly, a distinct lack of talent and coordination, coupled with the years of dedication and practice required, halted my progress as a guitar legend. So I happily settled for being a roadie.

The opportunity to listen to music for free and meet girls were why I entered the music business and not the world of insurance – and to think I could have stayed working in an engineering factory? I might even have made foreman.

America gave me a sexual education and I met some of the most beautiful women I have ever seen there. American girls were a breath of fresh air to a lusty lad in his twenties, as they did not have the hang-ups or put you through the pre-coital rituals and financial ruin of some English females. However, some American girls had to be harpooned rather than pulled. America does grow them big, and yet they make little attempt to cover up, resorting to 'leisure suits' and high-tensile, factory-issue, expansion textiles. An obese woman with a beer belly above and below her belt is not a pretty sight. These substantial ladies always wore the smallest fitting underwear, and it's not too difficult to see where Brian May got the song title 'Fat Bottomed Girls'.

Looking back at black and white contact sheets of a time when I could fit into 30-inch-waist Levis with room to spare, and when I thought International House of Pancakes was fine dining, the girls still look good. I'd try to remember all the girls I'd met on my travels in order of appearance – and marks out of ten. I just ended up getting confused – I should have made notes in the itinerary.

PLACES TO PLAY

The indoor gigs in America varied enormously, from traditional-style theatres holding a few thousand to vast arenas – the sports facilities or civic and convention centres that hold up to 20,000 plus.

The War Memorial Auditorium in Syracuse, New York, was quite unique in that it had a fixed proscenium arch, theatre-style stage and a cavernous hall. The novelty of this place was two small stars and stripes flags fixed to the walls either side of the stage. Before the start of the show, the house lights would be dimmed and the flags picked out by spotlights. Electric fans blew them in a gentle breeze, while a recording of 'The Star Spangled Banner' played through the house PA system.

Most of the audience would stand and sing along, some with hands on their hearts. Now there's patriotism for you!

In contrast to the older theatres was the grandeur of

venues such as the famous Madison Square Garden in New York City. This phenomenal building had its arena on the fifth floor, and to witness around 20,000 people moving excitedly to a rock band five floors up was remarkable. The concrete really trembled beneath your feet. Backstage, the hallways were lined with images of fleeting conquerors: grainy, bleached, black and white prints of Muhammad Ali and other great fighters, Mr Frank Sinatra picked out by a single spotlight, victorious basketball and ice hockey stars, plus a wealth of musical talent from Liberace to the Rolling Stones. To perform at The Garden meant you had made it in America – and New York welcomed you wholeheartedly.

There is something for everyone in New York and in whatever quantities you like – day or night. After one particular show at The Garden, the planned after-show backstage entertainment included female mud wrestling. When hearing the plans for this, Fred wanted to have male dwarves with moustaches in leather shorts to serve the drinks. In New York – no problem! We can get female dwarves with moustaches too.

Backstage at The Garden was usually a celebrity circus, with guest appearances from Bob Marley to Andy Warhol to Liza Minnelli. I joined the late tennis star Vitas Gerulaitis, with a mutual friend, for a 'lifter' in a backstage room. His death was a tragic loss of a very nice man.

The end of a particularly long US tour culminated in New York where we received a bonus in the form of green $100 bills, which were soon converted into a bag of white 'burble dust'. Several of the crew sat around a room high up amid the luminescence of Manhattan with a map of America placed under the glass top of a table. The coke was laid out to follow various routes from the east coast over to the west. You chose your combination of highways and freeways and then hoovered up the road. Geography – never my best subject.

'IT'S A BLOKE!'

New Orleans is an American city that conjures up the spirit of fun and good times, and many good times were to be had in the historic French Quarter; the small section of faded French façade with US polish, as if the future is desperately trying to hang on to a small part of its inherited past – before it's too late.

The Marie Antoinette Hotel (one of Fred's favourites), a regular place of lodging for rock bands, is located close to Bourbon Street, where there was lots of cruising of every kind. The one thing you could always be sure of seeing in the quarter was a transvestite or two. In fact, there were shoals of them and they were *very* convincing. New Orleans was teeming with TVs. There was a perverse curiosity from even the most hetero of the crew towards these 'Shims': is it or isn't it? One of the crew's full-blooded American ex-football players pulled the most gorgeous blonde at a party and whisked 'her' back to his hotel room.

Some of us had our doubts.

'So what did you do?' he was asked incredulously.

'Well, I was pretty out of it by then and she did look gorgeous, so I just asked for a blow job.'

'She' happily complied and our mate's formidable size

ensured nobody dared accuse him of being some kind of poof.

I was awoken early by members of the sound crew leaving the hotel on their way to nearby Baton Rouge. 'Ratty, quick, quick, get down to room 103 and bring your camera and flash!'

I smelled mischief in the air and duly responded, being hushed as I approached the door in question. The biggest and meanest of the crew had not appeared in the lobby at call time and his phone was constantly busy, so the rest of the crew resorted to hammering on his door, but still no response. They got a pass key and opened up to find what I was to record on film: two naked bodies passed out on top of the still fully made and unused bed. One was our missing sound guy and the other a beautiful young blond girl with pert breasts and – male genitalia!!

They were lying close together, his arm around 'her' and in the other hand a bottle of Jack Daniels gripped firmly by the neck. The phone was stretched tautly by its extended curly cable from the bedside table, and nestled on his black carpet of hairy chest. The curtains were drawn and the bedside lamps glowed, filling the room with a 'romantic' light. I had never seen anything like it and neither had the others. The intensity of my flashgun or whirr and click of the motor-driven camera did nothing to disturb the sleeping 'babes', so, with the shot in the bag, I scuttled off to pass on my experience to the rest of the band crew.

The tour manager had prints made – which were widely distributed. A different disgruntled and deranged transvestite approached our tour bus as it was leaving in the early morning, screaming and ranting as 'she' hammered on the door. We decided to keep the doors locked. 'She' then proceeded to rip the large metal silver eagle motif from the front of the bus – literally tore it from the riveted mount! With the silver eagle under her arm, she ran off down Bourbon Street, pursued by a very angry bus driver...

New Orleans is the city of jazz, so, in autumn '78 during Queen's appropriately named *Jazz* tour, there was a large Halloween party thrown at the Fairmont Hotel.

The party was full of press, media, record company people, VIPs, etc. who were to be entertained by all manner of exotic girls and performing acts, and there is a much-publicised photo of Fred autographing a girl's naked bum during this revelry. By now, I had been educated in this cross-dressing caper and given a list of clues to look for when determining the true gender; check the hands, the Adam's apple, and, of course, listen carefully to the voice. I took this advice and pondered on it as the object of my desire perched on my knee at the party tried to put a long wet tongue in my ear.

'Ratty, I'm telling you – it's a fuckin' geezer,' someone whispered to me urgently.

'No – really?'

'It's a bloke!'

I made my excuses and left.

Our crew bus was being filled up with barrow loads of booze wheeled from the party and the jolly atmosphere continued on board for the long journey to southern Florida. As we were preparing to leave, one girl already on board said she wanted to come along with us.

'Yeah, but is it a bird or a bloke?'

Somebody offered to confirm the true gender by checking up her long, flowing skirt – with his head. No problem to the lady. He exits the skirt and nods: 'Yeah, it's a bird – but look at this!'

In his hand was a backstage pass that she had secreted in her knickers. Why?

Now you don't see that every day. Another slinky, lingerie-attired blonde was invited to join us on our journey, but replied in a low baritone voice, 'I can't go to Miami in a slip!'

God bless America.

Queen parties were infamous, but one regularly feted story stands alone as incorrect. At that party in New Orleans, there were allegedly dwarves circulating among the guests with bowls of cocaine strapped to their heads for the consumption of the revellers. Complete bollocks! The erroneous story has no doubt been circulated to add drama to the Queen legend, and even Brian and Roger have stated they never witnessed the bizarre scene. Roger accurately said on record, there was a dwarf at the 1978 *Jazz* party in New Orleans, but he lay underneath piles of cold cuts and sliced meat – and quivered when people approached the table. That's it!

IN GOD WE TRUST

The excitement of touring the USA was tempered by an edge of menace, omnipresent across the continent. America has always been associated with violence, be it cowboys and Indians, gangsters or even Clint Eastwood movies. The assassinations of Kennedy and Martin Luther King were stark reminders from my early youth but they had been too geographically removed to really affect me. Now, however, I was older, somewhat wiser and walking on the 'grassy knoll' in Dallas itself.

I came from a village 'bobby on a bike' background, where if you'd been a naughty boy you'd get a 'good telling off' – or 'clip around the ear'. In America they might well shoot you. I was disturbed by the constant reminders of personal danger; doors in hotels with spy holes and security chains, convex mirrors in the elevators, thick plexi-glass screens in cabs that separated driver and passengers, signs that stated that the driver/attendant only carried $20 in change; cops and guards with heavily polished wood-handled guns on display, so near you could touch them. The danger was brought closer to home by a fatal stabbing, during a conflict between rival bootleg merchandisers outside a venue. Somebody died over a T-shirt? Madness.

The things in America that disturbed me initially quickly became the norm, but I never got complacent and was always aware that my marvellous cruise through exhilarating waters could quickly turn into rapids, where strong currents could pull you off course and drag you devastatingly on to the rocks. One distraction from the ever-present 'edge' in America was the fascinating variety of local radio stations. Many were purely rock oriented, which was great after having limited and mostly chart-biased radio back in England.

The US stations played continuous music, with little patter or interference from the DJs. You could regularly hear the stuff you would have to go out and buy at home. Great.

There were also countless other music stations catering for different styles and tastes. I was particularly amused by the Country & Western ones in the South where the accents were slow, lazy drawls that were both affectionate and abrasive.

The country acts had the most bizarre names and so did the songs. My three all-time favourites (artists unknown) were: 'I'm So Depressed I Don't Know Whether to Commit Suicide or Go Bowling', 'If You Want to Keep Yer Beer Cold Put it Next to My Ex-Wife's Heart' and 'I'm Going to Hire a Wino to Decorate My Home'.

Songs with titles that mean exactly what they say. In America songs by rock bands were sometimes challenged as having hidden meanings – satanic messages maybe? Spooky. America loves a conspiracy theory and one bizarre claim was that if a section of 'Another One Bites The Dust' is played backwards at a certain speed there is a message: 'Smoke Marijuana'. No doubt whoever came up with that absurd theory had done precisely that. Other 'coded' or alternative, subversive messages in Queen songs? Well I believe that 'Hammer To Fall' was about Brian's love of DIY – but with the worry that he might hit his thumb when knocking a nail in.

Lay preachers would broadcast on US radio and it was hilarious imagining the scenes as they 'healed' people live on air.

The Good Reverend would cure a minor ailment by a combination of the laying on of hands, vocal bullying and hysteria. Stiff necks would seemingly ease and back pain too. The Good Reverend greeted the sick, asked what ailed them, then stated that he would help their bodies to be cleansed and cured through God – and a donation to his particular church to continue God's work would be most gratefully accepted.

He introduced one woman on air, who told him she was blind.

Startled, the Rev enquired of her, 'Blind?'

'Yes, sir, that's right – I can't see.'

'Nothing?'

'No, sir – I can't see nuthin' at all.'

Pause – as you imagine the Reverend cursing his aides: 'How in hell did you let *her* get up here!!?'

He then whipped the congregation into a frenzy, proclaiming, 'We will all work together with the Lord to bring back your sight – do you believe?'

'YES.'

'You MUST believe!'

'YES.'

Amid terrific noise, the Reverend was shouting, screaming, and stomping.

'Can you feel my hands?'

'YES.'

'Can you feel the heat?'

'I can sir – I can.'

'Can you feel the power of the Lord?'

'I think so?'

'Can you feel the mists clearing?'

'No...'

'Ok, let's all work together with the good Lord to help this unfortunate woman. The power of healing – tell me my child, can you see the light coming through now?'

'No.'

Cut to commercial break and wait for the off-air fireworks to start.

North and South Carolina and Georgia were firework country, where all year round roadside stores offered a variety of loud and exciting, colourfully packaged gunpowder – some equivalent to about a quarter stick of dynamite. Lethal weapons. Were any safety warnings heeded by the mature responsible adults that we were? No. Two sides emerged and took up arms against each other – inside the tour bus. Small rockets and bangers were slid under the door between the lounge and bunk area and other exploding devices were thrown into areas of conflict by leaning out of the windows as we sped down the highway. One bus ride to Memphis in '78 was via firework country, where we eagerly stocked up. On arrival that evening, a group of us went straight to the parking lot to ignite our new toys, as others stayed in their rooms and fired rockets across the busy freeway. After a fine display that embroidered the balmy Tennessee evening, the air was punctuated by the 'whip-whip' sound and blue flashes of police sirens approaching – fast. Time to lie low.

Later, in the early hours, drunk and fuelled by the moment, we raided our arsenal and ignited Armageddon in the hotel corridor; rockets aimed at the far-end window, firecrackers under people's doors and whirly flying things that burned the carpet and crashed into the ceiling before careering out of control. Great fun!

We had already woken and seriously pissed off the guys who were on early call, when tour manager Gerry Stickells, having received phone calls of complaint, stuck his sleepy,

This was my view every night – looking down the Steinway grand piano at Freddie singing 'We Are the Champions'. John is in silhouette and, with the swirling smoke and dramatic lighting, it's an evocative image – one that I saw so many times and just had to capture. This particular photo was taken at the Budokan Arena in Tokyo in February 1981.

July 1982. Brian playing Roger's Fender Broadcaster guitar on the set of the 'Back Chat' video.

John with Kramer bass guitar on the set of the 'Play the Game' video in London, May 1980.

Roger on the set of the
'Somebody to Love' video
shoot at Wessex Studios in
London, November 1976.

Montreal Forum in Canada, November 1981 – the concert for the 'We Will Rock You' movie.

Above: The view from stage left as the band return to the stage amidst smoke and pyrotechnic explosions for the 'heavy bit' of 'Bohemian Rhapsody'.

Below: And the view from upstage right, showing the band and the audience. The backstage bar and set list can be seen behind the piano speaker cabinets.

Above: November 1982 – Seibu Lions stadium in Tokyo. This is an overhead view of Queen and back-up keyboard player Fred Mandel at Freddie's piano performing 'Crazy Little Thing Called Love'.

Below: Queen taking their bows after the final encore in the Budokan arena in Tokyo in February 1981.

Above: January 1978. The video shoot for 'We Will Rock You' and 'Spread Your Wings', shot in the garden of Roger's house in Surrey.

Below: The video shoot for 'Radio Ga Ga' at Shepperton Film Studios, November 1983.

Uncle Grumpy head out of his door, shouting, 'Quit it, you fucking guys – the cops are on their way!'

I heard the arriving lift door 'ping', and a hotel security guard emerged, immediately letting loose an enormous Doberman Pinscher into the hallway. I snapped my door shut. I don't like dogs.

The more Machiavellian among us would hold back some fireworks and stash them in equipment cases, to be retrieved for maximum effect later in the tour. Often at sound check to amuse the band. Crystal, Roger's drum roadie, used some of the tubular chrome drum fittings as launchers for rockets and incorporated a sophisticated sights attachment and handles to grip it with, like a mini bazooka.

Aiming for the hanging electronic scoreboards that are central to many sports arena venues was popular, but the combined displeasure of the house union officials and an irate tour manager curtailed this sport. Firework abuse was an example of young men behaving badly and without due consideration for others. However, we had members of the American crew who had experienced real fireworks – Vietnam. And I thought a 'Nam Vet' was somebody who worked with animals! Growing up in England post-National Service, it was easy to forget that somebody my age could be drafted into the US armed services – to fight foreign people, who may well shoot back at you!

No thanks.

I certainly found one or two of my fellow crew members to be damaged by their experiences in South East Asia; yet they revelled in setting up the pyrotechnics for Queen's show – and yelling 'Fire in the hole!' as they tested the mini explosions.

The idea of young guys travelling around America conjures up romantic visions of Kerouac's classic *On The Road*, or the film *Easy Rider*, but in reality for the crew it was often a case of travelling blind. Waking up on the bus, either outside or inside a vast concrete facility, daylight hours would then be spent in the dim interiors of these venues. After load out some 16 hours later, you would be back in the darkness, travelling through the night. If somebody brings up the US city Ames, Iowa (highly unlikely, I grant you) in conversation, then I can raise my hand: 'I've been there.'

'Really – what's it like?'

'Well – I don't actually know...'

One way of knowing where you were was when Fred took his first bow of the evening and greeted the audience: 'Good evening ————, how you doing tonight?'

The logical way to know where you were was from the tour itinerary or 'book of lies'. This guide to your life over the coming weeks and months was careful to state at the beginning: 'All information correct as of ————' and the term TBA: to be advised or arranged. And occasionally to be avoided. Tour itineraries were issued to every member of the touring party, relevant offices, plus families and associates back home. Each member of the band and crew was allocated a number, which was on your luggage tags, hotel room list and sometimes stage passes. Guess who was No. 1? No. To avoid arguments, usually there was either no No. 1 or tour manager Gerry Stickells had it, so the band numbers started at No. 2.

Fred was sometimes No. 2. *Not* something he was used to being.

THE BIGGER THEY ARE THE HARDER THEY FALL

Verdi's *La Donna e mobile* – The Woman Is Fickle – is pertinent to the most fickle rock mistress of all – America. After *The Game* album and tour in 1980, Queen were enormous in America; two number one singles, 'Crazy Little Thing Called Love' and 'Another One Bites The Dust', which was number one in every music chart except country, and the song adopted by the Detroit Lions football team. *The Game* album was number one and the very successful tour established them across the USA.

When you are on tour with a band that is No. 1 in America, you feel invincible – and wish it could never end. But it does.

In 1982, following the *Hot Space* album, Queen asked Billy Squier, a rocker from Boston and an old friend, to open the show for them, which he was delighted to accept. Billy had already enjoyed huge success with his *Don't Say No* album, guided by the triple 'M' partnership of Munich, Musicland and Queen's producer, Mack. The follow-up record, *Emotions In Motion*, which some of Queen had contributed backing vocals to, had just been released. On paper, this was a promoter's dream, which was sure to sell out, so working to tight percentages was not seen as a big risk.

Billy was a long-standing admirer of Queen and, though he could have headlined his own tour, he chose to get the high profile this large double bill tour would attract.

The Queen/Billy Squier package was an exciting prospect but somewhere, somehow it all went slightly wrong. The singles from *Hot Space* failed to penetrate in the US, and the album itself was not selling like hot cakes – more like soggy biscuits. While relaxing on our tour bus one evening before a show, I saw a recorded interview with Fred on local TV; a rare event, as Fred was not keen on doing solo interviews. During it he said he thought that the songs on *Hot Space* were good but the timing was wrong. That's fair comment as a lot of the album had a disco and dance feel, picked up from the phenomenal success of 'Another One Bites The Dust', and no doubt Fred was influenced by spending many hours in gay discos that pumped out music with *beat*. *Hot Space*, despite being well played and produced, was not what the American Joe Public wanted at the time from Queen.

Hot Space and its dangerous rhythms was also claimed to be ahead of its time. But regardless, it was a turning point; and, while it's easy to blame the record company, it turned out to be Queen's last for the Elektra Asylum label in America. The '82 US tour moved along but there were tensions, as Billy Squier's album was doing very well and his performances were also very well received. The US record-buying and concert-going public can have short memories and, although hungry for something new, they often resisted change in areas they felt sacred. *Hot Space* was not *The Game* and the figures spoke for themselves. America likes its rock bands to *ROCK!*

The tour was not a failure, it had just not reached the very high expectations that Queen demanded. The *Hot Space* tour finished in Los Angeles in September of '82 but Queen still had an engagement in New York to appear on the prestigious *Saturday Night Live* show. There were several days' break before the TV show, so, after organising splitting the equipment to go to Japan for the upcoming tour and New York for the TV show, I arranged to re-route my LA to New York flight via Seattle, and stay with an old 'friend' with whom I had reignited our friendship during that tour. I was given my per diem, and set off for a welcome break in Seattle. My gorgeous friend looked stunning when she picked me up from the airport in her E-type Jaguar.

It was like a scene from a 1960s film as I leaped into the white open-top sports car, with a smiling pale-skinned, raven-haired beauty in sunglasses at the wheel. We roared off down the highway laughing, as the wind blew our substantial hair.

Austin Powers? My Arse!

In Seattle, I discovered a Dobro guitar in a second-hand shop. The classic metal acoustic was in need of minor repair and on sale for only a few hundred dollars.

I had dreamed of having a Dobro since seeing Peter Green of Fleetwood Mac playing one on the opening to 'Oh Well'. These guitars were later featured by Dire Straits on the cover of their *Brothers In Arms* album. Iconic guitars.

My friend lent me the money and the guitar was later shipped to Queen's office in Los Angeles. When I next arrived in LA, I took my new pride and joy to show Brian May, having been invited to join him and his family for a day at the pool – very LA.

Brian was excited by the guitar, saying that he had always wanted one, and knew how to fix the loose plate inside the body.

One of my employers wanted it – what could I do? In

fairness, he could actually play it and do the instrument justice, and I wanted it for a whim, a trophy and a piece of rock sculpture. I succumbed. This happened often, this guitar 'divining'; I would sniff out rare or interesting guitars, buy them for myself, and Brian would then emotionally mug me for them!

FAREWELL, OLD FRIEND

After my Seattle sojourn, I arrived in New York, ready to resume my duties for Queen's *Saturday Night Live* performance. Hosted by comedian and actor Chevy Chase, this mix of comedy, interviews and music was one of the highest-rated TV shows in America. Queen played two songs over two slots; and as the title says it was live – no mimed TV studio posing here. The NBC studios high in the Art Deco Rockefeller Centre building in central Manhattan were heavily unionised, so we had to tread very delicately with the moving and setting up of Queen's equipment; officially being 'consultants' to the union TV and sound technicians. The warm-up act for the audience before the live show was a young and not yet famous Eddie Murphy.

As I was tuning guitars backstage, he paced up and down in front of me, practising his lines and jokes.

'All right, mate?'

'Yeah, man.'

Queen performed 'Crazy Little Thing Called Love' and 'Under Pressure'. Fred's voice was suffering quite badly, due to an excess of New York, but he persevered as always and the band played well under a great deal of intensity and scrutiny as the show went out to tens of millions of homes across the continent. Sadly this was to be the last ever live performance by Queen in the USA.

Queen and America deserved each other – needed one another maybe. Both were big, flamboyant, ambitious and uncompromising and it's a great shame their relationship faded like it did. In 1984, *The Works* album was not supported by a US tour; the first time Queen had made such a brave but ultimately suicidal decision.

The rest of the world was toured and *The Works* was very successful, but not in the big one – America. Maybe both thought they were bigger than the other? A mistress needs to be worked at and wooed. In short, effort has to be made. Just because you've seduced her in the past does not mean she'll welcome you warmly every time.

Flowers and chocolates are not always enough.

You should have kept in touch – and kept the fire burning.

CHAPTER FOUR

LOS ANGELES

(LIKE BARS OF CHOCOLATE – FRUITS, NUTS AND FLAKES)

Los Angeles – City of Angels. No. City of *Angles* – very oblique angles. Los Angeles is technically part of America, but it is unlike anywhere else. Anywhere. Once God had finished creating the world, they say, he picked the globe up and shook it a few times and all the loose bits ended up in southern California. Parts of Hollywood (Hollyweird), Beverly Hills, Santa Monica and the *Valley* are home to some of the strangest human beings on (or off) our planet.

There is a smell to Los Angeles that is unique. The moment you arrive at LAX airport it hits you: a mix of dry heat and automobile fumes. A sweet, acrid smell that catches in the throat. The other smells that make up LA are those of money, decadence and seared skin at the plastic surgery clinics. Oh, and the overriding whiff of bullshit. My introduction to LA and its beautiful people was abrupt. I'd heard about the wild women, parties, swimming pools and sunshine in LA, and couldn't wait to taste it all for myself. I'd even fantasised about meeting and wooing a glamorous female movie star. The closest I had previously got were akin to Rin-Tin-Tin or Champion the Wonder Horse.

The Continental Hyatt House Hotel – the Riot House as it was more commonly known – situated on the famed Sunset Boulevard in West Hollywood, had a reputation for wild and crazy times among resident rock bands. Night falls and the 'strip' crackles into life in paint-by-numbers neon. It never feels like night-time in LA – there is a constant glow wherever you are. Electric twilight. It was only a short drive down Sunset to The Rainbow Bar And Grill, the gathering place for rock 'n' roll's participants and disciples. Later, suitably happy and chemically balanced, we returned to the Riot House with some new female friends. A group of us gathered in a room and were sampling some California Gold grass, when I was asked by my companion if I would like to try something special.

'Yeah, yeah,' I answered with youthful gusto. 'What is it?'

'It's really wild! You snort it – it's crystallised embalming fluid...'

I started laughing. And my companion joined me, asking, 'The grass – pretty strong stuff – got to you, has it?'

'Yeah – it must have. I thought you said crystallised embalming fluid...'

'I did,' she said with sincerity.

'Bloody hell!' Just what did this stuff do to you? I had no wish for me, or any of my parts, to be preserved in some science lab jar. A new level of drug experience – along with

Angel Dust and the 'big one', Heroin – that I did not wish to scale up to.

A can of carbonated root beer, a large pack of Wise potato chips and a night in front of the telly watching *Happy Days, The Benny Hill Show* and *Gilligan's Island* will do me nicely, thanks. For a young country boy, it was all too much to take.

But LA has a habit of drawing you back.

One morning in 1976 in the foyer of the Riot House, I saw Paul Kossof, the guitarist from Free, with his current band, Back Street Crawler. I was a big fan of Free and excited to see a hero in the flesh. Tragically, a week later Paul Kossof died on a flight from Los Angeles to New York.

Los Angeles was an important centre for Queen as, along with their record company, Elektra, and later Capitol, our US office, run by tour manager Gerry Stickells and his GLS Productions, was based there – at Crossroads Of The World on Sunset Boulevard. Only in LA could you get an address like that! Elektra Asylum Records was on La Cienega Boulevard and only a few minutes' walk from where we usually stayed. Bryn Brydenthal was one of the rare breed of record company executives who made a big effort to be friendly to everybody on tour – especially me and Crystal. She would invite us to the Elektra offices and ply us with albums and other swag from the stable of artists on the Elektra label, including The Eagles, The Doors, Jackson Browne, The Cars, and Warren Zevon. We had no sway with the record company side of Queen, but Bryn always showed us great hospitality – and we reciprocated when we could.

LA was a good place to bring the family, so Brian, Roger

and John all bought houses – sorry, homes. (Nobody lives in a house in America; they live in a *beautiful home*.) Fred preferred New York and all that the intense east coast metropolis had to offer, so, although we did tour rehearsals in LA, the only Queen recording sessions were on *The Works* album at the Record Plant studios on 3rd Street. It was in the control room of the Record Plant that Fred said the most profound thing I ever heard from him. He was clearly feeling down when he arrived for the session and his mood didn't seem to lift, and it was clearly due to his love life once again. When somebody tried to cheer him up, he snapped. Standing sharply from his chair he shouted at the room and directed his comments towards Brian, Roger and John: 'It's OK for all of you – you have your wives and families – I can *never* be happy!'

Apart from the initial shock, I thought it was a terribly sad thing to have to say and I felt for him tremendously. Freddie had so many genuine people who cared for him and indeed loved him, but he still thought he could never be happy. However, I believe he did find some happiness in the last few years of his life.

TWO FREDS ARE BETTER THAN ONE

During those Record Plant sessions, Canadian musician Fred Mandel, who lived in LA was invited to play on several tracks on *The Works* album. Fred had been Queen's back-up keyboard player on the previous *Hot Space* tour in '82, and was highly respected as a musician and a person by all of the band, Queen's co-producer Mack and the crew. He was a phenomenal talent who worked with such speed and seemed to make his job look easy. It wasn't. 'Fred No. 1' was very impressed with 'Fred 2' and later invited him to play on his solo project *Mr Bad Guy*. Fred Mandel also played on other Queen members' projects, but his input on *The Works* was notable. He played the synth intro and solo on 'I Want To Break Free', and his keyboard skills contributed greatly to 'Radio Ga Ga', plus sections of 'Hammer To Fall' and 'Man On The Prowl'.

Two men often on the prowl in LA were Rod Stewart and Jeff Beck, who came to the studio one evening and started jamming with Queen – great stuff. A casual, spontaneous session where nobody was under pressure, or out to impress. Rod had met Queen before and, as he and Fred were both good friends with Elton John, he suggested that the three of them form a trio and call themselves: Hair, Nose and Teeth! Rod would hang out with his cronies at the nearby Coronet pub and we sometimes took refuge there too.

Another nearby escape from the tedium of studio life was Oskos on La Cienega. It was a famous disco of grand proportions, but diversified on some evenings – with female mud-wrestling bouts. Other times, we got some relief from recording or rehearsing music – by going to see other bands! At the downtown Sports Arena, we all saw The Who: Me, Crystal, Jobby and all of Queen, including Fred.

It's the only time I have ever seen Fred in an audience! The band sat in the middle of a general audience area on the floor of the Sports Arena. They were not surrounded by minders or security – quite remarkable. They just really wanted to see The Who.

I saw The Cars at the Sports Arena with John, and with

John, Brian and Roger we went to The Forum to see Robert Plant, AC/DC and Supertramp, amongst others.

My favourite venue was Disneyland. A lifelong ambition to visit was fulfilled in early 1977 as the ban on men with long hair entering Disneyland had been lifted. I got to see Mickey and friends, plus an interesting encounter in the caves on Tom Sawyer's island – when the girl I was with started to interfere with my trouser area. Uncle Walt would certainly have disapproved, and must have turned in his grave, liquid nitrogen or wherever his final resting place may be.

CRUISING – NOBODY WALKS IN LA

An LA highlight has to be cruising in a big American car down the palm-lined streets with your arm out of the window taking in the warm Californian sunshine. In the summer of 1980, I was doing exactly this in a hired station wagon one late afternoon down Santa Monica Boulevard, with the radio tuned to KLOS, my favoured FM rock station on 95 point something. I was on my way to pick up a complimentary 4x12 speaker cabinet for John Deacon, from a store that dealt in Sunn Amplification. Feeling good with the world, I lit up a cigarette and tossed the match. Soon, I was aware of the familiar sound of LA police sirens and in my rear mirror a black and white cop car was indicating that I should pull over. Having seen many US TV cop shows I knew what to do: stay still, be calm and keep both your hands on the steering wheel. But what had I done?

The LAPD version of John Wayne sauntered up to the open window, bowed down, removed his mirrored sunglasses and drawled, 'Was that your cigarette you threw out of the vehicle, sir?'

'No – no I, I did, no it was, was not...?'

Looking into the car, the cop saw my burning ciggie in the ashtray.

'Oh, right, okay - it was the match then, was it, sir? Are you aware that's an offence in the state of California?'

I decided to play the stupid and apologetic foreign tourist, so replied in a false cut-glass English accent:

'I am most terribly sorry, officer, I just did not realise.'

'Well, sir, we have big problems with forest fires in our dry climate. It's state law.'

'Yes, of course, officer, I perfectly understand.'

'Can I see your driver's licence, sir?'

'Certainly – it's right here in my bag.'

I leaned over and urgently delved into the shoulder bag lying on the bench seat.

CLICK!

I looked around and saw that, about six inches away, a large LAPD issue handgun had intruded into my personal space.

'Nice and slowly, sir.'

I handed over my licence and the cop looked at it, turned it over, looked again, turned it around once more and then rubbed his action-hero chin.

'Mmmmm – English, huh?'

'Yes, correct officer.'

'Well, sir, may I suggest you use your ashtray in future.'

With that pearl of wisdom, he was gone. My tense bottom disengaged itself, and I selected 'D' on the automatic and carefully drove on down the boulevard.

As an American driving licence was an official form of ID and a Californian one a particularly cool item to flash down the pub back in England, on the advice of John Deacon, I decided to get one. When I first went to America, I wasn't legally old enough to drink in some states and was regularly being 'carded' for my ID. There was also the added bonus of using a California drivers licence to rent cars outside of America and not get nicked for parking tickets. I set a time in our LA schedule to take the test but had not planned on going out on the razzle with John Deacon, ending up at The Playboy Club in Century City, the night before a 9am driving test. I spent a lot of time talking and drinking with an actress from *The Loveboat* TV show – who I think was slightly famous – but isn't everybody in LA?

After little sleep, I blearily drove to the Department of Motor Vehicles, joined the line for the multiple-choice test paper and duly paid my 30 bucks. If you fail this written test, you just join the back of the line, pay again and try once more. 'What should your course of action be if a person holding a white stick or a cane walks suddenly into the road in front of your vehicle?' Two of the suggestions were: swerve wildly on to the opposite side of the road or kerb to avoid them, or wind your window down and shout at them to get out of the way!

I had the required number of ticks in the right boxes and for the road test I was told to drive my car into the street outside the building and wait for my examiner. My very large examiner came out of the building towards me, looking bemused. She approached the open car window and informed me I was facing the wrong way in a one-way street!

With the examiner installed in the passenger seat, she then explained in a scripted voice how the test was fair, equal and I would not be tricked in any way. I nodded compliantly and set off with my 100 driving points intact. As the test progressed points were deducted for driving errors; a minimum of 70 points being required to pass. The driving part of the test took about ten minutes and I literally drove around the block a few times.

Approaching a cross street, I was asked to 'turn left here please'.

I waited for the oncoming traffic to pass, and then turned perfectly into the street. My examiner just stared at me and said, 'You just turned on a red light.'

I had completely missed the hung traffic light suspended on a cable overhead.

'I thought you could turn on a red light in California – if it was safe to do so?'

'No, sir, that's a right turn, and by the way, your accent, are you from England?'

'Yes, madam, how observant of you,' was my clipped reply.

'Oh, well, I guess you don't know too much about this stuff.'

We then drove straight back to the test centre and she passed me with 80 points!

If I'd failed, I could have joined the queue, paid the $30 and tried again.

I then had my mandatory mug-shot photo taken, but, as the machine only took a single shot of you, I had just one chance of looking like a criminal, moron, child molester or grinning buffoon. I went for the look that incorporated all four, with a touch of Keith Richards on a bad day thrown in. The finished photo had the startled look of somebody who has just woken up in LA, thinking the rigours of the night before has made them feel wobbly on their feet – when in fact it was just another minor tremor – an earthquake! Something I experienced on a few occasions, but I was never sure which was which.

PASSING THROUGH

LA is home to The Rock Beasts: a species of young women who savour rock 'n' roll and the lure of its attendant trappings. These girls held records for squeezing the most flesh into the least amount of spandex, the biggest back-combed hairstyles, the most nasal accents and the supreme honour of fitting more sequins and studs per square inch on black leather or vinyl than anybody in the known world. The Rock Beast held a craving for drugs, specifically the soporific types such as Quaaludes, that gave them their permanent grin and rubber-limbed movements. The den of the Beast tended to be a scruffy apartment in West Hollywood where the large refrigerators in their kitchens would be covered with 'scalps': stick-on backstage passes from every band that had ever been through town. They were indeed very social animals and by remarkable coincidence knew all my friends who worked for other bands…

I once met such a girl in The Rainbow, called Bamm-Bamm. Her nickname was apparently derived from the baby in *The Flintstones* cartoon show, but I had heard it as 'bang bang', which seemed pretty accurate to me. One bright, late morning she asked me to drop her off at work. We jumped into the rental car and screeched out of the underground parking lot like they do on TV cop shows, and she instructed me to drive west on Sunset towards Beverly Hills. As we entered an exclusively wealthy area, she asked me to pull over into the next driveway. I stopped the car in front of a pair of imposing metal gates and was told to lean out of the window and talk into the rock? I looked over and saw a piece of fake stone with a small pattern of holes in it. Talk into a rock? What's the protocol for conversation with pieces of geology? However, we had already been spotted by the cameras mounted on the entrance and a voice crackled through the rock politely asking how they could help. Bamm-Bamm leaned over me and shouted into the rock who she was and who she had come to see. The gates magically opened and I was then instructed to drive slowly up the drive to the front of the house and not to leave my vehicle. I asked her what this was all about and she casually told me that this was Hugh Hefner's Playboy Mansion! She got out and disappeared through a large wooden door of the mock castle. If doors could talk... I was spellbound. Instructed by men in black with walkie-talkies to keep driving, I followed the route down the other side of the estate, and out of another set of automatic gates and back on to the street. I was taken aback – I had been in the legendary domain of Playboy parties and the experience felt like a fast-food drive-thru.

'Anything on the side with that?'

I don't know what Bamm-Bamm did on-the-side at the mansion, and I never asked, but I presume she had not been invited for her flower-arranging skills.

Beverly Hills, Hollywood, Santa Monica, Venice Beach: LA place names sounded glamorous to an English boy more used to Factory Road or Abattoir Avenue. One exotic street name was Cahuenga, which was apparently the name of an American Indian princess. Cahuenga was the location of one of the many film and TV facilities that were available in Tinsel Town, and Queen were booked into one of the large sound stages to do rehearsals for the summer 1980 *Game* tour. On the adjacent stage to us, a car photographer was shooting pick-up truck ads. During a break, I walked out of our sound stage into the Californian sunshine – BANG! Something hit me in the head and I went down. Had I been shot? This was America...

Dazed and spinning, I looked up to see the car photographer and his team leaning over me, showing great concern – I had been floored by a frisbee! My eye was already swelling and changing colour as I went back to our stage to sit down. 'Here, man, take a few hits on this,' said Doug the photographer. 'It should chill you out.'

I was offered a 'Brain Dart' – a small joint of Californian grass. This stuff was so strong I had to go and sleep off the combined shock experiences inside Roger's foam-lined gong case. Despite bending my face and my mind, Doug and I became firm friends and still remain so today.

STAR QUALITY

When in LA it was not unusual to see stars of stage, screen and vinyl: Henry The Fonz Winkler, apparently a big fan of Queen, stood quietly in awe at the back wall of a sound stage watching the band rehearse, and The Rainbow Bar & Grill was always good for spotting rock people.

Stevie Nicks was stumbling around The Rainbow one evening, when Crystal called her over: 'Hey, Stevie, you owe me $19.95.'

She came over to the booth, waving her arms in her mystical stage manner, and dumped herself down. She sprawled over us drawling: 'Whaaaaat?'

Crystal replied, 'I bought your last Fleetwood Mac live album – and it's crap. Give us me money back!'

John Belushi was spotted there the evening he sadly died, and comedy actor Robin Williams also frequented The Rainbow in his wilder days.

Somewhere at the end of the rainbow is a crock of gold. But in LA it was usually a crock of shit. Los Angeles can really eat people up and spit them out without compassion or prejudice. This city is the fountain of youth – if you can afford it. The obsession with looking young can be aided by extreme exercise, dedication and behaviour that excludes any alcohol, tobacco, drugs and enjoyable food. It seems ridiculous to me that you make all these sacrifices, and yet still breathe the stifling, filthy, polluted air. No amount of colonic irrigation, crystal aura therapy, rebirthing analysis, rune reading or flotation tanks are enough to counter that. A very common LA way of retaining youth is via the chequebook and specialist doctors. Plastic surgery and remodelling is popular with residents of all ages, and it usually shows. There is a theory that all the plastic surgeons in southern California get together and pool all the bits they have chopped, snipped or lipo-sucked. From this cornucopia of fat, flesh and tissue, they then allegedly construct the faces of the hosts for daytime TV quiz shows.

And for the rejects cable TV shopping channel presenters. Allegedly.

If you survive LA's smog and medical bills, there is still the small matter of being shot, mugged, knifed or sued to contend with. Sued is probably the worst, and the most common. Or counter-sued. I understand you can have your birth sign legally changed by deed poll if your planets are not harmoniously aligned.

California is very strict on drink driving, and commendably so, as Queen's upper-class English lawyer found out. Returning from a South American tour to Los Angeles for business, he was stopped in his convertible rental car on his way home one night in Hollywood, though he hadn't had a drink. The legal eagle was not eagle-eyed but naturally slightly cross-eyed. To make matters worse, he had recently picked up an eye infection. The cops pulled him over and did their standard talk but the state of his eyes convinced them he must be over the limit. Then they hauled him out of the car and took him to jail, not buying his pompous explanation of: 'Don't you realise I have Venezuelan conjunctivitis!' Whatever his condition was, he no doubt found a night among the dregs of society a sobering experience. Just like public school?

Rock shows in LA are an exercise in circus. *The* place to play was The 'Fabulous Forum' – the LA Forum, a huge indoor arena and home of the LA Lakers basketball and the Kings ice hockey teams, located in Inglewood, about half-an-hour drive south of Hollywood. The capacity was around 18,000 and most of them were on the guest list. If you played a three-night residency, probably only two of the concert's tickets were actually paid for. OK – I'm exaggerating – two and a half. On the 1980 *Game* tour, Queen played an unprecedented four nights at the venue – and could have sold more. The after-show parties were at the in-house Forum Club and packed with major and minor celebrities, plus assorted pretenders, hangers-on and poseurs – a normal night out in LA.

I was approached by an allegedly important middle-aged woman who was full-on Californian – to the power of 10. She quizzed me: 'HI! You work on stage with the band – right?'

'Yeah, something like that missus.'

'I just *love* the way you interact with Freddie, the understanding and synchronicity you guys have together is perfect – truly wonderful. Beautiful.'

Had she been at the Crystallised Embalming Fluid? Did she mean me crouching below the piano until it was time to hand or receive Fred's microphone on a stick? She enthused about the lights, and how they were: '*So* eighties.' It was 1980.

LA is serious about its bullshit and I believe you can now major in it at college.

During one of these post-show Forum parties, we put firecrackers into a massive glass bowl of hot chilli dip that had large shrimp creatively arranged around the rim. After ignition, we beat a hasty retreat back to Hollywood as the mini explosions had redecorated the surrounding area. Little did we realise at the time that we had invented a new LA art form – Performance Catering – after Jackson Pollock.

I got my 15 seconds of fame in the LA Forum when Fred

spontaneously and embarrassingly introduced me to the audience during the song change to 'Crazy Little Thing'. After putting his guitar on him, I was tightening his mic which had slipped on its stand, in the full glare of a dozen or more spotlights.

To keep continuity with the audience during this unscheduled pause, Fred announced, 'This is Ratty. His real name is Peter Hince and he has been with me for years – allow me to introduce you all to him. Come on – take a bow, dear.'

I scuttled off stage as quick as possible but was followed to my hiding place and illuminated by all the roving spotlights. I was suffering serious stage fright as Fred continued: 'He's not looking so good this evening – you haven't washed your hair have you, dear?'

'Crazy Little Thing Called Love' was the only song in which Fred played guitar on stage – a 12-string Ovation acoustic – which was one of Brian's back-up instruments. He had been persuaded by the rest of Queen and me to play guitar on stage after the song was released in 1979 – as it would add yet another dimension to the show, and give him another prop with which to communicate with the audience. However, Fred posing with an acoustic guitar never really cut it – macho guitar hero poses required a different type of guitar.

So one day I approached him: 'Fred – you look a bit poofy playing that acoustic guitar on stage – it doesn't work.'

'Do you really think so, dear?'

'Yeah – it's not really rock and roll – posing like that with an acoustic. It's – poofy'

'Poofy? Well, we can't have that!'

'No – so what about playing a Fender Telecaster, like Brian does during the song. The feel of the song is very '50s – the era of the Telecaster. Brian plays a black one – and I know how much you like using white on stage – I'll get you a white Telecaster.'

Fred nodded positively: 'Very good – arrange it then for me, Ratty.'

So I did. I bought a very nice maple-neck white Telecaster in New York, which he tried on the '82 *Hot Space* tour, but he didn't get on with it – he said it felt far too heavy. It was a remarkably heavy-bodied Telecaster, more like a Les Paul in weight, so after a few tries we went back to the acoustic.

When we got back to London, I called the UK Fender office and they invited me to their warehouse where I inspected every white Telecaster guitar on the rows and rows of industrial grey shelving, until I found the lightest one. They varied in weight considerably, and the one I chose was only fractionally heavier than a large acoustic. Unfortunately, it was not a great-sounding guitar and the intonation and harmonics were poor – but it was light! I chose the string gauges as Fred, despite only using his fingers and never a guitar pick, could break strings with the force he played.

He played with this guitar from *The Works* tour on every show. The original heavy telecaster was kept as a back-up.

In LA, we all needed some recreational back-up, and a haven of sanity from 'loonyville' was Barney's Beanery in West Hollywood, a down-to-earth bar and restaurant famous for its selection of world beers, homemade chilli and for featuring in *Colombo*, the TV detective show, where the dishevelled sleuth (rather like a roadie) would eat his beloved chilli dish in one of the booths. The management at Barney's had produced a T-shirt that had printed on the front: 'The Original Barney's Beanery' and on the back: 'Faggots Stay Out Of Hollywood'. I wore one as a bet in the dressing-room area at a 1976 LA show at The Santa Monica Civic, as all the 'luvvies' minced about. It certainly got a reaction… Even the matchbooks at Barney's were printed with 'Faggots Stay Out'. It was a very different era.

TIME TO GO

Los Angeles is a magnet for many alternative lifestyles and religious cults. Some never made it out of the airport.

'Would-you-like-to-buy-a-lovely-orange-flower?' some simpering bald tit dressed in a dyed bed sheet would ask at LAX.

'No – I'd like to buy a large vodka and orange!'

'Peace and love – brother.'

'Rock 'n' roll – mate!'

'Hare Krishna, peace and love.'

'Harry Ramsden, salt and vinegar!'

Time to get out of this 'La La Land'. 'Boarding pass, please – aisle or window seat – as long as it's in smoking!'

CHAPTER FIVE

JAPAN

(TALL YOUNG MEN AT LARGE)

We flew west out of LAX – to the east, across the big blue bit on maps usually referred to as the Pacific Ocean, and from one foreign place to another. Los Angeles had certainly been an alien encounter, but what lay ahead was equally strange – and intriguing. Japan in the mid-1970s was still a novelty, a journey into the unknown and an exciting bonus to life on the road for the few bands invited to play there. Queen were big in Japan, even before they ever arrived.

'You won't like the food,' a veteran of one previous visit nodded sagely on the JAL flight to Tokyo. He was right. The immaculate, smiling doll-like stewardess passed around trays of cold rice, raw fish, purple pickles and seaweed. Raw fish! Now, I didn't mind a rare steak – but raw fish? It took the smile off my face. And the hot towels we were graciously served with took the grime off my face.

Wherever we went in Japan, we experienced the polite ritual of being given a small handkerchief-size towel, either hot or cold, and sometimes fragrantly perfumed, to dab your face and wipe your hands with. For grubby roadies they were very handy – but it's not the done thing to use them for your armpits in a restaurant.

Clean and very keen, I was feeling excited and expectant as we descended into Haneda airport, with the sprawling blanket of the lights of Tokyo sparkling below. A ceremonial gong went off in my head, announcing Peter Hince's first arrival in Asia. Soon I was witnessing what I imagined Beatlemania must have been like. Queen, who had been up the pointy end of the Jumbo Jet, were being escorted through thousands of hysterical, screaming fans by their personal Japanese security: Samurais in cheap suits with what looked like white plastic National Health hearing aids. Brian May was towering above the throng like some curly-topped beanstalk; Fred, Roger and John in stacked heels, platform soles and 1970s hairstyles were also giants among the Japanese. The hordes of fans followed us to the hotel, where more uniformed security kept them at bay. I felt like I was in a movie; it was all somewhat surreal and I was so enthralled with everything I was experiencing that I never noticed any jet lag. Pure adrenaline took over.

A four-fold sensory bombardment followed, with more strange and suspicious food, sights both bizarre and serene, shrill noises and pungent aromatic smells. I soon encountered a fifth – which were very firm and accommodating indeed.

'Watch out! There's a high rate of VD in Japan,' the wise

old sage told us. The opening line from any Japanese doctor you saw, for any ailment, was: 'You have discharge?'

'No I can't hear, my ears hurt, a problem on the flight over here. It's very painful.'

'Aaaaahhh – your ears pop when you fry?'

These were the days when Benny Hill and his particular type of humour reigned supreme. Jingoism? I didn't have any idea what it meant back then; foreign people were there to amuse and entertain. Xenophobia? No, isn't that a Japanese wind instrument?

ESPIONAGE

The following muted phrase spoken in English by a Japanese female was heard from the room of one crew member, as he entertained his new 'special friend':

'You may ownee be loadie – but you are lock star to me.'

Pause to visualise the guy's huge grin that followed her remark. The young lady continues: *'I am not gloopie – I have feerings too.'*

This information was obtained by using a Tokyo Spider; a small radio microphone and transmitter, discovered while scouring the electronic-goods stores in the Akihabra district of Tokyo. By tuning in on an FM radio/cassette recorder, the conversation could also be saved for posterity. Once the bug was fixed in place, usually behind the curtains, and a sound check done, we went out clubbing. On returning, the sniggering, drunken ensemble would gather in a room on a higher floor and tune in. With the recording complete, we would retire with great anticipation for the following day's Queen sound check, when the recorded tape would be played once everybody was gathered. Queen appreciated wicked mischief. They really loved it as the victim was forced to listen to the highlights:

'I am not a Playboy, baby – I think you are really special. Would you like to stay?

'OH REALLY?' The crew would all shout in unison.

'Of course I can introduce you to Freddie and Brian'

'OH REALLY?'

'No, I'm not married – I don't even have a girlfriend. I've been waiting for somebody really nice – like you.'

'OH REALLY?'

'I'm tired, we don't have to do anything – just go to sleep. You can trust me.'

'OH REALLY?'

Cue – huge rounds of laughter.

AWAY FROM HOME

Though all this exotic Japanese exposure was stimulating, it was at times a real comfort to experience something familiar – and thankfully the Japanese drive on the right side of the road – by that I mean the *correct* side – the left. Japanese courtesy was followed to the letter as the rear door of taxis opened automatically for you when the car pulled up. It was comforting too to see things written in English: McDonald's, Shakey's Pizza and English Pub. I know – sad, wasn't it? The familiar publications of *Playboy* and *Penthouse* were available but, when opened up, it was found that all the women's 'front bottoms' had been scribbled over by teams of Japanese women armed with black felt-tipped pens. No display of pubic hair was allowed in Japan, though Japanese 'top shelf' material, which had a particular penchant for showing young-looking girls in white underwear bound and gagged, was freely available.

The cultural contrasts continued; Queen shows followed a very different pattern in Japan by starting much earlier, usually at 6pm and there was never a support act. The early start was so that the predominantly young Queen audiences could travel home on public transport in good time, and a large percentage of the fans were still in their smart school uniforms – something that was deemed rather attractive by some of the quieter members of the crew.

The visual impact of a Queen show was reduced, due to pyrotechnics not being allowed at all, while a total black-out was also vetoed by the strict authorities, the venue exits having to be clearly lit and visible. So, as the band crept on stage in this twilight, they could easily be seen by many of the audience, which lessened their grand entrance. A certain singer was not at all happy in his luminescent white stretch 'Mercury the winged messenger' outfit: 'Ratty – get those lights turned off or I'm not going on!' Sound familiar?

He did go on and the place went crazy. Japanese audiences were wildly enthusiastic, yet remarkably respectful. No steel barriers or battalions of bouncers were needed to halt any rush to the stage, just a rope or tape strung across neat and evenly placed posts. Like a queue in the post office. Very civilised. The honourable Japanese and their custom of bowing was taken to task by the dishonourable crew; prior to the show, a group of us would walk on to the stage, stand in a line and bow to the audience. The first few rows, having seen us, would stand up and politely bow back. We repeated our courteous gesture, getting more and more people to respond until the crowd caught on to what was happening, laughed and applauded. (Some nights we went down better than the band!)

They showed their appreciation by throwing things towards the stage during the shows, mainly paper streamers, confetti and colourful ribbons but also toys and gifts, with many cards of goodwill and confessions of undying love for Freddie, Brian, Roger or John. These tokens would be gathered up and put into boxes for the respective band member – 'member' being a common term used by the Japanese: 'Have members arrived? Which member do you play with? My favourite member is...' John Deacon was very popular in Japan and certainly Queen's biggest member in Japan. I know, I'd seen him in his tight trunks at the swimming pool.

These gift boxes and their contents (most of them) would be delivered to Queen's dressing room for after-show perusal. 'These are very nice, but where are the Sony TVs and Kawasaki motorbikes,' quipped Roger. Queen: multi-millionaires who were certainly not adverse to freebies or saving a few quid on a camera, digital watch or tape player. 'Could you just *slip* this in with the gear for me?' Many of the gift items from fans would be stored in the equipment or wardrobe flight cases for return to England, where in the sanctity of our warehouse at Elstree Film Studios, we spent many enjoyable sessions blowing up the cuddly toys with pyrotechnic flash powder and fireworks. Until you have slit open a small stuffed-toy penguin, filled it with flash powder, stuck a rocket up its rear, bound it tightly with gaffer tape, lit the blue touch paper, retired to a semi-safe distance and then watched it sail through the air finally to explode – you just haven't lived. Sorry, Brian.

For the crew, just touring Japan was a bonus itself and, when shows in the famed Budokan arena in Tokyo were sold out, the entire entourage got a bonus from the promoter. Queen's tour promoters, Watanabe Productions (aka What A Knob End), gave out ornately decorated envelopes with the Queen logo and colourful Japanese graphics. Inside were several hundred Yen (about £2). 'It's the thought that counts', and yes it was a nice keepsake, but where were the Sony Walkmans, Seiko watches and Nikon cameras that the rival promoter handed out to his visiting bands and crews? As the Japanese crew did all the physical loading and unloading and trucking of equipment, it is fair to say we had a relatively easy time in Japan compared to the band, who not only had to perform as usual, but also had a demanding schedule of interviews, TV, photo sessions, promotion, and the opening of supermarkets etc. And all with a polite smile.

When we arrived at a venue, a swarm of travelling Japanese crew, who took copious notes and drew diagrams of all the gear, would even have set up Queen's 'Back Line' of amplifiers, speaker cabinets and drum kit. Unfortunately, they set it up back to front and also measured the distance from the back of the stage – not the 23 feet from the front! Everything about a Japanese show was very orderly and efficient with legions of extra local crew, caterers, truckers, interpreters, travel and promoter reps, all constantly milling around.

In the early days, when the band were younger, leaner and

keener, they would play extra afternoon matinee shows at 2.00 pm, as the six o'clock show had sold out 'due to popular demand' as the saying goes. Some of these venues were large gymnasiums, which held a few thousand people. Travelling outside of the Western-influenced Tokyo to more school gymnasiums (tight white shorts and undergarments) and poignant sites of the nuclear explosions, Japan became even more foreign. This was the mid-1970s and many local inhabitants, who had never seen tall Westerners with long or blond hair, stopped in the street to gawk and point. They probably hadn't even seen *Starsky and Hutch* on TV. Or flared jeans. To travel, we took flights: All Nippon Airways – and all Nip Off again! – or buses and the Shinkansen (bullet trains), to places with some familiar names: Hiroshima, Nagoya, Osaka, and some not so well known: Himeji, Yamaguchi, Fukuoka and Kanazawa.

At the local nightclub in Kanazawa (where?), aptly named Zoo, we were made welcome with free entrance and complimentary drinks. Top place. After a few more rounds, when some of us drifted over to start talking to some local ladies, the management politely asked us to return to our table. Why? We were not causing any trouble (yet), the girls weren't complaining about our behaviour (yet), so what was the problem? Club policy dictated that: 'you must only sit at the first table that you sat at when you entered, and only with the people you arrived with. You may stay sitting where you originally were or you must leave without paying.'

Fine by us – see you at the hotel, girls. Getting girls back to your hotel room outside of Tokyo, unless they were registered, was very tricky and involved fire escapes, disguise, bribery, corruption and diversionary tactics to allay staff. If you did succeed in getting young ladies to your room, you could almost guarantee that they would stick to you like a rash, following you around on tour like a lap dog.

THE SEX POLICE

One evening in provincial Japan, The Sex Police struck! This self-righteous force consisted of those who had not pulled that particular evening and their task, fuelled by envy, was to stop or interrupt any activity by those who had got lucky. When they burst into the room of this particular victim, they did not catch him *in flagrante* but fast asleep... on my own – my companion having already left. She had to leave early as she was working; haunting houses by the look of her. Jet lag was regularly used as a scapegoat for ending up with The Dragon Lady of The East, resplendent with her dyed red hair, black lips and nail polish. An awesome sight: 'I'm telling you guys – she wasn't *that* bad.'

This particular lady was known as Ed the Spread, because she appeared to put her make-up on with a plasterer's trowel. Fuelled by adrenaline and not to be denied their fun, The Sex Police picked up the mattress, stripped it of the bedclothes and carried it complete with occupant, also stripped bare, to the hotel elevator, which was then dispatched to the ground-floor reception. When the automatic doors opened, it was just in time to greet a welcoming party of elderly Japanese ladies, who were at the hotel for a wedding. It turns out that a mattress is a very heavy and awkward item to grab quickly to hide your modesty, particularly if elegant, elderly Japanese are looking on incredulously.

Some of the female fans we met had a charming habit of leaving you with a novel memento in the form of their school badge. These metal lapel badges were beautifully crafted items, some in the shape of a heart with Mount Fuji lightly embossed, and on the reverse some etched Japanese characters. Head girl? Certainly top of her class!

ROOM AT THE INN

The band and the crew stayed in different hotels. Japanese hotel rooms, like the Japanese, were compact and often there would not even be enough space to leave your suitcase open. I hasten to add that the band did not stay in rooms like these. Many crew hotel rooms had plastic bathrooms, where everything was moulded into one piece: toilet, bath and basin, and there were illustrated diagrams of 'stick men' to show the Japanese how to use a western toilet as traditional 'squatters' – a hole in the ground – were the Japanese standard.

Staying and travelling separately in Japan, we consequently saw very little of Fred, Brian, Roger and big member John apart from shows, although we did catch the occasional glimpse of our employers at parties or in nightclubs.

During a Japanese tour, there were usually several stays in Tokyo and I sometimes stayed over with big member John in the spare room of his suite in the New Otani Hotel or Keio Plaza in Shinjuku, when we got in late from clubbing.

The clubs in Tokyo were great; we could go there and be treated well in spite of being young men behaving badly. The band were lauded at The Lexington Queen in Ropongi, a swish place frequented by western fashion models, but crew activities were mainly at Byblos in Akasaka, which was a disco laid out over several floors, with a DJ in a 'space pod', which travelled in a perspex tube between the various levels. Visiting bands and their crews were given licence to be as lively and boisterous as we liked – but without being physically destructive or violent. It was always in the back of your mind that every Japanese bouncer is probably some kind of martial arts expert.

Big member John, who was the only member of Queen I have ever seen being truly active on a dance floor, would love to 'pop up and bop in Byblos'. That's some tongue twister – particularly after the passing of a sake bowl the size of a UFO. A rhythm player with real rhythm, that's big member John. Upon entering Byblos, tickets were issued for your (watered-down) drinks; 'Delightful King' for guys, 'Beautiful Lady' for girls. Weekends were 'Delightful Saturday' night in Byblos. The club had a raised VIP section; a round table with curved bench seats around it. One evening, a famous Japanese actor came in flaunting some porcelain-skinned girl on his arm. He slid into the VIP area, where he ordered champagne – horrifically expensive in Japan. Unbeknown to the actor, the drum roadie from another rock band, feeling the effects of his excessive evening, had crawled under the seating for a recuperative sleep. The Japanese celebrity was served his bubbly in a stylish silver champagne bucket and was popping the cork when, suddenly, this dishevelled figure crawls out from his hole and throws up into the champagne bucket. He then crawled back under the bench and went to sleep. The stunned actor and his girl understandably decided to leave.

Through my Japanese girlfriend, I once met a local gangster in a Tokyo nightclub. He owned it – and several more. As we got talking, he told me that he hated Americans but loved and admired the English, because of our island race culture, proud military heritage and respect for our royal family...

'Hello, old chap – Peter Hince, the second Earl of Hammersmith and Fulham – so charmed to meet you.'

We got free booze, free food, a key ring and a free lift home. Japan seemed to be full of non-discreet clubs and bars – as they boldly flaunted neon signs outside. This magnificent, cultured country held ribald amusement for young men out for a good time back in the days before political correctness, and the way the Japanese interpreted English was a source of great fun – as in the names of some of the clubs: Image Lash, Club Goose, Refreshment House, Club Open, Club Brain, and, though I never encountered it, no doubt there was a Club Foot. A young Japanese sported a T-shirt with a slogan that read 'Let's go drive – New York – Los Angeles – okay?'

However, there were many wonderful diversions in Japan that did not include taking the piss, clubbing, sex and alcohol, so with plenty of free time we visited shrines, temples and palaces and, ever braver, trying the local cuisine.

The delicacy in Sapporo of having tiny, live baby eels in your beer is not my idea of fun, but the Japanese bodyguards revelled in crunching the heads before swallowing. Brian May was so horrified by this that he released his eels back into the adjacent ornamental stream.

I was personally horrified by some Japanese 'seafood' in

Osaka, where I witnessed an enormous whale being towed up a canal by barge. On top of the whale were several Japanese workers hacking at the corpse with axes.

Japanese nights brought the streets and seafood to life in neon-clad automatons, as giant crabs snapped their rotating pincers overhead, alongside fluorescent pink, smiling and singing shrimp. In vast hangar-like amusement arcades and Pechinko Halls, rows of people sat transfixed at machines, as thousands of metal balls rattled through channels and holes – occasionally vomiting out into the *win* tray. Weird. Then I saw the Mole Bashing Machine! This mechanical *amusement* involved hitting the heads of plastic, replica moles with a mallet, as they randomly popped up from their holes – a direct hit causing a squeak of pain and points on the board.

Japanese cities had convenient vending machines that perked up at night, in order to sustain the inhabitants with everything from beer and sake to toothbrushes and used schoolgirls' (white) underwear. These vividly illuminated machines became an amusing diversion as I staggered back to my hotel. The two drinks I just *had* to try from these machines were 'Tasty Drink' (no explanation, just a Tasty Drink) and 'Pocari Sweat'! I've no idea what a Pocari is – let alone if it perspires. This was supplemented by 'Diet Pocari Sweat'. Both were sweet sports-style drinks and actually not too bad with vodka – when there's nothing else. Even in our advanced state of drunkenness, we avoided the strange dried seafood snacks on offer from the machines. Desiccated squid wotsits? With ice cream? One popular Japanese dish we enjoyed was Shabu-Shabu: meat and vegetables cooked in boiling water inside a traditional pot. But it was the name that struck a nerve in the crew's funny bone. 'Shabu-Shabu' was used as a phrase of greeting or reaction, accompanied by a rapid twisting and shaking of the hand in the air as the arm moved in and out from the body – a Masonic roadie handshake.

We didn't understand Japanese but, when we spoke quickly in tour buzz words or roadie slang, our parlance could not be understood by anybody whether in Japan or New Jersey.

SCRUBBERS

Twentieth-century commercial icons sat alongside the traditional symbols and customs of Japan, one of these being the Bath House. Bathing may be an ancient and regular ritual in Japan but is not *quite* so regular with road crews. The full Bath House treatment was arranged for the entire entourage after a 1979 gig in Hakata, and the particular place chosen by the promoter had the novel name of The Hole In One Club. The Japanese have an obsessive passion for golf, and inside the club were 18 'holes', small wood-fronted cabins that looked like the entrance to a sauna. The hallways were covered in green plastic fake grass and the numbers of the 'holes' printed on triangular golf flags that could be turned to show the room was occupied. On the ground floor was a sparse dentist-style waiting room where we perched nervously on the edges of our hard chairs, before being summoned upstairs.

This was a totally new experience for me, having previously relied purely on my 'charm' to pull women – of my choice. I now felt the dread akin to having root canal treatment. I needn't have worried. My 'caddy' took me and my driving woods to Hole Eight, where the tiny room was split into two sections, a dry part, with a small single bed, mirrors, compact fridge with cool drinks and a dresser that had bottles of whisky and glasses full of cigarettes on offer. The raised section was the wet area with a deep bath, tiled floor with drainage grilles, a wooden 'U'-shaped stool and a *serious* high-pressure hose. With interchangeable nozzles. My hostess spoke no English at all and yet communication was quite clear as she bathed my body completely.

She then dried me down and got me sitting on the novel little wooden stool, where she started the 'treatment'. She continued alternating between this 'treatment', which brought tears to the eyes, and dumping me back in the bath, to which she added fragrant oils and beautiful rose heads. My oriental scrubber meticulously washed my hair and even brushed my teeth, before unrolling a thin rubber mat, similar to one used for aerobics, and spreading on to it warm oil, honey – and me. Then back in the bath! I think I played a par four. When I was squeaky clean, I sailed downstairs to a room of broad smiling faces. I had apparently missed out on an in-house speciality, including menthol, but I didn't care. I was feeling as cool, calm and collected as I ever had. And certainly the cleanest.

Reports filtered through a few years later that the place had burned down – maybe it was all that attrition and friction?

COMRADE RATSKI
After the end of the '82 Japanese tour, which finished at the

Seibu Lions baseball stadium in Tokyo, the gear was trucked to the docks south of the city, for customs clearance and loading into sea containers for the ten weeks' shipping back to the port of Felixstowe in England.

Three representatives of each department – Queen's gear, sound and lights – left the Akasaka dormitory hotel in the very early morning with Mako our interpreter, to guide us to the commercial port of Sakuragicho. We arrived to find the gear already unloaded and spread around a bonded warehouse in this vast complex. Allowing unsupervised handling of the gear was never a concern in Japan, as the labour teams were meticulous in their treatment of equipment. Our promoter's rep and appointed customs agent were in attendance, nodding and bowing, with the promise that Japanese customs officers would arrive soon.

While waiting, we took an unscheduled wander around the dock area to the dismay of our disciplined Japanese colleagues. Big international ports intrigued me; they were truly fascinating places with vessels from all over the world. Splayed against the concrete dock were goods and produce from exotic corners of our planet: weird-shaped fruits of arresting colour in wooden crates and high-tech electronics passing through in the other direction were reflected in row upon military row of shiny new compact cars bound for commercial invasion across the Pacific. In the near distance was the centrepiece – an enormous Russian ship with a gold hammer and sickle emblem against a red background, standing proud on its black funnel, as it caught the autumn sun. I had never been to Russia or seen anything quite so Russian (apart from the gallons of vodka we consumed) and was intrigued to see something real from behind the Iron Curtain. The customs officers duly arrived and without any delay or inspection stamped the paperwork for Queen's gear first. As I loaded the sea container, the highly efficient local crew blocked the wheels of the flight cases to the wooden floor and battened everything securely down, to protect against the onslaught of both the Pacific and Atlantic Ocean crossings.

Having finished my packing and other responsibilities, I suggested I return immediately to Tokyo, in order to catch the JAL night flight to London. Mako our interpreter said I could get a taxi at the main gates to take me to the station for a train to Tokyo. She would write all instructions for me in both Japanese and English so I would not get lost or confused. When we had first arrived at the port, our taxi had taken us in through the gates to the warehouse where our gear was lying. Now, though, we had no quick way of getting back to the entrance, which was not even visible beyond the hundreds of warehouses and cranes. Mako, in efficient Japanese manner, rallied the dockworkers, and finally they produced an ancient 'sit up and beg' lady's bicycle. Mako was the perfect business host and insisted that I ride the bicycle and she would walk beside. Being the perfect English gentleman, I couldn't accept. Mako being the perfect Japanese host insisted. Eventually, we compromised by taking it in turns for a short time but it was not very efficient; so I put Mako on the saddle and stood up on the pedals and propelled us forwards. It was hardly reminiscent of the romantic scene in *Butch Cassidy and the Sun Dance Kid* as we skewed and rattled past gawping and grinning dockworkers on our journey to the gates. It was all great fun and we reached our destination intact and both fell off the bike laughing. Mako, trying to stifle emotion behind her hands, pointed me towards a waiting taxi.

I said my goodbyes, but as I walked past the gatehouse the security guards leaped out to urgently halt me. Mako immediately skipped over to intervene, and eventually after a lot of oriental protocol it was explained to me that the guards thought I had jumped ship and was a deserter from the Russian vessel. I couldn't stop laughing at this, but they didn't – and demanded my passport. I didn't have it. Then Mako improvised, apparently telling them I was in the music business by the way she was miming playing lead guitar. I then remembered a laminated backstage pass in my jacket pocket. So, I offered this, and Mako took it and presented it to them as if it were some ancient talisman.

It worked a treat and I was given a double security guard bow before heading on my way with the white-gloved taxi driver to the station.

Arriving back at the hotel, I confirmed the flight and packed my bags with newly acquired Japanese swag of electronics, kimonos, woodblock prints and a collection of plastic food used as displays in restaurant windows. A cab took me to the far Narita airport and, as I was checking in, I spotted Fred and Phoebe, his personal assistant, with their posse of martial arts bodyguards. I went over to Fred's troupe and was invited to join them in the first-class lounge (I was travelling roadie class). Fred adored so many things about Japan and had stayed on to do some shopping – not for a new Sony TV or Nikon camera but antiques and art.

He was a man of superb taste (with the exception of one or two of his stage and video costumes) and had a fabulous art collection of the highest quality at his Kensington home. The JAL flight to London was via Anchorage, Alaska, where the plane landed for refuelling. Apart from viewing the impressive snowy mountains through the windows, there was nothing to see except a ferocious, stuffed giant polar bear standing upright in a glass case.

There was no first-class lounge available when transiting through Anchorage, so I sat on a bench in the shadow of the huge bear with 'cuddly bear' Phoebe, and Fred squeezed between us. Hardly SAS security: a large, camp, ex-Royal Opera House wardrobe 'mistress' and a scrawny, bedraggled roadie, but it did deter most of the curious who were pointing at us from a distance. Fred always preferred to remain anonymous, but would never refuse an autograph if asked.

Crystal, Queen's drum roadie, was gleefully signing autographs for a circle of young Japanese female fans on the bullet train platform one morning, when the precision-timed doors swished shut, leaving him stranded. We laughed. We always laughed at each other's misfortune. Japan was the first (and only) place I was asked for my autograph. I was a little embarrassed.

'You're joking?'

'No – I ruv roo, Latty.'

The Rat is a symbol of good luck and fortune in Japan and 'The House of the Rising Sun' remains a big hit for me.

CHAPTER SIX

ROAD DIVERSIONS

(ALL DAMAGE MUST BE PAID FOR – OR WILL BE DEDUCTED FROM YOUR PER DIEMS...)

HOTELS

On tour, hotels were your temporary home-from-home – but without having to clean up afterwards – which was very handy. Queen stayed at the most exclusive five-star palaces available and, if there was no suitable hotel where we were playing, then they would commute from the nearest 'civilised' city. Despite meticulous planning, one, two or even all four guys in Queen would sometimes move out and stay in another or separate hotels – because the toilet paper was the wrong colour, the lifts were too full of guests, or the Hanging Gardens of Babylon were not visible from the sweeping balcony of their penthouse suite. When staying in hotels during touring or recording, Queen would naturally wish to remain anonymous, so a system of aliases was devised that was also used on luggage tags and room lists:

Freddie Mercury: Alfred Mason.
Brian May: Chris Mullins or Brian Manley.
Roger Taylor: Roy Tanner or Rudolph de Rainbow.
John Deacon: Jason Dane or Judge Dread.

The crew, who did not use aliases (though it could have been useful at times) were housed in more durable chain establishments, such as Holiday Inn, Marriott and Trust House Forte – from which Queen were banned during the 1979 UK *Crazy* tour due to incidents in Liverpool, and a particularly raucous tour party in Brighton.

In the mid-1970s, a Holiday Inn hotel was considered a real treat, and in the USA, enthralled by all things American, I found that the bed in my room offered a service called 'Magic Fingers' which was activated by putting a quarter into the coin slot on the wall. This would cause the bed to tremble gently for a few minutes. It gave me a queasy and mildly disorientated feeling, an effect that could also be produced by spending considerably more than 25 cents on alcohol.

The bathroom had a personal message from the maid: 'Dear Guest' told me that the toilet had been sanitised for my protection, and a white cellophane band had been stretched over the seat – inviting me to try and piss around it... There were powerful and controllable showers that made washing almost fun, rather than the limp dribble of the handset attached to the H&C taps back home. When you have spent as much time in hotels as I have, you never need buy soap, shower caps, bath foam or sewing kits, ever again.

IN-HOUSE ENTERTAINMENT

Days and nights off while on the road could tax the recreational imagination; after being so intensely active, it could be difficult when there was nothing to do for the evening. Unusual behaviour was not unusual at all: drunken, hairy-arsed lighting guys walking through reception in ladies' underwear – the more modest sporting a dress. High riggers scaled the outside of a 30-storey high hotel for fun, and 18-stone soundmen would wear *Playboy* rabbit ears or vampire teeth in the restaurant. For reasons of practicality, crew hotels would be close to the show venues. It may have been convenient, but these places were often way out of town or in depressing grey areas next to a busy motorway or industrial park. There was not a lot to do except laze around our rooms watching TV, drinking, smoking, playing cards and having a good moan about the miserable life we had chosen.

When congregating in a hotel room, it was always advisable to avoid offering your own, as the aftermath could result in damaged accommodation that smelled like a mixture of a stale brewery and somewhere for curing fish. Bored, we devised original ways of amusing ourselves, which were generally at somebody else's expense. Obtaining a pass key to another room was one way: rearranging the furniture or hiding until the occupant returned with a new 'friend', then bursting out and catching them *in flagrante*. This was best accompanied by wastepaper bins full of iced water and a camera. Sachets of ketchup and mustard with the corners cut off were placed under the front of a toilet seat and it was hoped the victim would need to sit, and then be rewarded with streaks of sticky red and yellow sauce down the backs of the legs. As back-up, there was always the cling-film-over-the-toilet-bowl prank.

A technical trick that caused mayhem in another Forte hotel was to open up the control panel in a hotel lift and switch the connections around. All the floor numbers outside the lifts were taken off, and also switched around. The result was that if you selected floor eight, for example, when the doors opened the number on the wall indicated three, though you were actually on floor six. Chaos. The manager, on the verge of a breakdown, threatened to throw us all out, although he couldn't actually prove anything.

The Rotterdam Hilton was regularly the scene of mischief, as we were always 'lively' during trips to Holland, due to the quality of illicit merchandise available. After returning from one show, our choices of fun were limited to the expensive nightclub next door – full of businessmen who no doubt thought Barry Manilow was cutting-edge – or the nondescript hotel bar. So, wide awake, bored and with nowhere to go, we resorted to opening the tiny door flaps in the corridors that lead into a room's wardrobe, where you leave your shoes on painted foot prints for the porter to take away for cleaning. A square metal key was needed to open the flap – we improvised with a large flat-bladed screwdriver. What next? Swap the shoes with other rooms? Could be fun? Why not try and crawl through? More fun?

The space was very tight, and with a few grazes and chaffed ears only myself and Dick 'Dirt Ball' Ollet, our electronics boffin, were skinny and wiry enough to manage it. Now we had proven that it could be done by getting into our own rooms, the next step was to get into a room where one of the quieter crew members would be sleeping. Dirt Ball crawled in through the targeted hatch like some dishevelled commando, and once through he very rapidly came back out of the room's main door, slamming it and instructing us all to beat it – sharpish, and don't wait for the lift, take the emergency stairway. It was not one of the crew rooms, as it turned out. As he appeared through the wardrobe for his grand entrance, he had woken a man and his wife who were innocently occupying the room. They were obviously in shock – was this a robber? The wife's lover? Certainly not hotel security...

There is a lot of stereotyping of rock bands' behaviour in hotels, which usually includes damage and the image of televisions being thrown from windows. Some of it may be true, but it still has to be paid for. Rich rock stars can afford it – road crews generally cannot. Although an innocent party, I personally own a section of fire hose from the Holiday Inn in Toledo, Ohio. My share of the damage bill was $20 I believe. Also in Ohio is Cleveland, a grey industrial city on Lake Erie. The city is often referred to as 'the mistake on the lake'. Once home to Richfield Coliseum and the powerful stage workers' union, now home to the Rock and Roll Hall of Fame – and once upon a time to Swingos Celebrity Inn. Swingos was an early themed hotel and a retreat from the industrial Mid-West, where they gave out T-shirts to resident bands, had a dayglo pink fur-covered piano in the bar and tolerated rock 'n' roll behaviour in the brightly painted, gaudy rooms. Fred had the pink suite. True. Swingos was where I invented the 'Doctor's Comfort' cocktail on 22

January 1977. After scouring the corridors late at night with a bottle of Southern Comfort procured from John Deacon's onstage bar, I couldn't find any cola in the vending machines to mix it with. So I chose Doctor Pepper.

'This guy'll drink *anything*,' my female companion remarked.

But drunk with a glacier of ice from the huge dispensers on every floor it was numbingly effective.

After a final night's European show in Basel in summer 1977, several of the crew were both numb and financially lighter as a result of the large damage bill presented by a disgruntled tour manager a few days later. Per diems withheld until further notice. The high spirits began after the show in the Sporthalle, for an end-of-tour party involving the usual strippers, girls in leather flailing whips by strobe light and some audience participation. Thankfully, the booze was all provided, as the cost of a drink in a club in Switzerland can cause a coronary of the wallet. The revellers were still going strong when they returned to the crew's hotel and the second floor was trashed, a covering of broken glass filling the corridor. I was, on this occasion, an innocent bystander and resting in room 208 the whole time. I was enjoying sweet dreams, having been smitten all day by a lovely young Swiss lady.

We subsequently enjoyed a long-distance love affair, but I knew the writing was on the wall when I discovered her ex-boyfriend's machine gun, pistol and live ammunition in her Zurich flat. Young Swiss men had to do a year's military service and every year afterwards return to camp for a few weeks' refresher, all paid for by the wealthy Swiss authorities. 'Just keep your guns and ammo at home lads!' I don't see the idea catching on in Britain somehow. The Swiss may be pacifists, but it was time for me to leave.

Back to Basel – where the hotel manager was surveying the damage and taking notes with a staggering and very drunk stage manager who had assumed the role of responsible representative. They paced the corridor together and counted the broken light fittings:

'Look! There's two more there,' the stage manager pointed.

'But they are *not* broken?' exclaimed the hotel manager.

BASH – right hand. SMASH – left hand.

'They are now!' the stage manager giggled hysterically.

The Swiss, not usually known for their sense of humour, did not laugh with him.

If you ever win the lottery and decide you fancy causing a bit of mayhem in a hotel, can I suggest that, if you do decide to throw the TV from a window, you make sure you have the set switched on and attached to a long extension cable. This way, when it hits the deck it will give off a bigger and better bang, causing lots of sparks and colour, and may fuse a whole floor of the hotel into the bargain. This is not recommended if aiming for the swimming pool. Or people.

NOT FILM PEOPLE – AGAIN!

Despite their reputation for planning and meticulous work, Queen videos were sometimes produced quite spontaneously, and a few were done in the middle of a tour as 'live performance' clips. This meant the crew might have to give up days off or free afternoons to prepare the live set-up when we'd rather be off smoking backstage.

There was plenty of smoke and pyrotechnics for 'Tie Your Mother Down', from the *A Day at the Races* album. It was shot in February 1977 in Miami the day before the show at The Sportatorium – affectionately known as The Snortatorium, because of the plethora of South American substances available in southern Florida. Fred was wearing the oversized, shapeless white boiler suit that he started the current show in, before stripping it off to reveal a skintight white leotard. At his request, I had been sent out to scour London to find a boiler suit that was several sizes too big for him, which I finally located in an army surplus store in Euston. Fortunately, that was my only main contribution to Queen's stage wardrobe.

We used the live venue of the Forest National in Brussels twice – once for 'Don't Stop Me Now' in 1979 and years later in '84 for 'Hammer To Fall'. 'Another One Bites The Dust' was shot in 1980 during an extended sound check at The Joe Louis Arena in Detroit, and 'Fat Bottomed Girls' at The Convention centre in Dallas in 1978. 'Save Me' was shot at Alexandra Palace London on the '79 *Crazy* tour.

Video and film crews were always seemingly overstaffed, which was possibly a union requirement, but, whenever they entered our domain of the live show stage, they were often a pain. There seemed to be little consideration or respect shown for us, the set or the band's gear, and they would take ages to get anything done. There were very well-spoken girls and boys with clipboards rushing about trying to appear important. A couple of dozen of us could break down the entire show and load it into five 40-foot trucks in well under four hours, whereas a huge video crew would take forever to sort out a large van or two. Unlike the video crews, we did not have the luxury of regulation refreshment breaks after a certain amount of hours worked, or get paid 'golden' time for working extra hours.

That age-old adage 'the show must go on' was paramount to us, and it did go on despite any problems or setbacks. We would work till it was right and ready and not stop for a union tea break. We were bigger than that.

'I WANT IT BIGGER'

As Queen got bigger so did their show, and as the band were always looking ahead, spare time on the road would be spent working on ideas for the next tour's show. Queen were renowned for pioneering lighting rigs, and Fred, especially, would work closely with the lighting designer during rehearsals on the look and dynamics of the show. The brief was always the same: have lots of lights – more than any other band – and make them move. The 1977 *Crown* tour was the first lighting rig that moved and the following year brought the Pizza Oven or Italian Flag which, with its vast banks of green, white and red lights on a fan-shaped grid, generated enough heat to cook any pizza of your choice. This design was approved by the band in the dressing room after a show in the Deutschland Halle in Berlin, using a pack of cigarettes and a human hand to demonstrate its construction and geometrical movement. Notes were possibly made on the back of that cigarette pack. Shades of *Spinal Tap*...

The two computer-designed outer lynch-pins of the main grid were remarkably heavy and difficult to transport. They were affectionately referred to as Marie and Francoise, which was a term derived from lonely nights on the road, with no company for the night. Once in bed, you held your hands out in front of yourself asking: 'Who shall it be tonight – Marie? (left) or Francoise (right)?'

When this rig was first constructed in rehearsals in Dallas, a curious visitor came by to see what we were up to. Genesis were in town, as they had commercial interests based in Dallas. Genesis roadie Geoff Banks, knew Crystal and me, and asked if Phil Collins could have a quick look at our new lights – to see if we really did have more than Genesis!

Genesis – in the beginning: When formulating new ideas for Queen stage sets, the designers and production managers never consulted the people who knew Queen best and were closest to them on stage – their personal crew. Much time and money was wasted on ideas that may have looked grand and, on paper, worked fine, but they were never going to work in a practical way – especially things that restricted Fred's onstage fluidity. My voice was dismissed as being 'just a roadie' but I could have easily saved them, and the band, a small fortune – had they listened.

The 'dickmobile' is one idea that never saw the light of day, and was actually dreamed up by Fred (possibly in one of his more 'fuelled' moments). His idea involved a large pink, phallic-shaped container, like a fairground rocket ride that would be hung above the audience and hidden by black drapes. Before the show Fred was going to put on a disguise (false moustache?), and be ushered through the audience to a secure area, where he would climb a rope ladder and clamber into the device. As the house lights dimmed, Fred and his 'dickmobile', illuminated by spotlights, would be propelled over the raised heads of the audience towards the stage, directing a powerful beam of light from the end of the 'dickmobile', which was on course to enter a fibreglass pair of lips (with moustache?) on stage, where it would climax spectacularly.

'Fred – you must be fucking joking!'

Another of Fred's 'grand entrance' ideas was quashed immediately. He wanted to be carried on stage by Nubian slaves sitting in splendour upon a gold throne on an ornate platform – like Cleopatra. Another legendary Queen.

'Fred – I will look after your gear, run around for you, scuttle under the piano and risk life and limb for you – but I am NOT putting on a loin cloth and oiling myself up! And neither will any of the others in the crew!

So he settled for security guards dressed as Superman to hoist him on their shoulders and carry him on stage to perform 'We Will Rock You'.

All rock bands need a big drum riser (called a podium if you were Fred). Adjacent to the riser the rock band must have walkways, stairs and catwalks that protrude into the audience from which the more mobile band members would project. The whole set-up looked like a giant hamster cage with selected toys for the animals to play on. All that was missing was a tread wheel – but we all felt like we were on one anyway.

An expensive idea that lasted only two Queen shows in Europe 1982 was a raked stage which, using a principle from the theatre, gives the viewing punter a good perspective even from floor level. It looked quite dramatic, but, knowing Fred as I did, I gave it little chance of surviving. He liked to work on a stage with no hindrances, a smooth uninterrupted space; this raked stage caused problems, particularly during blackout or entry and exit – especially when he went to the piano. It was also hard on the Mercurial muscles and put a lot of strain on his ankles. After the first show in Gothenburg, Fred was not happy, so a lesser-angled version was tried for the next show in Stockholm. It still didn't work for him, which Fred angrily told the tour manager after the show: 'Stickells, I am not a fucking mountain goat – get rid of it!'

Edwin Shirley Trucking, Queen's European trucking company, got rid of it, and dumped it in their rock 'n' roll graveyard at Edwin Shirley's farm in Kent. Edwin himself was a loose cannon who could be relied on to show up anywhere, any time. A true rock 'n' roll animal, Edwin, known as Shambles, would fall asleep in his food at expensive band meals and get ejected from restaurants, clubs, bars and other places of evening entertainment for being too wild. He particularly enjoyed joining in with the backstage all-female mud-wrestling bouts. The only way his office could keep tabs on him was from the credit card statements that came in, showing which cities and countries he had recently visited. Great guy and sorely missed.

Another serious party animal no longer with us was the German promoter Mike Scheller. Like many of his countrymen, Mike worked hard and played *very* hard; he knew every nightclub and host in Germany and had a large capacity for enjoying life. On his birthday in 1982 which fell during two dates at the Sporthalle in Cologne, he threw a party after the first show at an establishment called the

Romer Bad – The Roman Bath. The place was in an uninspiring concrete basement below a parking garage in a suburban area. However, once inside, the decor was swish marble and mosaic tiles, and reminiscent of a Roman orgy venue. We were all instructed to undress and put on toga-style bathrobes. Everybody then congregated in the bar area beside a small, cold-water swimming pool. As we had all been tooting up and there was an air of anxiety, we became wallflowers – until after a few drinks, Trip Khalaf broke the ice by diving noisily into the pool.

Legendary in the wedding-tackle department, Trip's old chap was nicknamed the Home Wrecker, which really hurt if he smacked it on the side of your head. Things escalated into a huge party as there was just the band, crew and immediate entourage.

The girls were really into it, as they normally had to deal with fat, balding businessmen and clients from the 'extruded plastics and mouldings trade' or other boring blokes in suits. But, now, here was a group of young rock 'n' rollers who liked fun, and knew how to party. So, free from the restraints of business, the girls got into the spirit admirably. The premises had a small, raised pool where the water was bath temperature. Swimming in this with a few naked girls and a bottle of vintage Cristal champagne is a very fond memory. Even Phoebe, the male wardrobe mistress, and a confirmed bachelor, was doing the breaststroke alongside one of the record company ladies. I often wonder if it's like that in the after-match bath if you won the FA Cup at Wembley. Well, I had definitely scored a couple of times and one of them was surely going to put us into extra time.

So could I out-do (Sir) Geoff Hurst and score a hat trick plus one against the Germans in my personal version of the '66 World Cup final? There should have been medals awarded afterwards – all winners and no losers. The booze bill alone was a reported $30,000, quite a few bob back in 1982. Queen on tour meant larger amounts of everything. Big Time.

RELATIONSHIPS

The relationship between a roadie and his boss, who just happens to be a rock star, is like any other close or long-term partnership – it has its ups and downs. The ups include enjoying a laugh and joke in places like the Romer Bad. The roadie was effectively a technical valet, and, being the first in line, often took the brunt of his master's temper; and these moments could be the downs. Most of it was petty and could easily be shrugged off, but at times it could be hurtful and unnecessary. Once you accepted that musicians are not normal, rational people, then you would usually be able to deal with it. John and I were close as I spent much more time, especially socially, with him. He would confide in me, whereas Fred would rarely do that. John asked me on more than one occasion if my parents were still alive, as sadly he had lost his father when he was a boy. He was disingenuous at times about what he had achieved: 'You join a band... and then you get all this money! It's great.'

He told me he had considered becoming an actor – but it was too competitive.

Competition!? After all *you've* done John? We would listen to similar music together and he admired musicians with natural talent like Stevie Winwood. John wanted the voice of Steve Perry, singer with US rock band Journey. To be fair, he admits he wished he had any singers' voice. After he'd upgraded to a new model, he gave me his first Sony Walkman – the original blue cased unit, that were almost impossible to find or buy when first released in America.

However, despite my close relationship with John, I think the bond between Fred and me was somehow the deepest. Fred was almost nine years older than me, and that seemed to be a big gap. As I entered my twenties, Fred was almost thirty. I looked up to Fred, not just as a boss or famous singer in a band, but as a person. He was very intelligent, witty, humorous and of course remarkably creative. He was a single-minded man with great drive, who could often be dismissive, but would still listen to me. I would suggest things to him throughout the years and often get positive responses, and in some ways ours was an avuncular relationship. On the 1975 UK tour, when I had settled in working for Queen, I was told via management that Fred was very happy with me – which was at first a relief, but, of course, gratifying. He would rarely give direct praise, but once told me that he thought I was precocious. I didn't know what it meant then – I thought it might be offensive! When I learned what the word meant, I took it as a great compliment from somebody of Fred's stature. I had some great times and many laughs with Fred, though sometimes it could turn frosty between us. He could on occasion be very abrupt and dismissive, and virtually ignore people close to him, usually when stressed or if his love life was going wrong. When he chose to play 'The Diva' and not recognise my existence, I ignored him back, which would infuriate him further. But as always, these periods passed.

'How do you handle it with all those poofs and drama queens about?' other bands' crews would ask. The answer was with macho roadie bravado.

It was widely known that Fred was gay and so were Wardrobe Tony, Fred's assistant Phoebe and Paul Prenter, but everybody else in the regular entourage was straight. There were often gay hangers-on, including a bunch of leather-clad, moustached clones from New York that we dubbed 'The Pink Angels'. They sported stick-on Access-All-Areas passes on the back pocket of their very tight jeans. 'The Pink Angels' were led by a chap named Thor – and no doubt he was. Wasn't Thor the Norse god of thunder? Along with the 'Sisters of Perpetual Indulgence' – moustached men dressed as nuns, they all caused a storm backstage.

You have schools of whales, herds of elephant and a gaggle of geese so what would be a suitable grouping for a gay ensemble? There were many proposals but I believe a Huddle of Homos was the winner.

The sound crew built a barricaded pen from flight cases at the bottom of the stairs to the stage and put up a sign entitled Fort Faggot, in order to protect themselves from the outside, alternative world. The gay contingent always saw the funny side of these things. Fred may have been a gay man, but he was *our* gay man, on *our* team, *our* mate, *our* top striker and we cared for him greatly. We would support and stand up for him, just as we would for Wardrobe Tony who travelled with the crew.

At this point, you may have formulated the opinion that

roadies were disgusting, degenerate, foul-mouthed, sexist, chauvinist, bigoted, mindless oafs. Well, there may be a sliver of truth in that. The computer 'spell check' doesn't recognise the word 'roadie', but gives alternatives such as 'rude', 'rowdy' or 'toadie'. No comment.

Despite their excesses and ribald behaviour, the crew were professional and dedicated, and the partying never started until the show was finished and put away. Nobody was ever 'out of it' during the show; you could not afford to be with so many responsibilities. The Queen monster was a renowned well-oiled machine, and a very tight ship on the road. The crew were rightly proud of this and many of the freelance sound, lighting and production guys were in big demand elsewhere. I was approached with tempting offers by several big acts, despite not being on the transfer list.

Like a football team, a crew is made up of all character types, weak and strong, and everyone was fair game. Home and away. You need a solid defence and backbone, discipline, commitment, work rate, dedication to the team cause and spirit, tempered with striking individual performance. Having personal crew who are frustrated (failed) musicians is never a good idea, as they tend to spend their time jamming just to prove they are musically competent – and annoying everybody else intensely. It is far more productive to have a roadie with no musical aspirations, who knows the gear inside out and can fix problems immediately. In any case, guitars were tuned electronically on strobe tuners. I knew enough bits and riffs to do John's and Fred's sound check, and a similar number of chords to those splendid fellas Status Quo. Possibly one less… You could never have had a Queen fan on the road crew – it would simply not work. I, and others in the crew, liked some of Queen's music, but not all of it. We were objective, and as such highly professional – somebody who is obsessed with the band could never detach themselves like that. I seriously doubt if a fan would ever tell Freddie Mercury he was being stupid and to fuck off!

I did – and it was justified.

A fan might know by heart every lyric to every song he'd written. I didn't, but did carry the full catalogue of Queen album sleeves or published sheet music to refer to when needed. More than once during a show, when he had a mental blank, Fred asked me what the chords were to a particular song. Fortunately, a lot of Fred's songs were written in E flat, so that's what I would suggest. He always seemed impressed I knew.

My limited musical ability was unexpectedly put to the test during a show in America, when John caught my eye and beckoned to me in the middle of a song. He came over to his electronics control rack and shouted in my ear, 'I'm bursting for a piss – I've got to go!

'Right – OK, I'll sort it.'

Whatever that meant? I found his minder, who was on the back corner of the stage, and we agreed that as soon as the song finished he would whisk John straight off stage to the nearest rest room. I got John's attention and gave him the thumbs up – miming that when the blackout came at the end of the song (I did a cut-throat sign) he should come off stage and I would take his guitar. I mimed that by using Air Guitar – or Air Bass actually.

This seemed a great idea – except nobody else in the band, the other musicians, knew – especially Fred. The song ended, blackout on stage and John rushed over and thrust his bass towards me before skittering down the steps and dashing off with his minder into the concrete corridor at the back of the arena. The audience were showing their appreciation and Fred was taking bows and thanking them.

'Hey – you guys are great!'

More applause.

'This next song is one written by John Deacon.'

Fred turned and gestured to where he thought John should be. He wasn't there. Meanwhile, I changed John's bass for the one he would (hopefully) be using in the next song.

'This song is for all of you who like a bit of boogie – are you ready?'

The audience acknowledge that they are.

'Are YOU ready!!'

The audience was but John's wasn't. Fred looked at me with a puzzled frown that says, 'Where the hell is John?' I responded by giving him the thumbs up – no idea why I did that… so he introduced the song: 'This is "Another One Bites The Dust"!'

Roger started the beat and the band expected John's classic bass line to kick in. It doesn't, and there's still no sign of John.

I have a Musicman Stingray bass guitar around my neck – and it's live. I know this one – it's quite easy, I had played it in sound check with Roger and Brian. But I have no discernible talent for proper playing. That doesn't stop me.

'That's it – I like it – I like it!' Fred chants.

143

'Oh God!' I groan.

'Come on – move it move it.'

Fred again.

After those initial few bars, John returns from having a piss and the bass is returned to its rightful owner. John was relieved, but nowhere near as much as I was!

HEALTH AND EFFICIENCY

That incident certainly hardened my arteries and gave me palpitations, but staying fit on the road was taken for granted as we were all young men in what we thought to be peak condition, and, no doubt, at that age felt immortal, taking on everything thrown at us – and winning. However, there were the usual colds and flu to contend with plus occupational knocks, scrapes and bruises, but the show had to go on and so did we, with adrenaline, stimulants and B12 vitamin shots. Queen themselves, although just this side of immortal, were also susceptible to ailments, and in the 1970s when we played a lot of back-to-back shows some had to be cancelled because Fred's vocal chords and nodes were suffering badly. In '77 John slipped in a hotel shower, smashing through the glass door – aahh! Scenes from *Psycho*. He played the last few shows of the tour with his stitched hand strapped up and painkillers running around his system. Brian's health was a little fragile and in the early '70s he had suffered with stomach ulcers and hepatitis.

Brian May and his good friend Eddie Van Halen partied together in 1982 when the bands found themselves in the same hotel in Portland, Oregon. The Queen band crew, who had also been invited, were challenged by the steroid monsters posing as Van Halen's security and refused entry until identification, invitation and verification were resolved. American rock bands often go over the top, taking themselves far too seriously, and some are escorted by as many men in suits and dark glasses as in a presidential motorcade. 'Security' all had walkie-talkies with ear pieces and it was comical to hear the conversations:

'He is leaving the room, he is now approaching the elevator... the doors are open, it's clear – we are on our way to the lobby – standby everybody.'

Give us a break!

Brian was not really the same hardened party animal as Eddie Van H, and, as a result, was in the bathroom on his knees, calling for 'hughie' and 'buick' on the great white porcelain telephone. At some point he slipped and cut his head, spilling a bit of claret. He was rescued by John 'Tunbridge' Wells, his minder (without walkie-talkie or even a transistor radio), who assured Brian he would not let him die.

'A picture of health' is hardly a phrase you would use to describe Brian 'Jobby' Zellis, Brian May's roadie, as he was slight in build with wiry little legs, pasty faced and poorly looking. He turned up one day, his usual refugee-looking self and sporting tight black Max Wall 'ballet' trousers, and a new white leather jacket with a high stand-up collar, studs, sequins and other sparkly bits. Trip immediately nicknamed him Elvis Belsen.

Now, nobody likes injections and everybody loathes the idea of big needles injected into your bum. On the '76 US tour, it was discovered that one of the roadies from The Cate

145

Brothers support band had contracted hepatitis, so the whole entourage had to be checked by a doctor and then get a shot. This unwelcome news was given at the Auditorium Theatre, Chicago where, post show, we had to wait for our turn. When my number was up, I waited in the corridor outside the dressing-room-cum-temporary-surgery, as Fred came out rubbing his hip. His expression was half grin, half scowl – what was he trying to say? Inside, the doctor rummaged in his black bag and, without looking up, told me to drop my jeans and pants to my thighs and lean over the end table. As I did so I saw his reflection in the dressing-table mirror. Oh my God! He was coming at me with something the size of Thunderbird One. That was the first – and last – time I ever bent over in a dressing room.

One condition that I and several others suffered from was 'gig butt', which is referred to in medical reference books as chaffing or nappy rash. The constant movement and sweating of a day's toil in tight denim caused a very sore bottom crease and crotch, despite regular showering and the application of talcum powder. A simple remedy that I found worked perfectly was to smear the affected area with Vaseline petroleum jelly. I had a bad case of 'gig butt' after load out one night on a tour of Europe and was not looking forward to driving our hire car the eight hours or so to the next destination in that condition. I slipped off to the toilet with my jar of Vaseline, but got some very funny looks from a few of the entourage who had seen me entering the gents lavatory with a large tub of lubricant, especially as I was Fred's roadie. In fact, because I was Fred's roadie, many fans thought I was also gay. I quickly countered that rumour by announcing that I was certainly not gay – but my boyfriends were...

All the concerns about hearing damage caused by rock concerts are not without substance, as my hearing has definitely been impaired by being in close proximity to the raw source on stage. There was no concept of health & safety back then and rock shows in general are not a healthy environment to be exposed to for years on end; the smoke, dry ice and pyro dust are on a par with being a chain smoker or an asbestos miner. The intense physical toll on the body and all the bumps, knocks and scrapes in extremes of temperature, combined with irregular working hours and meals, make it a tough young man's vocation. It's a vocation for tough young men, who drink the flight to Tokyo dry of sake and then fill their immigration forms in as The Archbishop of Canterbury. Or in a similar state upon entering Australia, when asked if they had a criminal record, reply, 'I didn't think you needed one any more.' ('Come with me please, sir. We can have a chat in my room. Are you allergic to latex rubber?')

Among that same bunch of tough young men were the guys who complained about breaking a fingernail when loading a truck or that the rain was ruining their new satin tour jacket and that they had no mains adaptor for their hairdryer.

And they had the nerve to call Fred a poof!

IT'S A HARD LIFE
Touring toughens you up physically (if you work hard enough) and certainly mentally. It also protects you from the

outside world and its realities. Receiving personal letters in hotels was exciting but slightly unnerving, as only the few people who held itineraries back home would know where to write to. During an occasional phone call to my mum, I discovered that my favourite uncle was ill and would not be getting better. My dad's elder brother had been one relative I could always identify with, because he was unconventional, played the fool and didn't take life too seriously. He had also been a bit of a rascal who liked the ladies. I was naturally upset, but touring spared me hospital visits, facing family members and the reminder of what appeared inevitable. Later in the tour, I received a letter from mum telling me he had died. Again, touring spared me more grief and the unpleasantness of a funeral. Insulated by my other family, rock 'n' roll, I avoided the intensity of personal drama and events, sometimes only seeing my family once a year.

Unless you made a huge effort to catch up, current affairs, world disasters or sporting achievements would pass by unnoticed when on the road. When Margaret Thatcher won the general election in 1979, we were on tour in Japan and I watched some of the news footage on TV in my hotel room, but it felt surreal, in a strange language, with manic presenters and weird, colourful graphics.

We lived in a parallel universe on the road, genuinely not knowing the days of the week – but what did it matter? We didn't get weekends off, had no other agenda to adhere to and were beholden to the tour itinerary. My life was geared to being in permanent transit and I was totally dedicated to Queen. Their career spared me many of life's domestic worries: no wife, kids, car or even plants to water. My utility and other bills went directly to the bank for payment, my suitcases were left leaning against the wall on one side of my bedroom, and I knew my passport number and US visa details by heart. I was always ready to leave...

My rock career, though hard work, was relatively easy; I was footloose and fancy free, so just followed the master's tune and my salary went into the bank every month. But looking back with the wisdom of experience, I now realise just how difficult it was for the band, balancing the pressures of fame and enormous expectancy with a home life. Families and relationships can easily take up most of your energy and devotion, so how do you cope when you just happen to be in one of the world's biggest rock bands? Something has to give along the way. It's often easier to make decisions when you are young with fewer responsibilities, but it is also easier to make mistakes.

Generally, I was happy doing my job and when the tour was going well – and you were pulling – the world was a marvellous place. But then along came days when you just wanted to jack it all in and do something else. These were known as the 'days of doom'...

CHAPTER SEVEN

DAYS OF DOOM

(WELL, WHOSE FUCKING FAULT IS IT THEN?)

O n the road there were occasional days when the gods conspired to make things as difficult as possible for us; when the gremlins, goblins and gollum's cohorts are released en masse from their evil lairs, and all science and logic are over-ruled to bring chaos, panic, tantrums and a very unhappy Mr Mercury.

The main reason for a 'day of doom' was equipment malfunction, but when you consider that on a Queen show there were literally billions of individual electrical component connections that were subjected to constant travel, temperature change, vibration and intense use, then it is not really surprising that something goes wrong eventually. However, try telling Fred that, when his microphone is cracking up.

CHICAGO: CHICAGO STADIUM, 28 JANUARY 1977

This was one of the coldest winters in US history, and, despite some of the 'tough' crew wearing tights (sparkly ones raided from Elton John's wardrobe trunks at our Elstree warehouse) under their jeans to keep warm, it was bitter – it actually hurt to breathe – and that wasn't because the tights were too tight. The truck carrying the Clair Brothers' sound system and Elton John's Steinway grand piano, which Fred was borrowing for the entire tour, was blown off the road during a blizzard en route from Canada to Chicago. This was a big tour for Queen, as they were now starting to play the big arenas. Chicago was a major city and the huge Chicago Stadium a true rock 'n' roll venue, covered by the press in detail. Despite the problems caused by the weather, Queen insisted on making a big impression for their first performance at the home of the Chicago Blackhawks ice hockey team, so a sound system was scraped together, including equipment imported from a rival sound company over the border in Canada. The weather was so cold – about minus 40 degrees with the wind chill coming off the lake – that electrical cables and leads became so stiff they could not be laid out properly and risked breaking internally. The vinyl flooring that was used to cover the supplied stages and give a smooth surface was folded solid and cracking. Spirits were not high and the rented piano was not as grand as the grand Fred was used to. I had managed to fit a pick-up to amplify it from the spares I carried but, as the band were taking the stage for the show, I was still adjusting the pick-up and the piano tuner was still tuning!

To their credit, the band never complained once and Brian

kindly thanked us all for our efforts during the show – which got a cheer from the crowd. To be fair, rock audiences – and US rock audiences in particular – will generally cheer anything: 'Thanks to our crew!' – big cheer. 'I just farted!' – cheer. 'This is a great rock 'n' roll town!' – bigger cheer, 'and you're the best audience *ever!*' – HUGE cheer.

The show was also marred by somebody throwing eggs on the stage, Brian slipping and falling from the smashed eggs. Fred got angry and threatened not to carry on if certain 'motherfuckers' didn't stop their behaviour. We carried on as always, and then loaded the gear out in sub-zero temperatures and cutting gales that sent a very sharp whistle up your tights. Are my seams straight in these…?

SAARBRUCKEN: LUDWIGSPARKSTADION, 18 AUGUST 1979

Saarbrucken was a one-off outdoor show in '79 during recording of *The Game* album.

Queen topped the bill, and it played host to many other acts including the late Rory Gallagher (who Fred adored as a guitarist – Taste, Gallagher's late 1960s band, were one of Fred's favourites and a big influence). The set was a rejigged one from the previous *Pizza Oven* tour and was to include many specials: fireworks, a water fountain at the end of the extended central catwalk, extra pyrotechnics and, of course, the usual enormous moving lighting rig.

The whole event started badly as the crew had missed the connecting flight on the small prop plane to Saarbrucken because they were all busy perusing the wares in Dr Muller's sex shop at Frankfurt airport.

Our bland hotel, adjacent to the Ludwigspark Stadion was a Novotel, generally known as a NO hotel. The sound check day was OK – but on show day it poured with rain most of the time, the crowd numbers were less than expected and none of the special effects worked: the fireworks, pyro or fountain. There was a total power failure during the show, and at the end of the performance the lighting rig seized, failed to move and all the lights went out. The only redeeming factor was that Roger had arrived with his hair newly streaked and dyed, but it had gone wrong and turned green.

INDIANAPOLIS: MARKET SQUARE ARENA, 11 SEPTEMBER 1980

The usual grand finale of Queen's live set (before encores) was a chain of pyrotechnic explosions along the front of the stage, which Fred would 'machine gun' using his wand mic. On this particular evening, I hit the individual switches to activate the effect but nothing happened. Fred freaked out. He had already been tense during the show as the onstage sound monitoring of his voice was not up to his high standards. The reason, partly psychological, was that the band's preferred monitor engineer, Jim Devenney, had already been booked to do a Fleetwood Mac tour along with Trip Khalaf, Queen's regular sound engineer, and would not be available until later in Queen's US tour.

Ray, Jim's replacement, was very competent but Fred, and to a degree the others, were struggling to get the balance right. Fred claimed that if he couldn't hear himself clearly then he had to sing harder and his voice would suffer as a result. (The simple solution of asking Brian and his 'wall of death' guitar amplifiers to turn down was not an option – he would only turn up again.) After the pyro failed to explode – Fred did! Rushing over to stage right where I had the ignition control box, he attacked it and me with his mic stand. I had never seen him like this – he was possessed!

Then during the first encore – and still very fired up – all hell broke loose as Fred smashed and wrecked anything he could find on stage, using his mic stand as a double-handed machete. Finally, he took out his wrath directly on the monitor console. Ray had jumped off stage as John threw his bass guitar at the console and Roger trashed his kit. The second encore didn't calm Fred down either. Particularly as he had to do it without any onstage monitors – which had all been turned off.

The local union crew, who had been operating the spotlights, raved about the show, as they thought all this was part of the act! Emotions run high at rock shows and heat-of-the-moment incidents do happen, and are as quickly forgotten, but this was too much – it had gone too far.

As we surveyed the onstage wreckage, Gerry Stickells tried to keep the peace on both sides. I was summoned to the dressing room and naturally expressed my disgust at being treated in this way. I only took on the responsibility of firing the pyro through loyalty to the band and because I knew the timing and songs so well – I did not set the fucking things up! It was the same with the strobe effects, drum riser lights and audience/platform lights: I operated those from a remote control. Again, not strictly my job, but yet more responsibilities I took on when asked, simply because I knew the timing and would get it right! Fred was not in a rational mood and wouldn't believe some of the things he had done, and insisted I raise my shirt to show proof of any injury he had caused. When I reiterated, 'You hit me, Fred!' he just said, 'Goodbye then, Ratty.'

The rest of the band groaned in disbelief at what was happening and I turned and walked out of the dressing room and back on stage to continue loading out. Ray and the sound crew had all quit in protest and it now appeared I was a free agent. Crystal said he was walking off as well and so did lighting designer Jimmy Barnett and other crew. Brian and Roger came out to placate us, giving assurances that Fred was very sorry at what happened and to please stay, but it appeared to be too late.

Why did Fred not come himself?

Gerry Stickells, ever the diplomat, told us to relax and enjoy the next couple of days off and see how we felt then. As I was loading the Queen band gear truck for what I thought would be the last time and filling my mind with other bands I might work for, Paul Prenter rushed up, as usual bright red, frothing and ranting.

'You mustn't leave, he needs you – you know that' was the message he barked in my ear as 'incentives' were pressed firmly in my hand.

The buses were loaded with cases of booze in an attempt to calm us down and buy us off. Predictably, we all got very drunk, stoned and fucked up on the overnight bus journey to Hartford, Connecticut. Retching into a stinking chemical toilet on a moving tour bus is not in any way glamorous, but demons needed to be exorcised.

Hartford was a short drive from where Ray (now a free agent) had a family beach house, so we hired a car and set off for a day of chilling by the water. The following afternoon, all of Queen showed up for sound check – including Fred who at that point in Queen's career very rarely came to sound checks, except for the first show or two of a tour and big outdoor venues. Fred's first action on entering the arena was to go out into the middle of the floor area where Ray was working, and briefing the new sound crew. Fred quietly gave his apologies to him and the rest of the sound crew.

A rare gesture – that was appreciated.

Fred did not apologise directly to me, but over the next few shows he gave me the odd wink, smile and gesture as if to say: 'Yes, okay, I know I was out of order. Can we carry on?' He also made the occasional remark, such as when I was preparing his onstage drinks: 'You're not going to poison me, are you, Ratty?'

'No, Fred – I'll just swap your onstage water for neat vodka and gin.'

'That's fine dear – I'll look out for it.'

We got over it.

MELBOURNE: SPORT AND ENTERTAINMENT CENTRE – 17 APRIL 1985

During a four-night residency with *The Works* show down under, a show was plagued – lights failed, speakers blew, monitors cut out and the biggest and most obvious malfunction to an audience – Fred's microphone – started to break up, distort and cut out while he sang at the piano. This had never, ever happened before. Immediately, I improvised and took his wand mic from under the piano, switched it on and held it up for him to sing into. As I balanced the mic precariously, Soundman, Tony 'Lips' Rossi, attempted to change the piano mic. This proved unsuccessful and, when Fred took to the stage for another song, the whole system had to be changed again. (The problem proved to be a faulty cable, remarkably unusual on a static microphone.) When Fred reached the dressing room after the show, he was furious about the microphone incident, screaming, 'And then all these roadies congregated around, pushing dozens of microphones in my face! I wouldn't have minded if they had been cocks – but this was ridiculous!'

Mr Mercury liked to be dramatic. Melodramatic at times.

He was still fuming long after the show, so we all took off for the Chevron Club to drown our sorrows, fuelled by poor-quality and very overpriced Australian cocaine.

We were comforted by the direct charms of the local 'Ozzie' girls and went back to our hotel to carry on numbing the pain. When my companion and I finally crawled back to my room from the rooftop swimming pool at about 5.00 am, she introduced me to a few indigenous phrases pertaining to the sexual union between man and woman: 'Do you want to slime?', 'Have you arrived yet?' and 'That's some "fat on" you got there!' (This does not mean overweight.) Then, when in the midst of our passion she called out, 'Oh, Ratty, me fanny's on fire, me fanny's on fire!' I was so taken aback I fell out of bed laughing and did my back in; so spent the next day being treated by the tour physiotherapist.

CHAPTER EIGHT

RECORDING

(ROADIE KILLS POP STAR)

Despite those rare Days of Doom on the road, touring was vital to the success of a band, and fundamentally to promote their recorded music. So the next stop for Queen after global gallivanting was to think up and produce new product – their fresh pound of vinyl for the record company Shylocks.

Recording: a process performed in recording studios, where records are recorded for record companies.

Record companies: organisations where artists' records are manufactured, promoted and distributed.

Record company executives: a professor ran an experiment on how dogs' and their owners' behaviour echo each other. He took three people from different walks of life and put their respective dogs in a sealed room – each with 12 dog biscuits. After an hour, the professor returned and appraised the first dog, which belonged to an accountant. The accountant's dog had placed two biscuits next to three biscuits, and in between made a + sign from two biscuits. Over to the right was a pile of five biscuits: 3+2 = 5. 'Very good. A success.' Next, it was on to the civil engineer's dog, which had built a tiny 'A' frame bridge from his biscuits. 'Excellent. Proves my theory.' Finally, he approached the record company executive's dog, who had eaten all his biscuits, fucked the other two dogs, taken the rest of the day off, and on leaving asked if there were any printed T-shirts of the event going free.

No surprises there.

'Queen – that "Bohemian Rhapsody" thing? It was all right, a flash in the pan though – they'll never last.'

'Nice video, but yeah – that glam thing is over. Finished!'

The dogs (talking) bollocks.

Some of these oscillating record company people stuck their heads so far up the collective ass of Queen they could wear them as a form of hat. Or crown.

It's a remarkable thing; there are now as many record company 'executives' who claim to have 'broken' Queen, and seen the wonderful potential of the six-minute 'Bohemian Rhapsody', as there are currently people living in China.

And of course *none* of them *ever* wanted to edit it...

ALL PART OF THE JOB

During their career Queen used numerous recording studios around the world, where I spent countless hours trapped in timeless limbo. Was it exciting being one of the privileged few to be there as the band developed and recorded new songs? No, mostly it was bloody boring! And to think I passed my first year City and Guilds in mechanical engineering to hang around waiting, making tea, collecting Chinese and Indian takeaways and feeding parking meters for a quartet of talented musicians. I was wasted; I could have been a qualified turner and fitter by now.

Making records, just like film – another glamour industry – is often tedious and repetitive, as 'take after take' is put on tape until it is perfect. Then once more – just to be sure. During the recording of *A Night At The Opera*, I was taken on as a full-time roadie for Queen and spent my days and nights commuting across London to the various studios being used. I was picking up an antique harp for Brian to play on 'Love Of My Life', from an equally ancient woman in Barnes, south London, when I thought, 'Queen is a rock band – is this rock 'n' roll?' Then I listened to snippets of *Opera* being sung in the control room, and when I heard other sections of what was to become 'Bohemian Rhapsody' I thought it was going to be a new intro tape for the live show. Wrong – it was a rather successful single.

Various London studios were used for their different merits: live room, dead room, control room or even recreation room. The studio with the magic feel was Sarm Studios in Brick Lane in unfashionable Whitechapel, in the East End of London. The first 24-track studio in the city was situated here in a pokey basement. Despite this, Queen produced very innovative early material here.

Wessex studios was an old converted chapel in Highbury, north London, and the place where, in 1976, we first witnessed punk. The Sex Pistols were also booked in and doing their early recordings, when nobody really knew who they were. Johnny Rotten was sitting in the lounge area on a brown corduroy seating unit, wearing a lime-green, mohair jumper and ripped jeans. Safety pins were inserted in every available space and his hair was dyed a ginger hamster colour, spiked and lacquered. Despite this, he seemed a quiet, pleasant sort of bloke – he didn't snarl at me when I asked if I could change the TV channel, just shrugged and nodded. What was all this fuss about these guys?

One afternoon when Queen were working in the control room, Sid Vicious stumbled in, the worse for wear, and addressed Fred: 'Have you succeeded in bringing ballet to the masses yet?' (A reference to a quote Fred had made in the music press.)

Fred casually got up, walked over to him and quipped: 'Aren't you Stanley Ferocious or something?', took him by the collar and threw him out. So much for the mean edge of punk...

During those recording sessions at Wessex, Fred defied the ethos of punk and purchased his first car – a Rolls-Royce Silver Shadow. Mine was a rusty old Morris Mini. He was very excited and proud, so insisted that we should share in his delight. Fred crammed as many of us as possible inside the car and got his driver to take us for a spin around the leafy streets of Highbury. One of the crew pointed out that the silver lady mascot on the bonnet of a 'roller' was a target for thieves – and they were often wrenched off.

'I'd cut their fucking hands off if I caught them!' he said with some venom.

'We Will Rock You' was recorded at Wessex, the 'boom

boom chas' at the start of the song being recorded by all available feet, including the crew, stomping on some wooden platforms, while hands clapped the off beat in the cavernous room. The result was soaked in echo, multi-tracked and given some studio magic by engineer Mike Stone to create an introduction that has become an anthem throughout the rock and sporting world.

Early one morning, after a long 'We Will Rock You' session at Wessex, a very tired Brian was driving home at dawn in his new Jaguar XJS. There was black ice on the Marylebone flyover. Whoops! Brian was shocked, but unhurt. The car, however, was trashed and Brian's 'Fireplace' – his true pride and joy, the famous 'Red Special' guitar he built with his father – was in the boot. Fortunately, it only suffered some surface damage, but the light fibreglass case had been little protection. After a chat with Brian, I commissioned CP Cases to build something that would survive a truck being driven over The Red Special.

FANCY A CHAT?

Queen were openly very competitive and studio discussions often brought out petty rivalry with other bands' successes. Few were above criticism.

'I see they're doing three nights at Madison Square Garden.'

'Huh! They'll *never* fill them! *Never* sell out.'

'They already have, Rog.'

'Well – the tickets must be very cheap...'

'I love this band, the one at number one.'

'What! Are you joking? One-hit wonders!'

'I still like them.'

'What do you know?'

'That they've sold loads more copies than Queen's last single…'

'What! Never! Get EMI on the phone, now!'

Two artists above criticism were Jimi Hendrix and John Lennon. Two icons praised and revered by all of Queen for their work, style and attitude. Fred idolised Hendrix, and in the sixties had gone to see him play live whenever possible. He loved the sounds Hendrix drew from his guitar and would often try to emulate his hero, but, accepting he did not have Hendrix's phenomenal guitar skills, would bang an acoustic guitar and vocalise 'taka taka taka taka – chak chak' and other things like that.

Gerry Stickells, Queen's tour manager, had been Hendrix's roadie, then tour manager, until his untimely death. Often the one to talk Fred around when he was being 'difficult' on tour, Gerry was a good diplomat and Fred was impressed with his 'Hendrix history'. This is the man who told Hendrix that the Blue Boar service station on the old A1 was a place that all the bands stopped at.

'You mean like a club, man?'

'Uuuh – yeeeaaaah…'

Hendrix in his wild attire sauntered into the transport café, guitar in hand, expecting to jam with other musicians. He didn't get a jam; he got a fry-up with brown sauce and some *very* strange looks from burly lorry drivers.

COUNTRY ESTATE

The mid-1970s: the era of shag-pile carpet, droopy moustaches, rubber plants and rock bands using the country house studio – to get away from it all.

Queen used Ridge Farm, a family-run rehearsal facility in Surrey where the band, their partners and the crew all lived together. After ideas had been formulated for the *A Day at the Races* album, plans to go to Portugal with a mobile recording unit were cancelled, and we stayed closer to home – Richard Branson's The Manor in Oxfordshire. This was the sweltering long-hot-summer of '76 and it certainly was good to be out of stifling London in the fresh air of the country. In keeping with the Branson/Virgin hippy image, some of The Manor staff were Buddhists who chanted in the attic (we had thought the incessant droning that kept us awake was some old Steve Hillage or Mike Oldfield tapes). This was the first album Queen had produced themselves, assisted by long-standing studio engineer Mike Stone.

To relieve the pressure between recording sessions, there was a TV lounge where we could watch *three* different channels. In the days before video recorders we all had to be there on time – *The Benny Hill Show* was everybody's favourite. A different era. It was the Montreal Olympics that summer and dainty dashes were made, by Fred in particular, from the studio to the TV lounge to see the live finals of the various athletic 'dashes'.

One evening, during dinner at the grand baronial dining table of The Manor, there was a phone call from Freddie's girlfriend, Mary Austin. She had left The Manor earlier that day feeling unwell and returned to London. She now confirmed it was an ear infection. Mary was Freddie's long-term lover, who supported him greatly in every way in the early days of Queen. They were at that time living together at his newly acquired flat in Kensington.

A year or so later, they parted as lovers and Fred bought Mary a flat at the end of his road, so they would still be close. She was the true love of his life, and remained close, loyal and supportive until the untimely end of Freddie's life. Mary inherited the majority of Freddie's estates and royalties.

'I have to go now! I have to go to Mary!' he stated emotionally to everybody gathered at the dinner table.

Fred would need to be chauffeured because he never drove – never even attempted to learn. But he did have an opinion on motor vehicles, and, when shortly before recording at The Manor John mentioned he was going to buy a Ford Capri, Fred told him that model of motor car was not suitable for a member of Queen. John subsequently purchased a sporty Jensen interceptor.

With dinner over, I offered to take Fred, not in a sporty two-seater, but in a VW van – the John Reid Management vehicle that I was using.

I was shot a cursory glance of Mercurial disapproval. The manageress of The Manor diplomatically offered the studio car: a Ford Cortina estate.

With Fred sitting up front beside me, we set off. I felt a bit uncomfortable with the car's brakes, which were spongy and slow to respond. During the journey, we chatted about music and things in general, but I sensed Fred was tense – he really cared about Mary and wanted to be there with her as soon as possible. Approaching London at a roundabout on the A40, I changed down a gear and pressed the brake. Nothing. Oh dear! I managed to swerve and steer the car most of the way around the roundabout until it veered into a pile of drainpipes. As I fought to control the car, in my mind flashed the headline that might appear in the *Melody Maker*: Roadie Kills Pop Star. The car came to an abrupt halt, and Fred and I looked over at each other and confirmed we were both all right. Completely free of injury, not even a scratch or bruise.

Knock-knock.

'What the fu...'

Faces pressed up against the car window; gypsies, who often parked along this stretch in their caravans. They wanted to know if we were OK and suggested that if we were drunk or had stolen the car it was better to leave soon – before the police showed up. We were both stone cold sober and the car was off the road, so what next? Fred would take control – he would go for help!

Neither the AA nor RAC stood before me on the roadside, not even the elusive, stylish Queen megastar, but Fred, in his faded blue jeans, white clogs and an embroidered black silk kimono a Japanese fan had given him. He had not shaved for a day or two and his dark stubble was proud, his carefully tousled hair now blew free as he wandered off towards some lights in the distance to call Mary, and his driver Derek. As I waited for Fred's return, a passing motorist stopped and enquired as to my welfare and then kindly offered to call a tow truck from the next available telephone box to take the car away. No mobile phones back then. I waited. And waited. And waited...

After about half an hour, Fred returned and explained the situation comedy that had unfolded. He had knocked on the door of the first house he came to and was quickly recognised by the people who answered. They let him use the phone and offered him tea. He graciously accepted and then realised that, being Fred, he had no money on him (he never carried cash) to repay their kindness. The electricity meter ran out, so they had to go next door to borrow some 10p pieces to feed the meter and boil the kettle – then there was no milk for the tea, so another dash next door was needed! Next door recognised him too and joined the tea party.

When Fred's car and driver arrived at the scene, he reassured me he had called The Manor and somebody was coming to pick me up. We were both still suffering a little from shock as he took off for London, so I watched The Manor's estate car being towed away and chain-smoked while sitting on my sticker-covered briefcase at the side of the road.

The wagon train duly arrived: Roger, Brian, John, engineer, studio staff, crew et al. They saw a solitary figure on the roadside and asked where everybody – and everything – was? Fred had relayed the accident in his theatrical manner as being hideous carnage and a mass of twisted charred metal! The car brakes were found to be faulty, and the police took no action against me. Later, a music press interview offered Fred a dramatic opportunity to relate how the incident had affected him. He replied that his life had flashed before his eyes – and he had wondered who would look after his cats.

'And the roadie actually screamed!'

Fred commended me for getting so far around the roundabout and never held me responsible. I still drove him many times after that – even in an old Transit van!

ACHES AND A PAIN

Losing Fred would have been a disaster, as would losing an album's master copy, which held all work done to date. There was also a safety copy. Just like on a modern computer, everything was constantly saved and backed up. The master and safety copy were kept and transported separately – just like royalty.

Vinyl days, before sampling, were when musicians played and sweated hard in the studio. Roger, being a sweaty drummer, needed to be in good physical shape and was complaining of aches and pains during recording at Island Studios in London. A masseuse was located, and a very sexy-looking lady, in starched white uniform and high heels, turned up with her little kit bag. Screens were pulled together in the studio for an area of privacy and naturally the microphones were left 'live' for engineer Mike Stone to capture the moment. But she was a proper, qualified masseuse and Roger was genuinely relieved of the stiffness... in his back and shoulders.

Poor old drummers are often the butt of jokes.

'What do roadies, groupies and drummers have in common? They all hang out with musicians.' Guitarists weren't spared either, being generally fussy and pedantic. 'How do you know when a plane full of guitarists has landed? You can still hear whining when the engines have shut down.'

Bass players only have four strings to worry about so they generally keep quiet.

And of course we *never, ever* took the piss out of Fred...

SOUND TRACKS

As Queen became increasingly popular, their talent was noticed by the film industry, and offers to do 'movies' regularly came into the office. Queen were constantly busy recording their own music and touring, so film projects had to wait, until 1980, when the offer to do the soundtrack to *Flash Gordon* was taken – despite the fact that they were still recording *The Game* album in Munich and Roger doing a solo project in Switzerland!

Brian, a big sci-fi fan, was particularly keen on *Flash Gordon*, but it was interesting to see how Fred, John and Roger approached what was a creative 'carte blanche' with no strict format to follow. They were not being asked to produce 'songs' with verses, choruses and a middle-eight. As a musician it must have been fulfilling to use the inspiration from the visuals of the film and match it with your own musical input to create mood and drama. Ideas that had previously been kicking around and not fully fledged might be adapted, and styles and sounds that would not suit Queen's regular format explored. The soundtrack was done in various London studios, including Advision and De Lane Lea, which had projection and dubbing facilities for synching film and soundtracks.

Queen were synonymous with being creative and innovative in the studio, and as they had just begun using synthesisers during this period, they featured prominently, alongside traditional Queen trademarks of vocal harmonies and Brian's guitar 'orchestra'. The opening 'Flash's Theme' by Brian, with its pulsing, clunky piano intro was done at Richard Branson's Townhouse studios in west London. Brian was working on it late one night, but couldn't get the exact piano sound he wanted.

'What about using a pick-up like we do live?' Some keen fool suggested.

'Great!'

Getting the section of Helpinstill piano pick-up and it's ancillary parts to fit to the studio piano and blend with the microphone sound involved jumping in the van and making a cross-London trip to our warehouse at Edwin Shirley Trucking in West Ham. After waking up the night-watchman and scouring 2,000 square feet of equipment-packed space by torchlight, we finally arrived back at the Townhouse with the various component parts – some three hours later. The things you do for art...

The art of mastering sounds from a synthesiser was not particularly difficult – but making music from them was something else. However, the Flash soundtrack was a blank canvas for electronic 'noise'. Crystal and I did some experimental synthesiser 'noise' which actually got included in playbacks to the film producers! But not included in the final album unfortunately.

Subsequently, more film offers flooded the office, including rumours of a James Bond movie, and the invitation to do Sylvester Stallone's *Rocky III*. The story goes that Stallone wanted to use 'Another One Bites The Dust', but was denied, so 'Eye Of The Tiger' by Survivor was eventually used, as

Queen were too busy to do any original material. Latterly, many Queen tracks have been licensed for film and TV use, and I recently heard Fred's 'Somebody To Love' masterpiece in its original form, as the soundtrack to an ad for sofas and soft furnishings on TV. Oh dear.

I wonder what he'd think of that? I believe that had Fred lived, he would have no doubt continued to work and be creative – and I think film music would have been an area he would have embraced, once he'd hung his leotard and prancing shoes up.

CHAPTER NINE

MONTREUX

(NUMBERED ACCOUNTS, CHEESE WITH HOLES
AND HUMOUR BY-PASS CLINICS)

The first five Queen albums were all recorded in the UK. However, the ailing Labour government had a penchant for taxing wealthy rock stars higher and higher. Switzerland, a traditional home of tax exiles, had a studio in Montreux with a track record of recording top artists, so it was decided to spend a convenient period there during the company's tax year.

'Greetings from Montreux – beautiful but boring.' That's what my postcard home from Switzerland would say; after all, how many Swiss rock bands can *you* name? (World champion yodellers maybe, but none in the Rock and Roll Hall of Fame.) Switzerland has clean air and clean living. Orderly and efficient, it is a wealthy God-fearing and law-abiding police state. As for the packs of beer available in 1978, they were printed in three languages: 'sans', 'ohne' and 'senza' alcohol.

Not *quite* rock 'n' roll is it?

It is early summer 1978, and Queen are to spend some four months in this healthy, fiscal climate, writing and recording new songs that the record companies, accountants and hungry public demand. Rehearsals and recording will begin in Montreux, then on to Super Bear Studios in the south of France, to finish the vocals, overdubs and do final mixes. The plans for the US tour to follow the album are already in preparation, with Europe, a live album and Japan also pencilled in. Then some more recording to finish off the year. No pressure then? Queen – *This Is Your Life*. Welcome to the corporate spreadsheet and annual report and accounts.

The exciting appeal of rock 'n' roll was that you never knew what you would be doing very far in advance. I relished the element of surprise, but now the next year of my life was mapped out. But as always, it still held a few surprises…

JAZZ?

The pretty, chocolate-box town of Montreux on Lake Geneva – or Lac Leman as locals call it, has a reputation for its international Jazz Festival, held in the casino complex that had previously caught fire and inspired the Deep Purple song 'Smoke On The Water'. Housed in the side of the rebuilt concrete building was a recording studio that was used by rock bands in exile from the wicked taxman.

I had driven out in a Ford Transit to help 'prep' our time in Montreux. The back of the van was stuffed with last-minute personal effects, for what would be a long stay for the band and their partners and families. There were boxes of disposable nappies stacked in with toys and stereo systems and other items of home comfort. After a few days, the truck with the equipment arrived, followed shortly by the band.

For Queen's rehearsals in Montreux, we were booked into a classical ballet school that was on summer break. Situated in a steep, narrow, cobbled street, it was a very daunting load in for the required gear. Fred's Steinway piano, weighing over a ton in its enormous flight case, teetered precariously while being manoeuvred over the threshold into the rehearsal room. Creak – snap – crunch! Its industrial-strength wheels pierced the parquet floor, tipping it at a jaunty angle. Nobody was injured.

'Aaaah – look at that – all this damage!' The horrified studio manageress, who had booked the ballet school, screamed.

'I know – lucky, weren't we?'

'Lucky? Lucky! Do you realise, in order to get this place, I told the owners we had a small musical group in town who wanted to do *a bit of practice*. That's a beautiful antique floor!'

'Not anymore.'

The reduced Queen crew of just myself and Crystal, set about arranging an intimate and creative musical ambience; we put the gear in a circle, put Queen in the middle and left them to it.

'Tea – tea please' the call came down to the kitchen basement area – a haven from all the noise upstairs. Queen regularly took tea: Fred and Roger: milk and two sugars, Brian: milk and one sugar, John: milk and no sugar.

Local shopping produced drinkable local tea, a hand-carved Swiss pipe and some not so local 'Moroccan tobacco' to take to our secret hideaway in the ballet school. The lake and mountains looked *really* beautiful those summer evenings. Man...

After a Jazz Woodbine and armed with free passes, it was on to the Jazz Festival. Despite our enhanced state of mind, we still couldn't understand jazz. But I really enjoyed the performance of Ray Charles (once he recovered from walking into his piano).

CHALET SHENANIGANS

Queen's accommodation was dotted around the mountains; Crystal and I were in a two-bedroom flat, above a ground-floor flat that housed Geoff Workman, the studio engineer, brought in by recalled producer Roy Thomas Baker for the album. These flats were built on to the side of a stunning house in the mountain village of Blonay, and were owned by Monica, an attractive woman in her forties, who was a high-class lady of some note. The lady of the house got into trouble with the police for failing to register us as paying guests with the local authorities. Local bedtime was around 8.30 pm – but not for us. Rather than come to the door and ask us to shut up or keep the noise down, the locals went directly to the police and reported what they were unhappy with – us.

'Knock-knock-knock!'

I raised my weary head: 'It's that bloody Geoff, wanting to scrounge a cup of tea! Hang on, I'm coming!'

Yawning, I staggered down to open the door. Geoff Workman, who described the state of his eyes in the

TOUR STAFF

TOUR MANAGER   -   GERRY STICKELLS

ROAD MANAGER   -   PETE BROWN

QUEEN ROAD CREW   -   JOHN HARRIS

JAMES DANN

BRIAN SPENCER

PETE HINCE

BOBBY REID

CHRIS TAYLOR

RICHARD ANDERSON

CLAIR BROS. CREW   -   BOB WEIBEL

JIM OBER

DAVE COB

TOM FIELDS CREW   -   CHRIS LAMB

STEVE WHITMER

TRUCK DRIVER   -   GEORGE TRAVERS

WARDROBE MAN   -   DANE CLARK

HAPPY BIRTHDAY
'76
AMERICA

Santa Monica Civic

QUEEN

MARCH 11, 1976

311   6

BACKSTAGE PASS

MEMO RE: QUEEN

For security reasons, members of QUEEN will be booked into hotels under pseudonyms:

ALFRED MASON/FREDDIE MERCURY
BRIAN MANLEY/BRIAN MAY
JASON DANE/JOHN DEACON
ROY TANNER/ROGER TAYLOR

STAGE
PASS
PANTHER
PRODUCTIONS

QUEEN

KIEL

5/76

AUTHORIZED

A RON POWELL PRESENTATION

The tour staff page from the 1976 US Tour itinerary. The piece of paper stapled in gives the aliases Queen used when staying in hotels.

Above left: Fred with dancers on the set of the 'Crazy Little Thing Called Love' video shoot in September 1979.

Above right: August 1978. Fred with lover Mary Austin in the gardens of Eden au Lac hotel in Montreux, Switzerland.

Below: Puebla, Mexico in October 1981. Fred at the piano, which had a synthesiser on the top of it. Both keyboards are reflected in his mirrored sunglasses.

Above: Sound check at Velez Sarsfield stadium in Buenos Aires, Argentina in February 1981 (left) and in Puebla, Mexico in October 1981 (right).

Below: John dressed as 'Grandma' on the set of the 'I Want to Break Free' video shoot in London, March 1984.

Above left: London, March 1984 – Roger dressed as a 'smoking' schoolgirl on the set of 'I Want to Break Free'.

Above right: Roger at his silver glitter kit on the set of the 'Play the Game' video in May 1980.

Below: Roger makes clear his allegiance to the drums department at Musicland Studios in Munich, November 1981.

Above left: Cheers! Brian drinks a stein of Munich's finest beer at the Englischer Garten beer garden.

Above right: Brian on the catwalk during a guitar solo at the Montreal Forum in Canada, November 1981.

Below: Sound checking at Puebla, Mexico in October 1981.

This page and opposite: Scenes of work and play at Musicland Studios in Munich.

→20   →20A   4   4   5   →21A

LM 5063   KODAK SAFETY FILM 5063

→23   →23A   →24   →24A

SAFETY FILM 5063   KODAK SAFETY FIL

Brian 'resting' with
drumsticks – Munich,
1981.

morning as like 'red lace curtains', had remarkably transformed into two Swiss cops in bulging uniform and peaked party hats. One asked me in French why we were making a lot of noise, playing music every night and bouncing around on the balcony.

'Well – it's fun. Have you not heard of it here?'

He asked me what we were doing in Montreux, and when we were leaving.

'*La musique – dans Le Studio Mountain*. You'll be shot of us in a few weeks'

He then asked me for our passports. I obliged. After studying them, he replied that he was going to take our passports away for further checks. I snatched them back and quoted him in plain English the inscription inside a UK passport: 'We are subjects of Her Majesty and "are to be afforded to pass freely without let or hindrance" – so piss off!'

I slammed the door. They didn't try again, and just did a lot of muttering, took lots of notes – then waddled off to report back to Big Brother.

The Swiss are a very ordered race with clinical and squeaky-clean lives. We became a nasty blot on their beautiful Alpine landscape. Our truck driver hated the compulsive cleanliness of Switzerland so much that he would save up all the rubbish that he accumulated in his truck cab during a tour; cigarette packs, chocolate wrappers, crisp bags, papers plus the contents of his packed ashtrays. Whenever he crossed the border into Switzerland, he would throw the whole lot out of the window into this antiseptic neutral territory.

Nevertheless, Montreux did offer some diversions. The White Horse Pub was an English-style inn complete with dart board, and, when evening meal break was called, Geoff Workman would bolt from the studio and dash down Rue Du Theatre towards the pub shouting in his Liverpudlian wake: 'Come on, you're wasting valuable ale time!' No fancy haute cuisine band meals for Geoff, the self-appointed cultural attaché for Merseyside: Beer. Burger. Beer. Fries. Beer. Belch. Beer. Beer. Punctuated by several high-strength cigarettes.

The White Horse closed relatively early, and after being banned from the Hazyland Disco – thanks to the antics of Gerry Stickells on a flying visit – the only place for late-night recreation left to us was The Hungaria nightclub. It became known colloquially as The Vulgaria, which was fair. Trying to remove cigarettes from some drunken local's mouth with a stripper's whip was a nasty business. Medical facilities are fortunately very good in Switzerland.

The exiled Queen were now settled; the band and their respective families were enjoying mountain and lake-side life. Brian, Roger and John had all driven their cars over from England, and Derek, Fred's driver from London, had driven over the Mercurial Mercedes, but was not available to be daily personal chauffeur to Fred, so a driver was needed. The Mountain Studios office found Valerius Knobloch. Who? Valerius Knobloch, an American on his European Adventure. Valerius Knobloch – a joke or a bet? It turned out to be his real name, poor bloke. How unfortunate. It would be cruel to taunt.

Valerie Knob Rot.

'Val' had to drive Fred when required, including the two-hour-plus round-trip to Geneva, where the late-evening establishments Fred was drawn to were situated. Fred didn't care much for Montreux at that time, it was too dull for him. However, its peace, tranquillity and clean air, did give him some pleasure and comfort in later life.

DOWN TO WORK

The Mountain Studio was not big, certainly not a mountain – more of a mole hill – with a hallway the size of a postage stamp, a cramped control room and no lounge or recreation area. The studio itself was one floor above the control room and, again, small. Communication was by talkback and closed circuit TV cameras. For *Jazz*, we were lucky to have use of The Salon, a vast sectioned-off area of the casino arena. (It can be seen in the panoramic gatefold photograph I took on the *Jazz* album.) Little areas for separation of the instruments were constructed and centred around producer, Roy, working out, through some mathematical calculation with a pencil and some string, where the dead centre of the room was. Once the axis of the universe had been established, that's where the bass drum was placed and the rest of Roger's vast kit built around it.

The guitar booths had wooden floors to give a 'live' sound, and studio screen walls with a roof thatched from huge shaggy sheepskin rugs. These grubby, tatty old bits of fleece made the booths we had built look like a herd of Tibetan yaks. (Tibetan yaks giving painful birth, when Brian and his screaming guitar were inside.)

'Fancy a drink down the White Horse?'

'Yeah.'

A pint or two later, we returned; the Tibetan yak was still in labour.

'Yeah – sounds great, Brian! Wanna try another…?'

'Mmmmm? Yes, I think so… just one more take, just to be sure.'

'Fine.' (Fancy another couple of swift halves?)

We were effectively 'on the road' as far as the equipment went, and had very limited local resources for hiring or buying any item required on a whim. Consequently, we had transported a whole 40-foot trailer full of gear: dozens of guitars, drums, amps, effects, etc. – but not one synthesiser. In addition to our arsenal of instruments we added bicycle bells! Every bike shop in the area was scoured in order to build a collection of various tones and actions of bell, used on Fred's locally inspired song 'Bicycle Race'.

THE BRASS SECTION

As the town's most glamorous guests, in sleepy Montreux we held a strong interest for adventurous local females – all given unique nicknames:

Edam – a resident Dutch girl; The Lapin – a girl who wore a rabbit-skin coat and 'went' like one; Marty – a girl with large bulging eyes who resembled the comedian Marty Feldman; and the ubiquitous 'That bird you reckon you knobbed'. I did have a tender encounter with an Israeli stripper, who resided (honestly!) at the Hotel Eidelweiss. Julie Andrews she was not. I had to help her up the narrow staircase to her attic room with her 'equipment', which included a small set of carpeted steps.

Then there was Rachel (not her real name) – otherwise known as James Galway – who, like the flautist, had marvellous oral control talents while holding an instrument. She had a deep, sexy voice too: 'He is like a long flute, him – a saxophone, and he – a French horn!' (Lucky lad).

'Him – only like a piccolo!'

I once sneaked her back to the flat under cover of darkness, but we were locked out. Unperturbed, and spurred on by the desire to have a full brass section symphony, I drove the van under the balcony and we climbed on to its buckling roof. From here I tried shunting her up on to the balcony. She was *very* well built, and as she straddled around my neck trying to grasp hold of the balcony rail, I caught sight of our adversary – the old dragon from across the road peering aghast through her shutters.

Knock-knock... 'We are officers of the law!'

No need – I'd already been *punished*. She was a *big* girl....

There are many exclusive finishing schools in this area of Switzerland and lots of girls, big and small, from all parts of the globe. A Middle Eastern girl, the daughter of some mega-rich Arab, translated the words and gave the correct pronunciation to Fred's Islam-inspired song 'Mustapha'.

'Mustava piss – I'm bursting.'

'Are you bloody lot making fun of my song – again?'

'Us, Fred? Never!'

TAPED

A year or so later, Queen purchased Mountain Studios, but no major changes were made. Eugene Chaplin, son of silent comedy film star Charlie, who had spent his later years on a splendid estate in nearby Vevey, was still on the staff, and had invited us to spend the day around the pool at his beautiful family residence. A studio flat, decorated in Swiss 'punishment and correction' style, was added at staggering distance away from the studio. The Mountain Studio office, across the street from the casino, like all contemporary Swiss buildings, had a mandatory concrete nuclear fall-out shelter in the basement. These bunkers, with sealed doors, were required to be stocked with a certain quota of food and drink, plus bedding and supplies for survival when the 'bomb' dropped. The studio office used their nuclear shelter with some interpretation – for storing wine and skiing equipment.

Mountain studio was managed by Aileen, a lovely local girl who spoke excellent English. She told me she had been inspired to learn the language from an early age while listening to Beatles records. But without a scouse accent.

The original 24-track master tapes of an early Queen album were requested from the EMI vaults in London; they were needed for a particular sound, reference, effect or possibly just to settle an argument. Quite possibly. The tapes duly arrived via personal courier; a shy young English girl, who arrived late one evening. She was new to being a personal courier, and had nowhere to stay that night.

'Don't worry – we'll look after you, darling,' Crystal and I offered.

'No! There's a sofa bed in the office – she can stay there' Aileen interrupted protectively.

The master tape was immediately spooled on to the Studer machine and very quickly it became apparent that the tape did not hold the right album. It was not even a Queen one – it was Kate Bush! So much for those highly paid record company professionals, back in London.

'That's not snow on top of that Swiss mountain – it's my stash, man.'

'I see – and just how many Jazz Woddbines or 'sans' alcohol lagers have you had this evening?'

'Well, maybe a few – I think I've just seen Brian water skiing out on the lake...'

It's true. The not obviously sporty Mr May had mastered the art of being towed by a high speed boat with two bits of wood (not clogs) strapped to his feet. I was most impressed! I'd had a few tries and failed miserably – it was bloody difficult.

I might have found it easier on a sloping lake?

Another Brit residing near the local lake was Formula One racing driver Sir Jackie Stewart. He was a big fan of Queen and told John that their music sounded great inside a Porsche 928S, a road car he suggested John swapped his Volvo for.

'A Volvo – you drive a Volvo?' Sir Jackie said incredulously.

To be fair to John he was a dedicated family man – and a Volvo is a family car.

AU REVOIR LA SUISSE – BONJOUR LA BELLE FRANCE

Whatever vehicle you had, it was a long drive from Montreux via Italy to Super Bear Studios in the south of France – particularly with a very hungover Crystal and Geoff

Workman crammed into the front of the van with me. As we wound down the hills into Nice and our meeting point on the Promenade des Anglais, we could see the rich luminescence of Monte Carlo and Monaco below. Pulling the old van up outside the posh Hotel Negresco, we felt a little out of place among the Rolls-Royces, Ferraris and Bentleys. Liaising with David, our dashing leather-trousered studio contact, it was another hour's drive into the hills of Berre-les-Alpes to our destination of Super Bear. The 40-foot trailer of Queen's equipment could not negotiate the tiny winding mountain roads, so we had to decide what would be the minimum amount of gear needed to cover what recording remained. The trailer was left secure in a parking area, and many shuttles up and down the hairpin bends were required in a large Citroen van. After a long day in the scorching Provençal sun, the required gear was finally up, in place and the cases stored. It wasn't long until Roy Thomas Baker pulled a creative 'moody', claiming the studio room was too 'dead', and that he wanted the entire carpet taken up to reveal the 'live' marble floor underneath. All the gear had to be moved outside again, where there was little space; it was all very tight to manoeuvre and took ages. On cue it started raining. Then – *then* the room was deemed *too* live. All change again. Producers? Piccolo? Possibly...

As time became tighter for finishing the album and the upcoming US tour grew closer, the final mixing and overdubs would be done in shifts around the clock.

One night we were treated to some special astronomical event that Roy and Brian knew all about. Most of us were keen to see it and watched through a telescope. Shortly after, there was the most tremendous electrical storm that lasted ages. Brian took inspiration and using his portable recorder put on tape some of the thunder, lightning and rain effects for his song 'Dead On Time'.

During one late shift, while Fred was doing a lead vocal, he had taken a break to tinkle at the piano to find the key he wanted. While we waited for him in the control room, I told a raucous gay joke to Geoff, Roy and John – whose song we were working on at the time.

A sharp voice catapulted over the monitor speakers: 'What was the punchline again, Ratty?'

Out of my sight, Roy had purposely been leaning on the talkback button and Fred had heard everything through his headphones. I sank below the mixing desk waiting for the earth to open and thinking: 'That was a novel way of handing in my resignation. '

Everybody laughed loudly, Fred grinned and we carried on.

Oh, the fine line between humour and unemployment...

CHAPTER TEN

MUNICH

(I HAVE IN MY HAND A PIECE OF PAPER – FOLDED
INTO A SMALL ENVELOPE)

The tax year that had begun with recording in Montreux ended with recording in Munich. Munich was a lot more fun than Montreux. The Swiss are neutral. The Germans aren't. Taking sides tends to make life more interesting. München – heard the name, but where is it? Before I began touring, I had never visited Germany or any other country for that matter. My limited knowledge of Germany and its people was gleaned as a kid from *Commando* comics and war films, where I found useful phrases, such as:

'*Achtung – Englischer Spitfire! Englander Schweinhund*' and '*Zee war is over for you now, Tommy!*'

'Yeah! Eat lead, Fritz!' *Buddaa-buddaa-buddaa* (machine-gun sound effect)

When, during this period of my youth I had watched my dad, an electrician, poking around in the back of our tiny black and white TV, he would tell me he was cleaning out all the dead Indians shot by the cowboys. Presumably there were a lot of dead German soldiers in there as well? This was the same TV, with its standing magnifying glass screen positioned in front, that we huddled around on 20 July 1966 to see England's finest sporting triumph as we beat West Germany 4–2 in the World Cup final. All this partisan information only confirmed to a young mind with no notion of jingoism that England had to be a superior nation.

However, far from being a country and a race I held in suspicion – with their *Beetle* cars that made an annoying farting noise (the local district nurse drove one and I was always *very* suspicious of her and that ominous black bag) – Germany and its people became very dear to me. When you had spent your childhood in post-war Britain with older relatives who had taken an active part in the conflict, it was easy to be tainted by the lingering mood of bitterness. Bitter? No – only 'ein bier bitte!'

THE GAMES PEOPLE PLAY

In the late 1970s and 1980s, the Olympiahalle, adjacent to the Olympic stadium in Munich, was a regular venue on the European tours of major rock bands. Everyone hoped for time off while in Munich; and it wasn't just for the famous Beer Halls where you drink stein after stein of foaming ale, eat bratwurst, then fall over and puke! However, it was no problem, as installed in the toilets were hand rails to guide you along to the basins, and then metal handles to grip on as you throw up. All is easily flushed away with powerful water jets. Very efficient, very German.

During a bitterly cold 1979 Queen winter tour,

everybody was in need of some serious recreation to escape from our 'winter of discontent'. Munich came to our rescue and Queen were impressed enough with the city to spend the final six weeks of a year 'out' recording at Musicland Studios. The year had started with a Labour government (very high tax for high earners) and finished with Maggie Thatcher (lower tax for high earners), which suited Queen. Owned by Giorgio Moroder, the producer well known for his work with Donna Summer, Musicland had also played host to top rock artists such as The Stones, Led Zeppelin, The Electric Light Orchestra, Deep Purple and Rory Gallagher.

Queen had no current favoured producer or engineer as these sessions were to be experimental and a little looser than previous studio schedules, when there tended to be a fixed pattern of four of Fred's songs, four of Brian's, one of Roger's and one of John's, which were worked on exclusively until perfected. This was the first time Queen had gone into the studio without the pressure of a deadline, so for the Munich sessions they decided to produce themselves and use the freelance house engineer, an experienced local guy called Mack, who had done a lot of studio and live work for The Electric Light Orchestra. Queen and Mack immediately hit it off well. Mack was a Bavarian with quiet efficiency and great sense of humour (he knew and enjoyed every *Fawlty Towers* episode – including 'that' one). The final harvest of these Musicland sessions was the phenomenally successful *The Game* album, which Mack co-produced.

Located in the basement of the vast characterless Arabella Hotel, close to the trendy Schwabing district, Musicland was not an impressive-looking place. Entrance was through a black reinforced-steel door on the ground floor and down a flight of industrial carpeted stairs into the basement. The Musicland Bunker was not at all plush, but with its cheap, pine-panelled walls it had a warm, homely feel and, mixed with the atmosphere of the city, was conducive to recording some of Queen's best material. It had one small studio room, an adjoining control room, a sitting and dining area and a tiny workshop area (a large cupboard) for the maintenance engineer. Nicknamed The Office, this was the place for secret phone calls, secret deals and all manner of other secret things. In the underground corridor outside the kitchen was a table-tennis table, where Fred would trounce all comers with one hand behind his back or using his 'bad' left hand, when he was being really flash.

Other forms of entertainment were video tapes of the latest English TV programmes such as *Auf Wiedersehen, Pet* (very apt), the Benny Hill and Kenny Everett shows, plus *Top Of The Pops* and other music programmes.

Board games such as Monopoly, Risk and chess were also popular, but Fred would not involve himself in anything that he considered banal or inane and only concentrated on things that used his mind or direct skill and knowledge. Scrabble was a game he loved, and was exceptionally good at – having played since an early age with an elderly aunt, he told me. When the Scrabble board came out, it was a magnet to Fred and he would hover, interfering, or advising the current players. Usually he would insist we scrap the game and start a new one to include him. Whatever work he was doing was put on hold and thousands of pounds of studio time were wasted while Fred waited for the elusive seven-letter, triple-word square. 'Lacquers' was one word using all seven letters that particularly astounded him – as it fell into place on the triple-word square. It came from me!

However, the initial demand from Fred to get a Scrabble set for the studio was not received at all well. A German version was purchased, and he got very frustrated trying to make English words with the umlauts, accents and quite different letter construction of the German language.

'There's only supposed to be *one* Z tile in Scrabble – this version's got hundreds of the fuckers!'

'Lost in translation'. So an English edition of Scrabble was sourced and no expense spared in having it immediately delivered for Fred to enjoy.

Fred regularly did the daily word puzzle games in the English newspapers, striking one of his stage poses of raised arm and clenched fist, when he had solved the major nine-letter word from the box of letters – which never took him very long. Pumped up and excited, he would then offer to arm-wrestle all comers. However, he was the only member of the band not to try out the 'Gravity Boots'. This fad in the 1980s was for sturdy ankle clamps, that were attached to the legs and then hooked over a high bar – leaving you hanging upside down. It was claimed to be very good for the back, general health and well-being – well, I suppose it could be? I've never seen a sloth in a doctor's waiting room. The rush of blood to the head was very unsettling – back to the pinball.

During this period, I was becoming more enthusiastic about photography, and raided my savings and credit card limit to buy what I had long dreamed of – a Hasselblad 500

CM medium format camera. I had a state-of-the-art Polaroid back for my Hasselblad, which Fred was intrigued by. He had long loved the instant, creative process of Polaroid cameras and in the 1970s used his SX70 wherever he went. So, I was instructed to take a Polaroid using my hi-tech gear of Mr Mercury and his new addition – a moustache! He had cultivated it during the Munich sessions and, although he could see the result in the mirror, he wanted a two-dimensional record – to see what the world was shortly about to see. He excitedly waited while the Polaroid developed, and as I peeled the backing paper away to show him, he snatched it from me and immediately stated: 'Yes – I love it!'

He was in the minority at that time, I have to say.

THE GREAT ESCAPE

During the tax-efficient Munich sessions in 1979, I briefly went back to London to customs clear all the gear that had arrived back by sea from Japan and put it back in our warehouse. Having finished my professional duties, I was keen to return to the fun in Munich. Then I received a phone call.

'Ratty?' The office voice sounded a bit too friendly.

'Yes…?'

'There's something else for you to take back to Munich.'

'Is it heavy? Will I have to clear it through customs? Not English sausages!? – some of the band have been moaning they miss them.'

'It's Freddie.'

Fred, who was also in London for a few days, had nobody

to accompany him back to Munich. He never travelled alone; there was always somebody with him and in the adjacent hotel room. He craved company.

A first-class seat on British Airways was offered, so I dutifully agreed.

Unfortunately, a problem arose due to an industrial strike at Heathrow, and all flights were severely delayed. Anxiety was in the air as Fred had used up his allotted days allowed in the UK and needed to leave. Immediately.

I made my way to Heathrow, and hung nervously around the British Airways desk until I got positive news. When I did get a go-ahead for our flight to Munich, Fred was immediately sped down the M4 from Kensington to join me.

It was a sunny summer's day in London and a few glasses of in-flight bubbly were well received. At Munich airport, we were met by Peter, a local guy who was acting as Fred's driver, in a hired Mercedes. We cruised with smiles on our faces into the east of the city and our Hilton home. Fred was reinstalled in his grand suite and wanted to take a bath before going to the studio. I called Musicland and announced that 'his self' was safely back – and would shortly be joining them.

Fred was humming and tapping in the bath and shouting out the names of chords: 'D – yes, and C and G – Ratty, quick – come here!'

'Uh, you want me to come into your bathroom, Fred? I'm not sure about this.'

'No, no! Get me a guitar! Now!'

He emerged from the bathroom wrapped in towels, still dripping, and scurried into the living room of the suite where I gave him the battered acoustic that had been installed for these impulsive creative moments. Fred strummed away for a short time with his fingers – he never used a pick or plectrum. Seizing the urgency of the moment, we dashed to Musicland where a halt was called to whatever work was in progress. He summoned the band into the studio and enthused about this new idea, which they started to work on and record immediately. The song was 'Crazy Little Thing Called Love', one of Queen's most successful worldwide singles.

It was a privilege to have been there with him, but no matter how long I knew Fred, got to be accepted, trusted and cared for by him, you could rarely totally relax around him. Over a period of almost 20 years, we enjoyed many great social times together but there was always some kind of edge to it. Quite simply – Fred had an aura. It was always there, whether he was on stage in front of 130,000 people or picking his teeth at the breakfast table and moaning about his hangover. When he walked into a room – any room – you knew you were in the presence of somebody special. Somebody unique. Magical.

In Munich, I often witnessed Fred's magical way of summoning creativity. When he was looking for a word, a phrase, a chord, an idea, a memory or anything that could contribute to his work, he would bow his head and hold his hands by the side of his head, his fingers spread slightly. Then he would waggle his hands and fingers – as if they were vibrating. If sitting, he would put his elbows on the table and focus his eyes downward, all the time his splayed hands trembling and vibrating as if they were antennae tuning in to an unseen force. He would mutter to himself and it would not take long before he found what he was looking for and he would stand sharply and slap his hands together with a crack, usually with a loud shout of 'YES!'

It was quite remarkable.

Despite being in the constant company of Queen, I was not immune to being impressed by fame. I have met many rock stars and celebrities but I can say that none of them held the presence that Fred radiated – and yet he was actually quite a private and shy person.

SPARE CHANGE

Our activities in Munich required financing; studio bills went directly to Queen's Rain Cloud Productions office in London, but cash was needed locally to pay per-diems and fund other needs. Queen banked at Coutts – *the* Queen's bankers – where else? Prior to sessions in Munich, I went along to the branch of Coutts in Knightsbridge, situated across the road from Fred's favourite corner store, Harrods, to pick up the cash. I was registered as a signatory to receive monies approved by the accountants or John Deacon, who oversaw much of the band's fiscal arrangements. I parked the Ford Transit van around the corner from Coutts and sauntered into this historical banking establishment. There were lots of frightfully well-spoken people going in and out, and you could comfortably say that I looked out of place. After giving my name to the striped-tailcoated and waistcoated clerk, he decided not to press the panic-button, and took my ID and a sample signature. He shuffled off through a door into the back like some Dickensian figure, reappearing with wads of Deutschmarks on a silver tray, which he handed to me and asked if I required an envelope.

'Naaah, mate, I'll shove it all in my bag,' I replied, as I started counting the notes.

This did not seem to impress 'Jeeves', and he coughed a few times. I then presumed it was bad form and considered vulgar to actually count money in public at Coutts. However, I continued counting out the equivalent of forty grand sterling (a lot of money to be responsible for circa 1980). It was all there.

BORED AND LODGINGS

Home in Munich was the München Hilton, situated in an attractive spot next to the Englischer Garten with the Isar River running alongside – a good target for items thrown from our balconies. Those round aluminium covers that you get on room service plates to keep the food warm were very good aerodynamically. The four-star hotel was regularly used by touring bands, but we literally became residents, and I must have spent around a year of my life in that hotel. We took the same rooms and suites to make us feel at home. Fred and his personal assistant Phoebe inhabited the grand top-floor presidential suite which was known as the PPP (Presidential Poof Parlour), where the regal Mr Mercury held court. The next best available luxury suite was Roger's, which he shared with his assistant Crystal and was known as the HH (Hetero Hangout).

Brian stayed in a duplex suite, while John and I always had room numbers 826 and 828 or 828 and 830, with connecting doors. I installed a music sound system and a small TV monitor and video player for John, which entertained both of us. The management of the hotel were very tolerant of our behaviour, and the constant stream of weird and wonderful companions and guests filing past reception at any given hour. Stumbling in one morning at about 5.00 am, we discovered we had a football, so began kicking it around the lobby, trying to recreate our World Cup triumph of 1966.

The night manager came rushing up: 'My friends, my friends, please, if you want to play *ze fussball* then please play here,' he said, gesturing to the lobby area.

Where was the logic? I thought Germans were famed for it?

'Nein, it is better you play here because when you play upstairs you wake ze guests – please to continue!'

Some disgruntled guests did complain about the continuous noise coming from one of our suites (probably Fred's) so the hotel management immediately recommended that they leave. And don't come back.

We had a favourable deal with the Munich Hilton based on paying the bill on departure in full, in cash.

'Uhh, this is a bit embarrassing, Herr Manager – I can't pay the bill, can't even pay the extras. We've spent all the cash going out and… things. But I think the band are probably good for the money'.

'Ah, you had ze big fun! Ja? Kein problem, Herr Hince – you can transfer the funds – or just bring it with you next time.' He shrugged.

A hotel manager who for fun drove double-decker buses

around the Nürburgring race-track. Competitively. Now that's big fun!

As the hotel got to know our pattern of work and play, they would never send maids to make up our rooms until evening, so we could slumber uninterrupted during daylight. A delirious Paul Prenter once claimed that his stash of coke had been stolen by the maids and replaced with salt, and that another batch had gone 'off' – so he had to throw it away! This did not please Fred, who fancied some – but the cupboard was bare – Fred's cash surely having paid for it anyway. It is true that drugs can alter the mind... Little was seen of the hotel in the severe Bavarian winters, when we would come home just as it was getting light and go back out again as it was getting dark – and we didn't even get weekends off. It was usually mid- to late afternoon before we left the hotel for the studio and an English breakfast fry-up.

The musicians rolled in separately and Fred either dragged or bounced in. When he dragged himself in, he made no comment, just a grunt and you knew to keep quiet and give him Tabasco sauce with his eggs – to kick-start his day. When he bounced in, it was safe to ask how he was.

Sometimes he would ask first: 'Did you get fucked last night?'

'Yeah, as it happens I did'

'Me too! Me too!' he would cackle.

Forget the eggs, get the vodka out. Fred could handle it. I thought I could, too.

Munich '86 *Magic* tour. Back in the Hilton – party time! On the morning of show day I felt dreadful. I was now over 30 (just) and disappointingly my body did not bounce back the same way any more. I had already taken aspirin and a hot shower in an attempt to wake up, but this hadn't done the trick, so as a last resort to kick-start the body I had a glass of fizzy Brausen Tabletten Vitamin C, thoughtfully placed in the room's minibar. By the time I reached the lobby, my already upset stomach was having serious problems accepting the gaseous orange potion. I was going to throw up very soon – but where? Entering some bushes outside the entrance, I retched into my tour jacket. Oh dear. As I passed the concierge's desk on my way back in to sit down and recuperate, he grinned broadly: 'Are you feeling better now Herr Hince?'

While we are on this 'sick in Munich' subject... In 1984, preliminary rehearsals for *The Works* tour were in the Arri Film Studios where a new drum roadie for Roger was being introduced. 'Shag Nasty', as he was to be known, was taken out and shown the delights of Munich. 'Shag' seemed to be holding up well to his inaugural test, when Brian May offered him a lift back to the Hilton in his Mercedes. With Brian and Jobby up front, 'Shag' clambered into the back, where he lay down and threw up all over the seat.

Next day:

Roger Taylor: 'Shag, have you been tuning my drums?'

Shag Nasty: 'Oh no, Rog! I know how particular and precise you are about the kit and would never dream of changing your settings – I just tightened them up a bit.'

Employment terminated at the end of the tour.

LIGHT ENTERTAINMENT

To break the tedium of underground recording, we went out

in the evening, firstly to Cafe d'Accord in Schwabing, or Cafe München on Leopold Strasse, where the manager would delight in giving us a shot of the house speciality – a large bottle of regional schnapps that had a shrivelled viper in it. The viper was put in alive and the bottle capped. As the dying reptile reacted to the toxic alcohol, it spat its venom into the schnapps – charming! Local folklore deemed that if you drank a glass of this tipple each day you would live to be a hundred. Longer than the viper anyway.

That ritual was a prelude to going to the Sugar Shack, a club that did not play typical disco music. It was quite unique, and we had never found a night club that suited us like The Shack did. Situated over several floors of an old terraced building in Herzogspital Strasse it had, in the best club tradition, a discreet door in an alcove where, upon ringing the bell, a hatch opened revealing an anonymous pair of eyes that checked if you were worthy of entry. Once the door sprang open, we would acknowledge the staff and race up the winding staircase, edged with tiny lights, to the main room. The mood was dark and subtly lit around the bar and seating areas, with brighter lighting effects aimed at the central dance floor. The sound system was excellent and always loud, the music gutsy and rock-oriented. Bernd the DJ never spoke, and played continuous album tracks mixed with a few singles. His knowledge of music was impressive; the albums he played included tracks from obscure imported bands that we really enjoyed and wanted to know more about. A lot of inspiration was drawn by Queen from the Sugar Shack.

The Shack was a very 'up' place with fantastic atmosphere

that officially stayed open till 4.00 am. Our unanimous drinking preference was for Moskovskaya Russian vodka in the green-labelled bottle. What else could you ask for? WOMEN. Munich did not disappoint, it had some of the most beautiful, classy, chic, sexy, fun and accommodating girls in the world: The Hat, The Boxer, The Toucan, The Belgian Airline, The Budgie, The Biker, The Dustbin, The Secret, Legs, Harold's Bird, Horace, Bridget Bardot, The Gargantuan, Fang, The Tree, Shampoo & Set, Roy Orbison, Baby Baby, Mickey Mouse's Ears and The Top Barmaid. There was a laddish points system in place for scoring, with the highest accolade being a full five points for pulling a Sugar Shack barmaid. Brian has recently spoken about the 'deep emotional trouble' for all of us in Munich. And he's right. I was not in any kind of permanent relationship then, but I came very close in Munich – on a few occasions.

One of the guys who worked at the club – I'll call him Otto – was a tall, lean, tough-as-nails German who wore obligatory leather trousers and an open-necked silk shirt and gold medallion. A great guy with a dark past who would do anything for you, though he had a habit of breathing hot stale air against your ear as he barked at you in the din of the club: 'But listen, I tell you, I tell you!' Otto had spent time in prison, but you never asked what for, or how he got the scars around his body, barely visible in the club's dim lighting. There was rarely any trouble in The Shack.

We made frequent visits down the back stairs to his office for refreshment; producing some restricted imported substance, he would inform us: 'This one – he is a good one, you take him and you don't feel so much, then he creep up on you and get you – HA HA HA HA.' He was never wrong.

One major reason Queen enjoyed The Shack was that nobody bothered them for autographs, stared or pointed at them or made them feel uncomfortable with their status. They were treated well, but not as a sideshow. Fred would often show up late at The Shack, as the gentlemen's clubs he frequented closed earlier. Then 'family and friends' would stumble together down the back stairway and into the dawn light. Driving out down the one-way strasse, we'd be on autopilot returning to the hotel; however, one winter, when driving back in John's Volvo, we took the exit ramp up towards the Hilton, hit some black ice and began skidding wildly. I couldn't control the heavy car as it bounced dodgem style off cars parked parallel on either side, before coming to a halt. 'Don't kill us, Ratty,' I recall John flippantly saying. Fortunately unhurt, we got out to survey the damage when we were forced to skip aside to avoid another car that came sliding out of control towards us. This was repeated by other cars including Brian, and his roadie, Jobby, in a BMW. John's solid Swedish car was still drivable, so we continued the short distance to the hotel, and once inside congregated in Fred's suite for a soothing drink. Roger and Crystal came bouncing in, having seen the damaged Volvo, and asked what had happened. They then boasted that they too had hit the ice, but the combination of superior driving, the four-wheel-drive Range Rover and the magnificent drum department had saved the day! And as usual - they were being modest...

Inspecting the damage in the cold light of day, I noticed

that one of the Volvo hubcaps was missing. I told John that, as we had effectively done a 'runner', we had better try to find it. The Volvo was in a garage being fixed, and we returned to the scene of the crime under the cover of darkness in a rented car. After parking a discreet distance away, we scoured the frosty embankment, giggling like schoolboys. We found the hubcap and, still laughing as if we had been scrumping apples from some farmer's orchard, legged it back to the car, threw the evidence in the back and drove off. I reckon the hubcap now lies at the bottom of the Isar River.

FOREIGN AFFAIRS

Beware of Greeks bearing gifts – and grudges. Also beware of models married to mad Greeks – and one in particular. Dangerous liaisons and smitten by lust, there was a potential Greek tragedy for one of our team. One night, the leggy model shows up at a suite in The Hilton where we were all partying. She was black and blue from her husband's beating and he wasn't prepared to stop there, subsequently having a confrontation with his wife's lover one night in The Shack. Otto intervened and, after the Greek had left, said to us, 'I know him, be careful, he crazy, he always hold a knife, he not coming in here anymore – let it be. Let it be.'

Due to leave for London early the next day we endured a tense night, with 'Zorba' plotting violent revenge and damaging expensive motor cars. We did get out safely and our guy narrowly avoided being made into a Greek kebab.

I was involved in a love triangle with an angry DJ boyfriend who hid outside the Hilton Hotel watching his live-in girlfriend enter and then leave many hours later, while perversely another girl I was seeing was the secretary in the DJ's office. They found out. One of these girls I knew had introduced me to Tomi, a drug-dealing Russian defector. How he defected I never asked, but I suspect he was involved with the military; the army-issue handgun on open view in his apartment was a good clue. Shit! I don't like guns. What am I doing here? I'm a roadie – not into this kind of undercover, gangland nonsense!

The defector lived in a one-room ground-floor apartment close to Leopold Strasse, where I found him sitting cross-legged in the middle of his bed dressed only in his underpants (every time I visited him, that's all he ever wore). He had long, straggly curly hair, and judging by his eyes had not slept the previous night or even the one before that. Was this one of the Red Army's finest crack troops? Surrounding him in the small room were glass vivariums with creepy-looking lizards, chameleons and unidentifiable reptiles – and the tops to these tanks were open! He waved my concerns away and invited me to join him in a 'taster' from the lines laid out on a faded LP cover. After the buzz had taken hold, I pulled out a wad of blue 100 deutschmark notes and swapped them for black plastic 35mm film containers.

I subsequently visited him several times and it was always intriguing; there were rigid, staring people, who never spoke at all, secretive knocks on the door in the middle of the night, quick furtive exchanges of envelope for carrier bag, and coded phone messages. Once, when the cupboard was bare, I called up and the guy who answered said Tomi was not there. I mumbled in a faux code who I was, and asked when Tomi would be back.

'He is on holiday,' was the reply.

'So is he back soon?' I enquired.

'No, he is on a very *long* holiday.'

Aaahhhhh! The penny dropped and minor panic set in. I hung up sharply. I could only presume he was now residing in another one-room home, but as he never seemed to venture outdoors he probably wouldn't notice the difference until he straightened up – and realised he was in prison.

LA DOLCE VITA

In 1984, while in Munich recording *The Works*, Queen had finally accepted the annual invitation to top the guest bill at the San Remo Festival TV show in Italy. This national institution, with the highest ratings on Italian TV, was a showcase for popular Italian acts singing to backing tracks, who were then judged. The invited international guest acts who mimed their songs to playback. Despite being hugely popular in Italy, Queen had never played there, as during the seventies and early eighties there were often bans, riots, sabotage, theft and little chance of getting paid. With the political situation currently stable, shows were planned for the upcoming tour, and it made good PR sense to spend a few days on the Riviera and enjoy a bit of La Dolce Vita.

Early one bleary-eyed winter morning, I left the Munich Hilton and took a flight with Paul Prenter to Genoa to meet representatives of Queen's Italian record company and drive to San Remo, where we could visit the theatre and check it out. The technical side was my responsibility; stage set up, putting in extra lights, drum risers and so on, while Paul was to discuss arrangements for hotels, cars, the press, interviews, etc. Queen were top of the guest bill for the two-night show and as always keen to make a big impression. We had not been briefed, it was simply taken for granted that whatever was done had to be the best – and 'big'. We met our genial contacts and, as befits being in Italy, had a decent lunch.

After visiting the venue, it was decided that we would hire some extra lights, a drum riser and Ludwig drum kit from a company in Milan, and only bring with us from England Brian's and John's guitars, Fred's mic with 'wand' and a front skin with current Queen logo for the bass drum. Arrangements having been made, we drove to Milan. Before Paul left for London, he put in a request for some stimulants to be made available for our stay in San Remo. Apparently that was no problem.

Yours truly (sucker) would fly to Milan in advance of the show with a lorry load of lire and do the business, check all was well with the hired gear and then drive south to San Remo.

Arriving at Milan's Linate airport for my flight back to Munich, I wondered if all small Fiat motorcars should really be driven like Ferraris in urban areas. Having been frisked by machine-gun-toting security and subjected to a grilling and declaration of all my German cash, I was finally allowed through to buy my 200 duty-free fags. The gate marked on my Alitalia boarding pass gave the destination as 'Monaco'.

'Where's the gate for the Munich flight then, signora?'

A well-manicured finger pointed to the Monaco gate.

'No, love – Munich – in Deutschland – comprendo?'

An indifferent Italian shrug. Having given half my boarding pass away, I found myself being bundled towards the door and the waiting transit bus. Mild panic, and I'm looking for clues to our destination. 'Munich, München – Germany…?' I climbed the steps of the plane not knowing where I was heading, so asked the stewardess: 'Does this flight go to Munich?'

'Si, yes, it goes to Monaco – Munich.'

'Oh I see – it stops in Monaco on the way?' (Seems an odd route.)

'No sir, eeet eez a direct flight, eeet is same place, Munich and Monaco.'

Monaco turned out to be the Italian word for Munich. Very confusing this foreign language business…

The flight over the Alps was bad. Very bad. Bottles and bags came crashing down from overhead, but it didn't stop them from serving the meal. Now I know how important food is to the Italians, but a plastic in-flight snack – as you look out and watch the wings buckle by the glow of lightning flashes?

The total of Queen and their entourage who flew out to Italy from London for the four- or five-day trip numbered eighteen. Possibly a little excessive for a mimed TV show by four musicians! But hey – this was Queen – big band – first time in Italy – big impression. I left in advance for Milan with the few thousand pounds in lire of 'float' I had got from Coutts Bank. I was travelling with John's bass, Fred's microphones with 'wand' – which I had checked in, and a couple of fragile bass drum skins with the Queen logo as hand baggage. I also had different-sized spares in case the Italians got the drum dimension wrong. They did.

I had requested a window seat and made my way on to the Alitalia jet, where I asked for somewhere safe to put the drum skins. There wasn't anywhere. My assigned seat was already occupied by a large Italian woman, complete with black dress, a rosary welded to her fingertips and a moustache to rival Fred's. She did not want to move – in any language. I explained my predicament with the drum skins to the stewardess, and that I could store them flush against the edge of the window seat.

'Impossible – they must be checked in and travel in the hold,' she replied.

I tried again, this time using the name San Remo.

'San Remo?'

'*Yes – gruppo – musica: Queen.*'

Magic words. 'Mamma Italia', her moustache and matching armpits were dispatched to the back of the plane. My own mamma-in-law was Italian – but fortunately nothing like that.

Arriving in Milan, I collected the luggage, weighed up my options, and walked towards the green customs channel where I was curtly stopped and asked to open the guitar case and other bags. The customs officers held their hands up and looked at me as if to say: 'Are you having a laugh? Looking like you do, and strolling through the green channel with this lot?'

The magic words: 'San Remo – Queen.'

'*Ah, si, la musica bella.* No problem. *Benvenuto in Italia!*'

Pleased at avoiding another customs confrontation, I waltzed my trolley into the arrivals hall where I was greeted by my sharply dressed record company contact of the previous meeting. (He was in Armani – I was more Army & Navy.) As we had met once already, he thought that entitled him to kiss me. I was certainly not having any of that nonsense! I appreciate that the Italians are passionate people, but didn't they invent homosexuality? No – maybe it was the Greeks? Anyway, as I have indicated, I later married into an Italian family and have to regularly kiss men, women and moustaches. But not holy rings.

Squeezing into a metal box constructed in Torino, we drove into Milano. I was assured all was 'magnifico' and a meeting for the goods was set up. 'Splendido.'

Time for vino? No.

'You have dollars or pounds to exchange?'

'No,' I replied proudly. 'No need to change it: I've got it all in lire.'

'Are you crazy? It is illegal to import or export lire above a certain amount.' (At that time about £200.)

'Customs were fine, no problems – but then they didn't see the money.'

'You are very lucky, signore. They would have "confiscated" the cash, you would have definitely been fined, and probably detained in jail.'

Oh-oh-oh-oh-oh-oh-oh! Mamma Mia let me go!

That was close. I was then told how many millions of lire were required.

'Fine, it's all here – I'm ready to go.'

'Peter, it is better you don't come to this meeting.'

'No, sorry, pal, I don't hand over large wads of cash without personally seeing something back.'

It was then *clearly* explained to me who the people holding the merchandise were: dark suits – Sicily... something nasty left in the bed (something nasty was about to be left in my trousers).

'I'll stay here with a cappuccino then – got anything in English to read?'

Having earlier narrowly avoided an Italian jail, I decided to skip meeting the Mafia. Our man returned with a bag of rocks – like slithers of ancient Italian marble. Flaking some off, we tried it. There was no need to ask for any money back.

When I arrived in San Remo that night, Paul Prenter was up waiting for me, or, more importantly, for the merchandise. He commandeered it all and hammered at the rocks with a glass hotel ashtray on the hard wooden floor – smashing the ashtray as chunks of cocaine slithered across the room. He was on his hands and knees desperately trying to retrieve every morsel. It's a very nasty drug at times, cocaine.

The following day, the Queen entourage arrived and the festival turned into a big party. I was moved from my room in The Royal Hotel to a tiny cupboard in the hotel annexe, as some periphery person deemed more important *must* have a room in the main hotel. It was around this time that I began to consider just how much I was appreciated and valued, and whether I wanted to be a roadie any longer.

Blondie, a German friend of ours from Munich, had shown up in his official capacity as representative for Puma sportswear. He had custom-made a tight red singlet vest with a leaping white puma on the front for Fred, and was delighted when he wore it on stage in front of a TV audience of millions.

In those days, there was little sponsorship or hard endorsements. Queen would be given loads of sportswear from Puma, Nike and Adidas and would maybe wear it – or maybe not. No contracts were signed or heavy lawyers involved. It was very relaxed and low key – just the occasional promo photo. It was a different era.

Appearing in San Remo were other English artists, including Paul Young and Culture Club. I was surprised at how big Boy George was. Normally, the angles photos and film of bands are viewed from are low, making people appear larger and grander. Many stars and singers are actually quite short and slight. Not 'Boy' – he was built like a brickie's labourer.

The San Remo show was deemed a huge success for Queen and I wasn't surprised. Queen's popularity in Italy is all down to 'Bohemian Rhapsody'. There are many theories of what 'Bohemian Rhapsody' is all about, but I know the truth. Honest. On a couple of occasions I asked Fred, 'What's it all about then, Fred – "Bo Rhap"?'

He would twiddle his hands dismissively: 'Oh, you know, dear – this and that.'

That was revealing...

Actually it's all about Italy and Fred being influenced by the magnificence of this cultured country. Just think about the words: 'Mamma mia' – Italian of course. Galileo, Figaro, Magnifico? – all Italians. Scaramouche – a pizza topping from Naples. Fandango – a formula one racing driver for Ferrari. Bismilah – a fashion designer in Milan. And

Beelzebub was a striker for Juventus. The pathos of the grand mini opera is summed up: 'I sometimes wish I'd never been to Roma at all.'

Now you know.

BACK TO WORK – OCCASIONALLY.

Back in Munich, recording carried on (a bit) and discipline slackened. The studio was not exactly being used to its full potential, doubling as a breakfast cafe, chat room, meeting point, dining room, recreation area, video playback suite and occasional place to record songs. Once the basic tracks were laid down, you no longer saw all four members of the band together regularly. They would come in for their own songs, to collaborate or play on other songs, or just eat and meet. At times, members of the band would fly out to Munich, do a bit of work and fly home to London again.

Expensive, high-speed German cars were rented on a whim, and road-tested along the nearby stretches of Autobahn. The sophisticated ABS braking systems were also tested – to establish if they did avoid skidding when braking at high speed – on ice.

Ironically, on one occasion when we were not spending large sums of money for Musicland to be sporadically used – a few hours of studio time and producer Mack were urgently required. 'I Want To Break Free' had been chosen as the follow-up single to 'Radio Ga Ga', and John was to oversee mixing the 12-inch version. The problem being that Musicland was being used by somebody else. I flew out to Munich with John and, in the meantime, Mack booked a professional studio that he knew – Union Studios in

Allescher Strasse. The 'Break Free' mix with its slowly building intro on the synthesiser was so popular with everybody that the seven-inch single was held back and then released with this new version.

When John and I and the rest of Queen were back in Munich at Musicland to finish recording of *The Works*, we were once again installed in the Hilton Hotel.

Room 828 Muenchen Hilton Hotel. Knock-knock…

'Who is it? It's 5:00 am and I'm entertaining!

'Ratty, it's John.'

'Yes, John.'

'I'm fed up with all this – I'm off.'

'Back to London?'

'No – I'm getting away'

'Are you… leaving the band? Surely not going solo?'

'Well in a way – I'm off to Bali – tomorrow – today that is, but I need some cash.'

(*You* need cash?)

'Right… well, you're the boss, it's your money, and it's stashed in a flight case – we can get it when the studio opens for the cleaners. Bali? Fine, well, I've heard it's very nice – when are you back?'

'Dunno, I'll call you. I need a break. I'll check out, put my stuff in your room, can you, I'm travelling light. And I suppose you'd better tell the rest of the band – please.'

'You're the boss…'

Later that day: 'Fred – John's gone to Bali.'

Cue Mr Mercury leaping on to the dining table to sing 'Bali High' from *South Pacific*, in the grandest operatic style.

Apart from breaking the news that band members had

gone missing, my daily routine would include going upstairs to the news-stand in the Arabella Hotel and buying what was left of the English papers that were flown in. They did not arrive until around lunchtime, which was very convenient as we were never out of bed until at least that hour. I would also buy an assortment of international magazines for the band to peruse, and music publications in any language.

Fred discovered a double page spread of himself live on stage in one mag and flaunted it around the studio. He and the others would often criticise other bands' images.

'Just look at Sting! She's posing with her shirt off again!'

'How could they look good under a green spotlight? Like some kind of disease!'

Fred always wanted his newspaper horoscope (Virgo) read out to him daily and sometimes other signs (presumably people he was close to or interested in at the time). I read John's to try to find out when he might be back from Bali...

He eventually called, a week or so later, asking me to book him back into the Hilton, and could I pick him up from Munich airport. He showed up with peeling, flaking skin from severe sunburn, and was immediately dubbed The Snakeman.

Fred would either get very excited by the horoscope prediction or dismiss it as rubbish. He then asked for vodka. Not *a* vodka – just vodka!

Everybody drank vodka, which is apparently a 'clean' drink and good-quality stuff is easier on the system – so they say. The band all drank it with tonic, the crew with orange juice. We were younger then and our livers could cope – most of the time. Brian also enjoyed his vodka, but was never the best at timekeeping and particularly after a hard night. He did not smoke cigarettes, never did drugs and had a good diet; so he did make an effort to look after himself.

All the crew smoked and so did Roger, but Fred and John, both former non-smokers, started the habit in the '80s. Then Roger, after various attempts, eventually gave it up. I never thought Fred suited smoking. There was historically an element of cool and macho-style attached to cigarettes, but Fred didn't jam the cigarette in the corner of his mouth as James Dean did or bite on it like Clint Eastwood. Nor did he hold it up and let it smoulder as Marlene Dietrich and other Hollywood stars would.

No, I have to say Fred smoked cigarettes like a schoolgirl, puffing quite lightly and urgently on cigarettes and never leaving them in his mouth for long, before snatching them out with his fingertips. Naturally, he never bought his own, so would bum fags from the entourage.

Munich and its people and places inspired everybody and in particular one of Brian's songs:

'Dragon Attack' – *The Game* – 1980

Written by Brian May; inspired by Munich.

Take me back to that Shack any time!

CHAPTER ELEVEN

LONDON

(HOME SWEET HOME – ONE DAY IN
SIX FOR TAX PURPOSES)

FRED'S BED

From Munich to Kensington – via West Ham. Fred would often buy things on impulse, and usually very expensive things. In 1980, while recording in Munich, Mr Mercury had bought some Art Deco-style bedroom furniture – a period he was very fond of. The pastel pink and peach, shell-style boudoir set was to be transported back to England with Queen's studio gear, which involved me organising the paperwork to export the goods, transit them through other countries and import them into England. It was a real headache as it meant mixing Queen's equipment on a temporary import carnet with Fred's goods exported for importation into another country while passing through other countries... Bloody paperwork! These difficulties were compounded by having to travel at the weekend when some customs services were not available at border posts. The traditional route back home was via Frankfurt, cross into Belgium at Aachen then zip past Brussels to Ostend and the ferry to Dover. This was not an option, and a more circuitous route via Holland had to be negotiated.

More bloody headaches!

There was no real choice but to travel in the truck myself, leaving the others to a leisurely lie-in before conveniently jetting home club class later that afternoon.

'*Wish you were here!*'

As Gerry, the driver, and I wearily approached the German/Dutch border that evening, I asked him to pull over anywhere I could find a phone, in order to call the local freight agent who would meet us at the border. I spotted a bar, jumped down from the high cab of the truck, ran over the deserted road and entered. It was now nearing the end of a bright summer's evening, but inside it was quite dimly lit and empty, apart from three or four reasonably attractive girls. I asked in my half-decent German if I could use the phone and would willingly pay for the call. As I was making my call, the bar girl gestured to me – did I want a drink? By now my eyes had adjusted to the dim light and, as I viewed the surplus of red velvet furniture and gold fittings, it dawned on me that this was some sort of brothel and I was potential trade. The agent had told me to go directly to the border only a few minutes away, where he would meet us, so I made my apologies, handed over some deutschmarks for the call and with a tinge of regret leaped back into the truck.

Crossing Holland, into Belgium, we arrived at the port of Ostende in darkness – missing the final ferry. The words loyal, stupid and underpaid came to my mind as I attempted to sleep while hunched in the passenger seat of the truck, parked on the dock, waiting for the morning's first crossing. My mouth felt like a used jockstrap and an overall personal freshen-up would soon desperately be needed.

Arriving back in London with an equally sore back and attitude, we dropped everything in Queen's warehouse at Edwin Shirley Trucking in West Ham and I made my way home on the tube, still in my clothes of two days standing – literally.

Shortly after entering my flat, I got a call from Queen's office: 'Is Fred's furniture back and all OK?'

After confirming that it was, I was told that Fred wanted it delivered immediately. Thanks!

There was now a problem in the fact that I did not have access to the Queen Productions van because it was being serviced. No excuse – Fred's bed *must* be delivered at once! Paul Prenter insisted.

Dragging myself back across the width of London, I arrived at Edwin Shirley Trucking, who had agreed to lend me a VW van for the evening. With the help of Jobby, we finally arrived at Fred's, only to be told that everything was to be put into Mary's flat at the end of the terrace.

By this point, I was completely shattered and could barely keep awake after two days without any proper sleep at all. The furniture was being carried into the flat by Fred's driver and other beefy chaps, and I told Jobby that, as we were double-parked, I would pull the van around the corner and wait for him there. It was getting dark, so I fiddled with the van's controls to find out how the lights worked, flashing them on and off. I lit a cigarette and leaned back in the seat to relax, when suddenly a serious-looking guy knocked on the side window. I looked at him incredulously as I was so tired. When he flashed an official ID police pass, I wound the window down.

'Is this your vehicle sir?'

'No.'

'What are you doing here?'

'Waiting for somebody – so what!?'

'What's your name and address?'

As I gave my name and the Queen Productions office address, more of these menacing plain-clothes guys were milling around the van. They ran a radio check on the vehicle, and me, to see if I had any previous records. I was told to get out of the van and hand over the keys. I protested strongly as I did not like the way I was being hassled – WHACK! – I was pushed hard against the side of the van, which gave the dull springing sound of a person indented on sheet metal. I was then informed from very close range at high volume: 'This can be easy or hard': which did I want?

Easy was just fine by me. I opened the back of the van for them to view, and, save for a few bits of cardboard packing, it was empty. One guy jumped inside and checked around thoroughly, as another checked the front. At this point Jobby showed up and was asked if he knew me and could confirm my name and address.

He gave them my home address!

Great! I was now in deeper shit for giving false information. However, after a few urgent radio conversations, they lost interest in us and were off as fast as they came. I had managed to find out that they were Special Branch officers, and as we were in the wake of the recent Iranian Embassy siege in Kensington, which was two minutes down the road, they were on the lookout for anything out of the ordinary in the area. Flashing my van lights on and off in a Kensington side street close to the bombed-out embassy was unusual enough to warrant checking out.

HOME IS WHERE...?

Despite being hassled by the security services, it was nice to get back to London where people spoke proper English and the telly was understandable too. London was our home, or at least it was where we all lived occasionally between Queen's hectic touring and recording schedules. When the band were off the road, they rarely relaxed, and apart from family and domestic duties, were busy writing, doing interviews, photo sessions, arguing, planning and spending money. I was on permanent call for domestic and professional duties; hunting down new musical and technical gadgets, taking garden rubbish to the tip, delivering decorative items of excellent taste to Fred or Roger's houses, all manner of new and antique things to Brian's, and everything including the bathroom sink and matching French suite to John's.

I even had to fix Fred's telephone and his ancient hi-fi system.

'Isn't he wonderful?' Fred would coo to Mary Austin.

Mary was wonderful too; a delightful lady to be around. In fact, all of Queen's wives, girlfriends and partners, including David Minns, Joe Fanelli and Jim Hutton, were very cordial towards the crew. They enjoyed a drink and a laugh like us, and would always find time for a chat and bit of banter, wherever we were in the world.

In 1976, after the *Night At The Opera* tour, the band had finally seen some real money and moved out of their rented flats into the land of mortgages and property ownership. Fred bought a grand duplex flat in Stafford Terrace in Kensington, a few minutes' drive from his old flat in Holland Road, and I had been asked to move his 'bits and pieces'. An honour.

On the way to Fred's, I got pulled over by the police (something that would happen frequently to me through the years) near the famous Rainbow Theatre on the Seven Sisters Road. I was driving in a bus lane, which was an offence – having long hair and an unkempt appearance confirmed my guilt.

The bus lane law was new, and though not a custodial sentence or hanging offence was a hefty (in 1976) £10 fine.

Arriving slightly late at Fred's flat due to the protracted police paperwork, I apologised to Mary, and we shuttled back and forward between 'Chez Mercury' old and new. Mary was busily occupied with the administration of the utilities bills, etc, and Fred was out somewhere, spending his newfound wealth on lovely things and *objets* to fill his new abode.

One important item that I moved was a neat little blue metal toolbox – but this was Mary's, as she was the one who knew how to use a screwdriver or fit a fuse! When all was cleared at the old flat, Mary came up to me and furtively slipped me some cash, saying, 'Thanks for your help and here's something towards the fine, but don't say anything to Freddie about it.'

One thing you could always be sure of when visiting Fred's was a cup of tea, usually Earl Grey – and not in teabags. This was sophistication indeed for a roadie used to a 'mug of char' and I quite got used to the taste and aroma of the fragrant bergamot (unlike Crystal who described it as perfumed piss). Tea was always served in proper china cups – with saucers. However, it was not brewed by the Mercurial hand, it was always Mary, Joe, Phoebe or whoever was nearest to the kitchen.

TRANSPORT

Driving a Transit van around town in the seventies, with one or two of the other roadies in tow, we felt like Regan and Carter in *The Sweeney* – confident and irreverent towards authority – just getting the job done. Sorted! So Shut It!

A van may have been fun to drive around London in, but was not great for pulling birds. Hardly surprising, really, when you consider the disgusting state band vehicles get into. The front of a 'bandwagon' was always full of old fag packets, chocolate wrappers, bits of paper, crisp bags, cellophane, etc., while the ashtray overflowed with dog ends. The dashboard would be thick with grease and grime and you could confidently say it was a potential fire hazard; as poignantly demonstrated in my early days on the road with Phil and Richie, when we worked for Mott The Hoople. Sitting in a line at the front of a three-ton truck somewhere on a motorway, having eaten our staple roadies' diet of fried everything with beans plus extra beans on the side, Phil took over the driving. As Richie relaxed, he started to break wind profusely and, greatly amused by this, decided to set his farts alight. Slouching down in the seat with his legs stretched out, he could rest his cowboy-booted feet on the dashboard. He then lit a match and, holding it close to his denim-clad ass, farted long and hard. This methane propulsion caused a substantial flame, which ignited the cellophane and quickly spread to the entire dashboard and its contents. Panic stricken, Phil screeched over to the hard shoulder as we flapped about to put the fire out. The rest of the journey was spent with the windows wide open to rid us of the stench of old farts and singed dashboard.

Another tale involving van life and bodily functions was when driving through the busy centre of London I suddenly felt my bladder straining intensely. I had recently been prescribed some pills by a special clinic for a recurring 'water infection' and a side effect of the medication was that it regularly flushed the system out – I was bursting for a slash! Stuck in heavy traffic and racking my brains as to the location of the nearest public loo, I realised I was not going to make it. I pulled over with two wheels illegally mounted on the pavement in a major road, then jumped into the back of the van where there was a pile of parking tickets still in their weatherproof plastic bags. Crouching on my knees as the traffic rattled past, I managed to fill a few of the bags before securing the tops. Later that day the bags were dispatched from the van window at an appropriate target.

Queen always spent Christmas at home and one of the van's domestic duties was a seasonal pick-up from Fred's, to take delivery of a mixed case of booze he had kindly given to each of the personal crew. You would always get a card from Fred as well, my favourite being the day-glo pink one he commissioned with a black and white photo of himself from *Vogue* magazine on the cover. Inside was the printed inscription: 'Wishing you a Merry Christmas and a Happy New Year from the Preening, Pouting, Posing, Posturing Old Tart'. To this he added his personal handwritten message. Priceless.

EXECUTIVE ATTIRE AND ASSHOLES

Being a roadie has to be the antithesis of a career as a suited businessman, so why was there a fashion in the early seventies for roadies to carry black briefcases?

What would you possibly carry around in them? Head roadies would have expense sheets, receipts, carnets, itineraries, tickets, etc., but for the others it was a pretentious holder for cigarettes and sandwiches. And sometimes a spare T-shirt. The briefcases never stayed black for long as they were quickly adorned with stickers and labels. These ranged from promo stickers for music stores to stage passes from somewhere cool. As a roadie's career blossomed, the mosaic built up, and layers of stickers thickened, with the highest-quality labels displayed on top.

The thin paper decal for a hotel in Brussels was superseded by a silky, material backstage pass for a gig in Los Angeles or a bold QUEEN JAPAN TOUR 79. Cases would be flaunted around town and particularly around Tottenham Court

Road, Shaftesbury Avenue or Denmark Street where the professional music stores were.

I always sported my briefcase to the accountant's office, but not a Queen Tour Jacket – that was seen as total posing, to wear an embroidered satin jacket around London. It was acceptable on tour because it could help in pulling women. Being interesting by association was still interesting.

Queen's posh UK accountant Keith Moore thought he was interesting by association too. Moore was a tall, well-built man who wore oversized 'Michael Caine' glasses and had other music-related clients in his office next door to the Kensington Hilton. Although well-educated, he had little style or taste and, like so many at the time on the periphery of rock 'n' roll, was seduced by the glamour of the lifestyle. He once turned up at Madison Square Garden in New York in a startling white suit – and the man in the white suit looked far funnier than the Ealing comedy. At Fred's 30th birthday party at Country Cousins restaurant on the King's Road in Chelsea, he sat next to Crystal and me, desperately trying to impress a female companion with how cool and 'turned-on' he thought he was. He wasn't. At all.

My background was basic working class; accountants and lawyers never featured in my world; they were above me, and due to the inherent British class system I believed that they were somehow superior. I am now of a *very* different opinion.

The rot at the accountancy firm started when I discovered one of its employees had misled me over a flat I was buying, losing me both the flat and money, then disappearing in a sports car he hadn't paid for – never to be seen again. The

Above left: The Live Aid award presented to me by Queen.

Above right: With Brian May at his racks of AC30 amplifiers at Oakland Coliseum in California, 1980.

Below: Checking the neck of John's bass, USA 1977.

Above: Freddie sound-checking with an acoustic guitar at Morumbi Stadium in São Paolo, Brazil, March 1981. Queen played to 251 000 people over two nights – the biggest ever paying audience for a live show.

Below: August 1978. Roger at his kit in the 'salon' room of the Casino de Montreux, which was used as the studio room to record the *Jazz* album.

Above: John with his Musicman Stingray Bass performing 'Tie Your Mother Down' during a 'live' video shoot in Miami in 1977.

Below: Brian in the studio in Munich, 1981.

Above: Fred at rehearsals for the 1980 European *The Game* tour.

Below: November 1983. Freddie battles with time on the set of the 'Radio Ga Ga' video.

Freddie in the control room of Mountain Studios in Montreux. *Above*: During the making of *Hot Space* in 1981 and, below, during the mixing of the *Live Killers* album in 1979.

Above: The band with German producer, Mack, 1981.

Below: John with the 'other' Fred: back-up keyboard player Fred Mandel, 1982.

Above: One of Queen's three dressing room wardrobe trunks.

Below: Relaxing backstage with John Deacon after the first momentous South American concert at Velez Sarsfield Stadium in Buenos Aires, February 1981.

NAME Peter Hince
**ACCESS
ALL AREAS**

Above: My 'Rat' pass for Queen UK summer concerts in 1976.

Below: With one of my trusty Nikon cameras outside Mountain Studios in Montreux in 1981.

guy who fled was not a qualified accountant at all, but a petty thief who stole items from the office. But, more seriously, he had been forging two of Queen's signatures on company cheques and embezzling the money for himself. Subsequently, Queen gradually pulled everything out of the accountancy firm, then adopted a different system for looking after their finances and appointed a reputable firm of city accountants. When Peter Chant, the new head accountant, was checking how I filled in my expenses book, he said, 'This all seems fine – but what does B&C mean for cash paid out?'

'Oh, that? That's bribery and corruption.'

He laughed, then asked me, 'OK, but please do try and get petty cash slips signed when you can, and not by Mr Michael Mouse or Ivor Bigun.'

What happened to Keith Moore? Queen's former accountant subsequently served a prison sentence for stealing around £6,000,000 from the Geordie bass player Sting.

Ironically, I met Sting in the reception of Keith Moore's firm one day in 1977.

I was introduced by Andy Summers, a session guitarist who I knew from previous tours I'd done. This was the era of punk, and, now sporting dyed blonde hair, Andy told us they had formed this new band: The Police. 'Never get anywhere,' I concluded with Crystal as we walked back to the van. I will add in my defence that we had not yet heard them play. I felt the same on the Mott tour in '73 about Queen and I *had* heard them play – every night.

A career in a record company A&R department was not really an option for me.

POP STARS

John, Brian and Roger liked to watch other bands play in London. Fred never went to rock shows and would favour attending the ballet or opera. Or he was equally quite happy at home with the telly. He seemingly took little notice of other bands or upcoming trends in music, but was actually very aware. He was not a fan of reggae, but when asked, respectfully described Bob Marley as 'hypnotic'.

I went along with John to see Bruce Springsteen at Wembley Arena on his 1980 *The River* tour. It was a tremendous show and afterwards we went to the backstage bar area and had a drink along with the press and most of the music world of London, desperate for a piece of Bruce's time. Shortly after, Bruce's manager came over and asked John if he would like to come and say hi to Bruce.

'Sure – love to.'

We were led back into one of the many rooms off the backstage corridor, which was empty save for a few chairs, a massage table and the smell of athletic massage fluid. We were given a beer and told 'The Boss' would be along shortly. Bruce opened the door unaccompanied, and the three of us then sat and chatted over a beer for ages, while outside the whole of London's music world clamoured to see him. He was a truly nice guy and pointed out that he had a masseur to help keep his body toned for the gruelling schedule he undertook. There appeared to be mutual musical respect between him and Queen, as Roger, who had been to Bruce's show the previous night was granted the same audience.

A year or so later, I was in the Sunset Marquis, a quiet, low-key apartment hotel in Los Angeles, and passing through reception when I saw Mr Springsteen coming in. I caught his eye and he came straight over, shook my hand and said it was good to see me again and asked after the band. I was stunned!

He must constantly meet thousands of different people, yet he remembered a humble roadie he once met briefly while accompanying his bass guitar-playing boss. Top man.

HOME COMFORTS

Roger had houses in London but his preferred residence was in the Surrey countryside at Mill Hanger (dubbed Coat Hanger) complete with the rock-star lifestyle: swimming pool, go-karts, pinball machines, snooker table, juke box and bar were all available. One of his neighbours was Rick Parfitt of Status Quo, who had a small studio incorporated into his country residence. An impromptu session was arranged with Rick, Roger and John, so I drove down with John and his guitars in the splendour of a Ford Transit van. Rick had Porsches parked in front of his house, which he called his 'Giant Tonka toys'. After some ideas were put on tape, he suggested we went off to his local pub for refreshment; the route on foot had us negotiating crop fields and small country paths. The centre-piece of the pub's bar was a gold Status Quo album. Rick was clearly a regular, and beckoned Roger and John over to meet his landlord: 'See these two guys here?' Rick whispered closely to the guy behind the bar. 'They're almost as famous as me.'

Later, while I was driving John back to London in the van, we were apprehended by a sole policeman, who had been concealed in the shadows of a Little Chef diner. John, who had been drinking, seemed a bit nervous but I was completely sober, and as it was me driving I told him we had nothing to worry about. I was also used to being stopped by the Old Bill and dealing with them. The cop was concerned by the pungent smell he claimed was dope, and inspected the van's ashtrays thoroughly. The smell was just the van's dodgy old heater, with its overheated, rubber signature.

He never searched us...

Fred's magnificent house, Garden Lodge in Kensington, was a testament to his superb taste. It was full of wonderful antiques and art tempered with personal knick-knacks, Mercurial *objets* and photographs, but despite its grandeur it had a homely feel. There was no obvious visual evidence on display at Garden Lodge of Fred's day job. All the hundreds of platinum, gold and silver albums, plus the awards, plaques and statuettes, were tucked away out of sight.

On one wall of his kitchen was a large, modern, forgettable but expensive oil painting that Fred had picked up on tour in South America. It was very big, and I had suggested strapping it into the lid of the Steinway grand piano case to ship it home. Fred thought this was a good idea as he could get his new piece of art back to London quickly: 'But what about all those customs men and things?'

'Don't worry, Fred – if they ask, I'll tell them a fan gave it to you. They'd find it hard to believe you actually paid money for it.'

I was rewarded for my insolence with the Fred frown.

Visiting Brian's house in a quiet area by the Thames, I was offered the usual cordial cup of tea. While sitting in the lounge, I noticed a new addition, a semi-circular shelf, positioned halfway up the wall that it dominated. I asked if it was reserved for an item of beauty he had purchased or some newly won award. No, the shelf and its small orange velvet cushion was set aside for Squeaky, Brian's tortoiseshell cat, to sit on. Brian explained this as he brought in the tea and biscuits, balanced in a drawer from a kitchen cabinet! Apparently, he had builders in and couldn't find a tray. A guitar-playing scientist is hardly going to be the model of domesticity...

John lived quite modestly and, as the most anonymous of the band, he managed to keep a degree of privacy, which he wanted for his family. However, when he moved to a big Victorian house to accommodate his growing clan, I teased him that it looked like the layout of the Cluedo board. You always got a good cup of tea at John's.

MEN IN TIGHTS

One of the more unusual gigs I did was for Fred, when he appeared with the Royal Ballet for a charity show at the London Coliseum in late 1979. Fred's circle of friends included Wayne Sleep and Wayne Eagling, both respected classical dancers, and Fred was delighted to join them for this one-off performance. As to be expected, Mr Mercury would only accept the invitation if he was fully rehearsed. I was summoned, as Fred's performance for 'Bohemian Rhapsody' involved him singing while lying on his back, carried over the heads of the other dancers as they glided across the stage.

'But how can we do it, Ratty?'

'*We*, Fred?'

'You know, you know, the microphone and cable and all that – it'll get in the way, won't it?'

'Yeah.'

'So what can we do then?'

'Don't worry, Fred, *we* can get a radio microphone for you.'

'Oh yes – very good.'

I rented a radio microphone system, which in the far-off days of '79 were temperamental. I located the very best available and went to visit the sound technician at the Coliseum to check the place out and see if there were any 'dead spots' or if they had experienced problems using wireless mics in the theatre. It seemed to work fine and a 1/4 tape was specially mixed at the Townhouse Studios to be 'dropped in' during the opera section of 'Bo Rhap'. Fred would then sing live to the remaining backing track. The rehearsals went well and all were in good spirits backstage at the Coliseum on the Sunday night.

I'm sure Fred was nervous, but I was shitting myself. No matter how good the technology of musical equipment becomes, you should always get a spare. In this case, there was no spare available and I was not on stage to solve any problems, as I was in the mixing booth at the back of the stalls, charged with the task of mixing Fred's voice with the ambient orchestra and dropping in the tape at the vital moment.

Oh shit, he'll kill me if something goes wrong. How did I get dragged into this – stupidity or loyalty? The biggest headache was that the mixing booth was enclosed behind glass, and the sound only audible through small monitor speakers. This was certainly not rock 'n' roll – I needed to hear it from source. The house engineer in the booth with me changed into an elegant black velvet evening jacket with satin lapels to mix the show, while smoking cigarettes from a long 'Noel Coward'-style holder.

No – not rock 'n' roll, and I rather fancy he was a bachelor.

By the time of Fred's performance, I had smoked my way through a pack of Bensons, and then as he began to sing I rushed out of the booth and through the auditorium doors to hear it for real. It seemed fine but pretty quiet, compared to what we were used to. After a standing ovation for 'Bohemian Rhapsody', Fred began to whip the dinner jacket and evening gown crowd into a frenzy with a version of the freshly released 'Crazy Little Thing Called Love' single.

At the end of the concert, I went backstage to retrieve the microphone from the dressing room. I was pleased but hugely relieved that Fred's performance had gone well. His dressing room was overflowing with flowers, champagne and theatrical 'luvvies' as I squeezed through to retrieve the forgotten (and extremely expensive) mic that was left lying forlornly on a side table. I wanted to see how Fred was, but he was in his element, surrounded by baying admirers and so no acknowledgement or thanks were forthcoming. Nor was an invitation to the after-show party at Legends club in Mayfair.

Ah, well – it was my job. But still, it's nice to feel you're appreciated.

Fred enjoyed several non-gay London nightclubs in the '70s and '80s; apart from Legends, he would frequent The Embassy in Bond Street, Maunkberry in Jermyn Street and Xenon in Piccadilly, where on 5 September 1984 he held a party for his 38th birthday after one of the run of Queen shows at Wembley Arena. Earlier at Wembley, Fred had commandeered an extra backstage dressing room into which he put several of his ex-lovers, who had been invited. He then left them to get on with it... that mischievous old Mercury! His birthday was tainted by the publication that day in a tabloid of details about Freddie's private life. The beans had been spilled by a former personal employee. Most definitely *not* a crew member I will add.

MAKING MOVIES (LIGHTS, CAMERAS, FRICTION)

Due to the decline of the British film industry in the 1970s, the studio complexes around London were being utilised by other forms of modern entertainment culture – notably rock bands. Being there when Queen made the pioneering video for 'Bohemian Rhapsody' at Elstree Film Studios, north of London, was in retrospect quite exciting; and so was being in and around film studios generally. At that time, Queen were starting their new management era with John Reid, who also managed Elton John, Kiki Dee and Kevin Ayers. A shared warehouse with Elton John's equipment was available for Queen at Elstree Studios, but not long afterwards was commandeered by director Stanley Kubrick to be used as the kitchen in his movie *The Shining*.

It was a coincidence I maintain, but I was once asked quite firmly to move my Transit van, as I had parked in Mr Kubrick's private space.

'Here's Ratty!'

Lots of the sets for *The Shining* were at Elstree along with those from *Star Wars*, *Superman* and other big screen movies of the time. Great stuff.

After being turfed out of our second Elstree storage space, we moved Queen's ever-growing collection of sound and stage gear to Shepperton Film Studios, west of London in Middlesex, where we rented storage space from The Who and their company ML Executives. Whereas Paul McCartney and Stanley Kubrick had bought parts of Elstree Studios, The Who had invested in Shepperton.

It was common for big bands to rehearse at film studios, as the sound stages gave all the space and production facilities required for a major touring show. It was a surreal experience, as long-haired rock 'n' rollers ate in the canteen alongside 'aliens' and other actors and extras in their costumes. Pinewood Studios was a special place to rehearse, as it was home to the enormous 007 stage that featured all the giant sets used on the James Bond movies. And I think we all liked to imagine we had a bit of 'Bond' in our lifestyles – shaken but not stirred, with a definite licence to thrill.

Although the video for 'Bohemian Rhapsody' was regarded as a seminal piece of promotion for a new era of the music business, Queen did not take every video they did so seriously. The music video became a necessity, but also at times an inconvenience. The follow-up single to 'Bohemian Rhapsody' was done during rehearsals for the *A Day at the Races* album at Ridge Farm in Surrey. Bruce Gowers who had directed 'Bo Rhap' was brought in to film 'You're My Best Friend'. The location was the barn we were using to rehearse in. It was the blistering hot summer of 1976 and the barn had no ventilation apart from leaving all the doors open. So it probably wasn't a good idea to have a video that included hundreds of candles as 'mood' lighting. People were literally passing out from the heat and smoke, as everybody fled the barn between takes. The best song (in my opinion) on *A Day at the Races* and released as the first single was the superb and still to this day outstanding 'Somebody to Love'. This video was back to Queen being creative and innovative, using footage shot at Wessex recording studios in Highbury during the recording of the album, and editing with live film from the '76 summer free concert in Hyde Park.

Exceptions to the rule of 'live' performance or staged studio videos were for 'We Will Rock You' and 'Spread Your Wings'. These were both shot together in the grounds of Roger's newly acquired country estate. As the property was technically not yet his, and he didn't have the keys, we were allowed to use the grounds by the vendors but not the house. Or even the toilets if I remember…

Thick snow covered the ground, and it was bleak and very cold, which did not please Fred. While the video set was being finalised and between takes, Fred warmed himself up with tots of brandy inside his Rolls-Royce parked conveniently in the driveway. He wanted some gloves to wear, but there were none available and no wardrobe person either. As a joke I offered him my 'roadie truck-loading' pair. These were standard issue for the stylish roadie at the time; American rodeo gloves in light beige soft leather, with a drawstring to tighten them at the wrists. These would be bought at 76 truck stops in the USA and then fastened on to a dog clip with bunches of keys and other paraphernalia that hung from the belt loop on your jeans. Mine were filthy dirty, had gaffer tape repaired fingers and written on both of them in thick black felt pen to avoid any confusion of

234

ownership was 'RATTY'. Fred gratefully accepted my offer and wore them on the video.

The Game was the band's biggest album in America with two number one hit singles; 'Crazy Little Thing Called Love', the first single, had a video shot in a small TV studio in Dean Street in London's Soho. It was choreographed by Arlene Phillips of Hot Gossip fame. This was Queen getting back into 'theme' videos and the 1950s-style song had the band dressed in leather jackets and a motorbike used as a prop. It worked very well, as once again Queen changed their image and moved forward. As the band entered the 1980s, they did shift – from being a successful heavy-rock band to being an even more successful pop-rock band. It was just how things evolved. The quality remained, but they were certainly more commercial. They all now, with the exception of Brian, had short, sensible haircuts that your mum would be happy with. Brian was playing the new black Fender Telecaster I had got for him and was wearing some wraparound sunglasses that made him look like a tall insect. Between takes, Fred was having his hair greased down with KY jelly by a stylist, when he shrieked: 'What a waste', which brought the entire studio to a standstill with laughter.

There were two very fit female dancers who were dressed provocatively in black waistcoats with tight black satin shorts, black seamed nylon stockings, black suspenders and black patent high heels – a blonde and a redhead. Oh yes!

Is that too much information?

There were also two male dancers, who were very light on their feet. At the end of the shoot, the director wanted a shot with rows of hands clapping together, to use with the section of the song that featured handclaps. The catwalk that Fred and the dancers were performing on then had symmetric rows of holes cut in the top decking and the sides taken off, so the 'volunteers' could squeeze in. The side panels were then replaced to make it look neat, and on cue sets of hands appeared from the holes and clapped in time (some of the time). As a 'volunteer' who sat on a hard studio floor with my body hunched over and hands contorted over my head in a confined space I was not at all comfortable, but it did give me a wonderful view of 'blondie' and 'the redhead' as they wiggled above me. I seem to recall that the enticement to get the crew to be boxed in and clap was that we could keep the dancers' underwear after the shoot had wrapped – the *female* dancers' underwear.

The video for 'Play the Game' was done at the same studio. We had arrived with all the gear early one morning, only to be told that Fred was feeling unwell and the shoot was cancelled. The rescheduled video was eventually shot against a Chroma Key background, a rich blue backdrop that can be replaced electronically by different imposed backgrounds and effects during editing. The set was minimal, a small drum kit and riser and one small amp set up for John and Brian, and was reminiscent of a sixties TV pop show. John played a new Kramer bass he had been given by the company and Brian played a cheap 'Satellite' Stratocaster copy. I had bought two for him as it was planned he was going to tussle with Fred in the video and then sling the guitar across stage and begin smashing it. Not quite The Who.

The video opens with Fred's silver Shure stage microphone hanging in space, and in an attempt to make it look like a fancy radio mic I put a connector in it without the cable, and rammed a bit of wire coat hanger in to give it the look of an antenna. Fred appears to pop up from the bottom of the screen, and as this was the first video with him sporting his newly grown moustache he looked like a lost walrus surfacing!

Later in the video when he is covered in water, he really does become a 'bull walrus'. The 'flame'-coloured background idea for the video was an extension of that particular single's picture cover. I had taken some group shots of the band crammed on to a chilly balcony of somebody's room in the Munich Hilton. I was experimenting with some 'grad filters' that put varying degrees of tint and colour into the top of the photo – in this case, the sky. Fred liked the idea, but, when he saw the finished shots, which included ones I had done for fun of rushing water in the adjacent Isar River, again using the coloured 'grad' filters, he got excited. He held a group shot that had been approved up to a light bulb and slid different background shots against it. When he had shuffled the background into the desired position, it was secured with clear tape and sent to the Creem design company to get a composite transparency duped. That was the cover of the finished single sleeve and the image used world-wide for various other PR. So the background is actually coloured water, not flames as so many people believe.

While recording *The Game* in Munich, Queen would alternate between Germany and London, where they were recording the soundtrack to the *Flash Gordon* movie. And a resulting video was shot for the 'Flash' single at Advision studios.

Music videos were now what accompanied every Queen

single, and did at least spare the band from appearing on *Top Of The Pops* to mime in front of a bunch of badly-dressed spotty youths, who gawped at the artists on stage, while dancing (badly) out of synch to the playback. However, we did make a couple of trips to BBC Centre in White City, with a minimal amount of equipment, to perform 'Good Old Fashioned Lover Boy' in 1977 and 'Las Palabras de Amor' in 1982. I always hoped that Queen's dressing room was close to the one used by Pan's People; the resident female dance group who were used to interpret one song during the show – usually in skimpy outfits and using their lithe bodies in an appealing way.

How many adolescents have gazed at the TV on a Thursday evening, waiting for them to come on and thought 'Whooaaaah!'? I did. And they were even better in the flesh! There must be something about female dancers...

Hot Space videos were not particularly memorable; 'Backchat' and 'Calling All Girls' were done at the same time at a TV studio in Wandsworth, south London. A trip to Canada was arranged for the 'Body Language' video – which was originally banned for being too raunchy.

When 'Radio Ga Ga' was chosen as the first single from *The Works* sessions, Fred took assertive control – 'We must do a huge video, as the song deserves it and we have become a bit complacent with videos, so we must do it BIG – and spend BIG.'

The mammoth video was shot at a small TV studio in St John's Wood and at Shepperton Film Studios on a stage that had previously housed Queen tour rehearsals. It was another milestone for Queen, with a huge set and hundreds of handclapping extras from Queen's fan club, edited with classic black and white footage of Fritz Lang's *Metropolis* movie. In the 'Ga Ga' video there is one small shot that involved Fred parting a building with his bare hands. High on a scaffold, Fred stood in macho pose as the polystyrene set was pulled apart and the crumbling debris fell, as smoke swirled around him. The smoke effects were not working well so the assistant director called through his megaphone for more assistants to fan and waft the smoke with boards. Meanwhile, Fred was relaxing up his tower with a cigarette and the harassed assistant director sensed that Fred was getting impatient because things were not speeding along, so he urgently shouted into his speaking trumpet with a cut-glass accent: 'More wafters, more wafters – we must have more wafters!'

This sounded like 'woofters', at which point Fred giggled with laughter, tottering precariously on his high perch and shouting down: 'Me too, dear, me too!'

The video for 'I Want To Break Free' was done over two days at Limehouse Studios in London's Docklands and a studio in Battersea. This video was a brave tongue-in-cheek move by the band and was well received – except in America, and as they declined to do an alternative video for the US market it was an indication of the beginning of the end for the band's popularity there. This was tragic as *The Works* was a very good album and the live show that accompanied it was probably the band's best, and deserved to be seen by America.

The second day of shooting 'Break Free' was the dressing-up in drag day, and, while Fred could always be guaranteed to revel in such camp drama, the others got into the spirit surprisingly well. John was happy to be dressed as a grumpy old grandmother but drew the line at having the make-up artist apply currants and sultanas to his face to look like warts and moles. Brian, though convincing in his part, was probably not going to give up his day job to 'tread the boards', and Roger was just a bit too convincing as he shaved his legs for his part as a schoolgirl. The atmosphere in the studio was very good and everybody appreciated that rock stars with alleged big egos could make fun of themselves. It was a typical move by Queen to show that they were always striving for change and to surprise.

The following morning, I flew to Japan, accompanying John, Roger and his assistant Crystal for a three-week promotional tour of the Far East, Australia and Los Angeles for *The Works* album.

The other single from *The Works* was 'It's a Hard Life' – a grand pompous affair that the band hated – which was done at Arri studios in Munich. Fred might have loved dressing up in over-the top, theatrical costumes, but the others looked very uncomfortable in theirs. The whole look did not befit the direction they were going in. Fred's deep-pink, shiny and risqué figure-hugging outfit with large eyes and antenna attached made him look like an overcooked tandoori king prawn.

CHAPTER TWELVE

TRAINS, BOATS AND PLANES – BUSES, TRUCKS AND CARS

(MAY I SEE YOUR PAPERS, SIR?)

Queen were never in London for long, so itching for adventure we would be back on the road again. A peripatetic profession, the essence of touring is the constant travel, and moving of personnel from city to city. A vast range of transportation was utilised by Queen tours, from Concorde and private aeroplanes to cross-channel ferries and mini-cabs (there is no truth in the story that one of the crew thought that Hertz Van Rental was a Dutch racing driver). The band always travelled in style and luxury; first-class air travel and a limousine on terra firma. Separate limousines – one each.

During our extensive travels, the crew spent many long hours on commercial airlines; in the days when the non-smoking section of vast 747 jets was just a few rows at the back. These were also the days when airline stewardesses would share their Hawaiian grass with you – taking clandestine draws while crouched in the aisle when the movie was playing. Smiling and giggling, the airlines were not spared our special humour; the Belgian carrier Sabena was nicknamed 'Such A Bloody Experience Never Again', Australia's Qantas was 'Queers And Nancies Trained As Stewards', and America's Northwest was commuted to North Worst. In the USA, the band progressed from commercial flights to touring by private charter aeroplane, the first one they used being the Lisa Marie, a converted Convair 880 that had been Elvis Presley's own personal plane.

The crew travelled separately to Queen and generally in customised tour buses, which had evolved in America with the Country & Western circuit. One of our drivers was Sherri, an attractive, 'built for comfort not speed' southern gal, who took *no shit* from anybody and kept a stout police-issue nightstick under her seat in case there was. There wasn't. A bus driver we shared happy times with was Bob 'Hot Rod' Williams, a middle-aged man who had been a Country music star himself, and still loved going on the road. He gave me the business card of a friend of his: Rudd B Weatherwax, the trainer of TV dog Lassie. On the front is a photo of Rudd and Lassie and on the reverse Lassie's paw print.

The front of the bus housed a lounge and TV area, in the middle of the bus corridor was a toilet (sorry, *rest room*) and then towards the rear, on each side were the bunks; 12 in total, two or three high, into which we were slotted for the purpose of sleep. In the rear was a smaller lounge for hanging out. Playing cards became a pastime, not as you might imagine – a smoky poker school – but instead cribbage was the game favoured by all nationalities. The same card game that old men played in the corners of pubs. Tour buses were the crew's home-from-home for months on end, and the vast distances meant we would not see a hotel for days, and would have to resort to showering, shaving, shitting and shampooing in venue dressing rooms.

A small bag of necessities was kept in our bunks, with our main luggage stashed in the bay under the bus. Twelve drunken, sweaty males sleeping in a confined space highlighted the need for pine-scented air fresheners and fully open roof vents. Leaving your socks and footwear out was taboo, as was dumping in the toilet. Good bunk positions were claimed with the same fervour as German holiday-makers putting towels on sun loungers at dawn. Lower bunks (away from the toilet) were better, being closer to the centre of gravity, and didn't sway around like the top ones. It was advisable to sleep with your feet facing the front, unless you wanted a neck injury if the bus braked sharply. Disappointingly, there were no electric trouser presses onboard, so you would simply put all your smelly clothes at the end of your bunk, opposite your head. Removing your clothes on a fast-moving vehicle while tired and drunk is tricky, and a dozen guys of varying size and shape preparing for bed is funnier than a West End farce.

When undressing, it was like the scene in the showers after a sports event, catching a sly glance to see how you measured up against the others. The British guys sported colourful hipster briefs or Marks & Spencer's pants. The Americans, however, were very conservative in their choice of undergarment, which was reminiscent of what your granddad wore. The US 'smalls' were not. They were an ample, white(ish) garment, often thermal, with heavy stitching. This was the first time I had witnessed underpants with the waistband so highly cut that they could pass as polo necks.

A skill that had to be quickly mastered was 'bus surfing'; keeping your balance in the central corridor as the bus lurched towards our destination. Changes in speed could propel you into the walls, door well or windscreen. Another skill was to pee into the toilet of a bus that's hurtling down the highway, where aim was vital. All men know the feeling of a full bladder in the early morning, when your todger is a far different fellow to the acorn you went to sleep with. It has developed a mind and size independent of your wishes. Staggering into the bathroom, you prop yourself with one hand against the wall while the other holds something you are now proud of.

Aim is vital. "Oh shit! Missed again...'

The Bus Monster: A mythical beast that materialised in the depths of the night and *got you*. The result of an attack was a dry mouth, sore eyes, bunged-up nose, aching body, and a total lack of spark. You felt dreadful. The monster usually attacked during the first few journeys of a tour as you adjusted to living in this unorthodox manner. To counter disturbed sleep, a large tub of 5 mg Valium tranquillisers had been legally obtained, and doled out to those giving a Churchillian V sign from their bunks.

'Oooh, Matron – is it "V" time?'

'To the power of five or ten?'

'I'll be a devil – to the power of 15.'

'Nurse – the screens!'

Brian, Roger and John each took up our challenge to spend an overnight trip on the crew bus (once – and with their minder in tow). Fred was always promising, but sadly never did. I'm sure it would have been a lot of fun. Fred certainly liked his fun:

'Ratty, do you have any rolls of gaffer tape? I need to take some to the hotel.'

'Sure Fred, a case full – do you want black or white?'

'Oh – black! Definitely black.'

We used gaffer tape (black) to rig up curtains for privacy on our first US tour bus, which was basic, with converted metal army bunks. At this time, wardrobe mistress/master 'Dashing Dane Clark', an ex-dancer from Las Vegas travelled (rather quietly) with the crew. His bunk was directly below mine where notes would be left. 'Hi, Dane, come up and see me some time, love Ratty.' Not by my hand, I add!

We all got on very well with Dane, and he would cut the crew's hair on days off.

I once spent a tense night on that bus wondering if I was going to turn into a hairdresser or dancer, due to a pill I had taken. 'Who's up for some of these? They're really great,' someone had said. Being young and foolhardy I popped one. The laughter immediately started – I'd taken a female hormone pill and spent a lonely night lying on my back, regularly checking my nipples for growth.

For a trip from Vancouver, down the west coast of Canada to Seattle, Washington, just across the border in the USA, we were travelling in a substitute vehicle – a standard

Greyhound-type of bus, with no beds or areas to lie down on. It was an early-morning run and we were all dead tired, so Dick 'Dirt Ball' Ollet, our electronic guru, crawled up into the overhead luggage rack and flaked out. It was only after passing through immigration into America that we realised he was still up there. Dick was British and living in Los Angeles at the time, on a special type of US exchange visa. Unfortunately, as he had no US entry stamp to balance his exit stamp to Canada, he was in the eyes of the US immigration still in Canada and not residing on American soil. He would now have to re-enter the United States – but without leaving. He had also avoided being interrogated by The Fruit Police, who patrolled the Canadian/US border.

'You will surrender all apples, oranges and bananas and place them in the designated bins.'

'Yes, officer.'

'*And* those grapes – don't you try and hide anything from us!'

I believe it was five years' hard labour in Alcatraz for secreting a pineapple.

I had experienced 'illegal immigration' on the eastern border of Canada with Detroit. Two young ladies took Crystal and me sight-seeing around 'Motor City' in their motor – and unbeknown to us, across the border into Windsor, Canada.

'Don't we need a passport to enter Canada?'

Too late. Locals could regularly cross the border using their ID/driver's license.

'How are we going to get back into the US – don't they check?'

'Uh yeah – they do. Lie across the back seat – and keep your heads down...'

NEW FRONTIERS

Europe didn't generally give us those particular types of cross-border issues, and European bus drivers were resourceful and experienced. However, occasionally you were concerned by who was at the wheel. In the middle of the night, when the bus is parked on the side of the autobahn and the driver sitting at the wheel holding a joint in one hand and studying an upside-down German Falkplan map through tinted sunglasses, the term 'right man for the job?' comes to mind.

After driving all night and for most of the next day, all you want is to get into the hotel, desperate for a night in a bed that does not move, with sheets that do not resemble corrugated cardboard. Approaching the outskirts of a city, hope springs eternal that shortly you will be having a refreshing shower, swim or drink in the bar. But still that naughty hotel could be elusive. Spotting it in the distance we would shout in unison: 'Quick – after it, before it gets away.' Our driver then decided the best ploy would be not to drive directly to the hotel, but circle it a few times, then sneak up and take it by surprise.

Despite the international rabble of passengers on board, travelling through European borders on a bus was relatively simple: leave all the passports with the driver while we slept, with the added sweeteners of records and T-shirts being displayed on the dashboard, if required. However, this didn't work when travelling the 'corridor' between old East

Germany and West Berlin, that decadent island in the middle of communist utopia. This journey was always at night, and if asleep you were abruptly awoken by a machine gun thrust through the curtains of your bunk. *Guten Morgen!* The East German border guard would study your passport and transit visa closely, before taking them away to be processed. This procedure could take any amount of time, so the bus remained stationary, as did we, in vast hangar buildings lit by reams of fluorescent tube lighting that cast a sickly green mist. Angled mirrors on wheels would be thrust under vehicles – to search for stowaways. Once while we waited, an open-back truck full of Christmas trees was being searched, the guards plunging long metal spikes into the trees at random and waiting for the screams. Happy Christmas, comrades.

My 24th birthday was on a show day in Hanover and the birthday evening was spent on the tour bus going through the bleak grimness and bitter cold of January in East Germany, on our way to West Berlin. Brian May had wished me happy birthday and asked if I was having a party... With an extra six pack of beer and some cheese and onion rolls onboard, we were celebrating my birthday so much we didn't realise we had reached the border. The guards strutted on board to witness us watching the climax to a video. No, not that type, it was *The Dirty Dozen*. Probably not the best choice of film, as Allied troops were about to wipe out the German HQ with grenades, machine guns and heavy hand-to-hand fighting.

The summer gig in West Berlin was the Waldbuhne – 'stage in a wood' – which is exactly what it was. The Waldbuhne was an outdoor venue where the stage and covering were a permanent fixture but the audience was seated in the open air. This old amphitheatre venue was built at the time of the infamous 1936 Olympic Games, and located behind the main Olympic stadium. It is recorded that Adolf Hitler gave many speeches at the Waldbuhne. The construction had a narrow concrete tunnel that ran from the edge of the wooded area to the back of the stage, which was the access for the gear, and where Adolf used to arrive in secret, appearing magically from nowhere he would glide on stage. Positioned in the walls on the sides of the stage were slits, where snipers would sit and watch the crowd for troublemakers and opposers of the man with the moustache's new Reich. The whole place had an odd atmosphere and in summer was particularly hot and humid, and plagued by mosquitoes. Tony, the wardrobe man, and first aid kit holder, bought cans of spray repellent and tubs of cream to soothe exposed bodies. After sundown when the powerful lights in Queen's rig came on, it was a magnet for squadrons of flying insects and creepy crawlies to come out of their lairs in the dark forest – and descend on the stage. Fred was not amused to find a large moth he later described as 'the size of a fucking pterodactyl!' spluttering in his drink on top of the piano.

An American crew member on his first visit to Germany remarked, 'Gee this Ausfahrt place must be real big 'cos all the exits from the autobahn have a sign for it.'

On approaching the Scottish border, we told him to be ready to get off the bus with his passport (the immigration office being a motorway service station). Europe's diversity confused him from the moment he arrived:

'How are you enjoying England?'

'Its real neat, but I can't understand the money – it's confusing'

'Don't worry, we're off to Sweden soon.'

'So what money do they have in Sweden – dollars or pounds?'

'No, their own currency: Swedish krone.'

'Ah…? Should I change it all as I go round?'

'No just change what you need'

'So after Sweden it's Denmark, right?'

'Yes.'

'So what they got there, dollars or pounds?'

'No, krona.'

'They have Swedish krona too?'

'No, no, no it's *Danish* krona. It's a different country, then we go to Germany where they use deutschmarks.'

'Not dollars or pounds?'

'No!'

All European money was collectively known as Local Drachma or Drinking Vouchers and any loose change was Shrapnel.

There was plenty of shrapnel and fall-out from the regular fracas that took place around European show venues with counterfeit merchandisers. Often they fought between themselves, but the main issue was fans buying bootleg T-shirts and other 'swag' before they got into the venues where Queen's official tour merchandise was for sale. To deter and dispel counterfeiters, two-wheeled transport was hired (for cash): powerful motor bikes with chapters of local Hell's Angels riding them. The 'Angels' patrolled the outskirts of venues and politely asked any non-official merchandisers to kindly leave. Or something like that.

YOUR PAPERS PLEASE (YOU'RE NICKED!)

Due to there not being enough space for the crew on one bus, Queen's personal crew were sometimes given the option of fly-drive on European tours. Driving directly from the show in Dortmund to Paris, we found ourselves stopped by French border officials in the middle of the night. Suspicious? Possibly? A top-of-the-range white Mercedes with registration plates from Zurich driven by me, a dishevelled, unshaven and wide-eyed mess. The passengers were Jobby, a most unhealthy-looking individual with a Canadian passport; Mr Modern, a gangly youth with a scowl, strange haircut and British passport; and finally alongside me in the front passenger seat was Angelika, my German girlfriend from Munich.

'*C'est bon*, mate? Can we *allez*?' I quip.

'*Non!*'

The peak-capped French officers searched the car thoroughly, pulling all the carpets up and tapping door panels as if they were sending some sort of Gallic Morse code – or maybe honing a sense of rhythm? Nothing. Rien.

'*C'est bon* – now?'

'*Non!*'

We dragged our luggage into the border-control office under yellow lights that made our tired, drawn faces look even worse than we felt. Despite every piece of paperwork being in order, the French still insisted on searching our luggage. They quickly zipped up my bag. A handy tip: always put your dirty laundry on top, as only the hardiest will get past the barrier of roadie's old pants and socks, and T shirts that are a distinctly different colour under the arms from that of the body.

Searching my girlfriend's bags, they pulled her clothes roughly out, and she frowned, but, when they started handling her lingerie, she let loose with an unrelenting torrent of abuse in German. We were given a dismissive French shrug and waved away. Angelika growled in her Bavarian accent about those 'Fucking Franzosiche Aschlochs!' as we sped down the autoroute to Paris.

Who was I to disagree?

A Ford Granada is not as grand as a Mercedes and does not fit through the sliding glass entrance doors of the Dragonara Hotel in Edinburgh – no matter how hard I tried. A party was thrown after Queen's first show there in 1982, and as normal involved strippers, audience participation and copious amounts of alcohol.

After the party, I drove the short distance to the Dragonara Hotel, the car's sunroof being handy for dispensing the empty champagne bottles on route. ('There's no need to be gentle – it's a rental.')

Upon our return, as we tried to put the Granada into the lobby 'showroom', there were screams and sounds of breaking glass from Fred's suite as he and Bill, his chubby companion from New Jersey, were having a bit of a tiff.

That was not unusual.

Drunken driving is an inexcusable offence, and there is no justification for it at all – even in Ireland, where everybody drinks.

Ireland, the Emerald Isle, home to mystical castles, leprechauns and rented Japanese mini-vans – for the little people.

Arriving in Dublin after a delayed flight from Zurich, we had all been enjoying the craic from the free booze on board. I approached the car rental desk and explained that I was not the person in whose name the mini-van was booked, but honestly I really was the one authorised to pick it up. This posed no problem and neither did my out-of-date Californian driver's licence. I then enquired whether there was a minibar in the mini-van and what side of the road would they like me to drive on while in Ireland.

Show day and on our way to Slane Castle, we were stopped at a roadblock by the Irish Garda. I wound down the window and the grinning policeman squeaked: 'Mornin' to ye lads, are yus off tuh the concert?'

'Yes.'

'Fine, so where's the stuff, then?'

'What?'

'The stuuuhfff, where is it then, where d'ya have it?'

We can have some fun here.

'Sorry – what exactly do you mean?'

'The stuuuhff – ye know droooogghs – we're the drooogggh squad.'

'Oh, the *stuff*. No, we don't have any, we're working at the show up at the castle'

We flashed our passes.

'Ah, I see now, but are yuh sure yuh don't have any stuuuhff?'

'No, we're sure to be sure.'

With a salute we were allowed on our way. We didn't have any 'stuff'. Only a pint or two of the black stuff.

In the 1970s, having long hair and being in a vehicle that you probably couldn't afford was like a beacon to the British police. The brand-new rented VW minibus I was a passenger in was stopped by Somerset's finest. I panicked slightly and, before the cops approached, quickly downed the contents of a plastic container where I kept my stash. I swallowed the speed tablets but the joke 'Dracula' blood capsules that were also in the container remained lodged in my mouth. As the police started asking the usual questions the capsules started to melt and fake blood began trickling to the corners of my mouth.

'What's wrong with your mate? He looks pale – and he's *bleeding?*'

'Uuh – just had a tooth out,' somebody replied.

I didn't sleep at all that night, and ended up in a local nurses' home, being nursed.

DRUG RUNNER

The tour bus was a necessity in America but regulations delayed its introduction in Europe, so in autumn 1975 for the UK *Night At The Opera* tour, Queen and crew had a standard coach each to travel around Britain. During a day off travelling from Newcastle to Dundee, the coach was flagged over to the roadside and plain-clothes police ran on shouting: 'Drug squad! Everybody hands on your heads – now!'

They were no doubt looking for the 'stuff'.

The cops stayed on board keeping a close eye on us all as

the driver was directed to the local police station. The search of the bus resulted in the huge haul of half a joint and two small wraps of amphetamine.

During questioning, I was asked to roll my sleeves up so the cop could check for needle marks! He said to me, 'You *look* like you take drugs, and you may not think it, but up here [he tapped the side of his head] is a mind ticking over faster than you could comprehend.'

'Really...?'

'We can get your visas cancelled – stop you going to the States and Japan.'

As I was led out, I saw Fred being questioned. He was in full 'glam' kit in those days; short fox fur jacket, satin trousers, sash, black painted nails, lots of jewellery and carrying his vanity/make-up case.

'Do you take drugs, Mr Mercury?'

'Don't be so impertinent, you stupid little man,' barked Fred in response as he snapped shut his vanity case and strode out.

It's true, Fred did not take drugs – then.

Many of us did, and the search by the north-east's crack squad of 'top men' was not particularly thorough. However, we were all very curious to know why the police had mounted such a massive operation. When quizzing some of them as we were released, their reply was: 'be careful who you travel with'. We assumed this was a reference to a runner who I'll call simply Dan (not his real name), who had been fired from the tour. A tenuous friend of one of the crew, he didn't last long, as he became dazzled with rock's glitz and glamour. In Preston, as a gesture, the tour manager gave him some cash and train fare back to London. Dan was not amused, ranting how he would get his own back. He did – he burgled some of our houses. However, when Dan attempted to rob Richie's home, he broke into the wrong house by mistake. BIG mistake. Richie's neighbour was a local villain who sported tattoos of spiders on his tongue – and was currently out of prison. We never heard from Dan again...

CHAPTER THIRTEEN
SOUTH AMERICA

(IT'S *HOW* MUCH A GRAM?)

D an simply disappeared without a trace... South
America had a reputation for people disappearing;
subversives and high-profile people who could command a
large ransom. Queen: wealthy, famous and decadent rock
band – good idea to go?

The 1980s saw Queen taking on new challenges; however,
South America was still a dark and daunting destination
that, although often dangled, never materialised. The money
and guarantees were never as forthcoming as the enthusiasm
or promises from the Latin entrepreneurs and promoters.

So, surprisingly, it was announced that, following five
shows in Tokyo during February 1981, *The Game* tour
would be extended to Argentina and Brazil.

Wanting to remain self-sufficient and not reliant on any
local equipment, we took everything with us, including
scaffolding and necessary staging, and for the world's

longest air trip from Tokyo to Buenos Aires we had at our disposal a chartered Flying Tigers 727 cargo plane. The Queen crew all flew to Buenos Aires via New York on a scheduled Pan AM flight, and were surprised to find Fred was on board; and more surprised that he was sitting in economy class. He had stormed off an earlier flight from Tokyo on discovering it was a DC10, a type of aircraft that had recently been involved in major accidents. He hadn't known he was on board a DC10 until he was comfortably relaxing in his first-class seat with a glass of something expensively bubbly. He freaked out and refused to travel on the flight, which was delayed while his baggage was unloaded. The next available non-DC10 flight was ours, in which first class was full.

Leaving Fred to enjoy himself in The Big Apple, we flew on and, after spending an exhausting 23 hours in the air, landed on a blindingly bright Buenos Aires morning. This was our first visit to South America and nobody quite knew what to expect. But we hoped. Though not a drug-producing country, Argentina was in the general area of the coca bush and so there would surely be piles of cheap supplies? Or, as a predominantly Catholic country, would there be lots of hot and lusty suppressed señoritas willing to keep us occupied? We had received strong warnings about both. Argentina had a military Junta and the omnipresence of armed troops and security vehicles was a sharp reminder. For the sake of a bit of toot and some hanky panky, I decided I'd prefer to keep my fingernails.

What did Argentina hitherto mean to me? Plenty of beef (which they sent 'corned' in tins to Britain), the Tango and that England had beaten them 1–0 (Hurst 78) in the brutal quarter-final of the 1966 World Cup at Wembley stadium, when their captain, Rattin, was sent off for foul play. The Argentine team were later branded 'animals' by Alf Ramsey, the England manager. They're probably a bit excitable down here, I surmised.

Permission for Queen to play in Argentina was granted by the then president, Viola, and political motives obviously crept into play. With an election coming up, he may have been thinking about the young persons' vote. But despite bringing the first major rock shows to Argentina, Viola didn't last very long afterwards.

Buenos Aires was a city familiarly European in style and with its wide avenues and cafes, reminiscent of Madrid. We spent a few days recovering from jet lag and acclimatising to the heat and humidity by exploring the neighbourhood. After being released by the authorities for taking photos in the harbour area and warned not to wear tight shorts downtown (another detainable offence), we got the go-ahead that the gear was now cleared; some form of import bond, fee or non-returnable sum having been paid to the *right* people.

The crew were driven to a far corner of the Ezeiza airfield where the lonely figure of the Flying Tigers cargo plane stood, the isolated area containing the single aeroplane creating the atmosphere of a hijack situation. Under a blazing hot sun, the pallets of gear were slowly unloaded and transferred into sea containers on flat-bed trucks. I was becoming rapidly hotter and redder – the discovery of spent live ammunition shells on the concrete plain raising my colour and pulse even further.

All Queen shows in Argentina were in football stadiums that had been built for the 1978 World Cup, the opening show in Buenos Aires being at the Velez Sarsfield stadium. The enthusiastic local crew would not really believe that the shows would be allowed to go ahead, convinced that things would be cancelled at the last moment. Broken promises were something we would get used to, and the term 'no problem' is no longer something I take seriously. Corruption, lying and false assurances were mandatory. For the crew, working, travelling and living conditions were grim, but despite all the setbacks the shows were a huge success, the world's press witnessing the energy-packed opening night in Buenos Aires.

Gerry Stickells, who had visibly aged during this period, was asked by a journalist from the British tabloid press how he felt after this pioneering show. He replied, 'After the countless months of negotiations, organisational and logistical problems, inadequate facilities and resources, the "local" factor plus the ever-nagging possibility of "the surprise element", that, overall, it was a huge relief!'

The unimpressed hack replied, 'So what do I write for people to read back in England? "Queen's tour manager says that the first ever major rock show in Buenos Aires felt like having a piss"?'

The crew all understood that things would not run as we were used to, and Queen themselves (who were used to being pampered in five-star luxury), did not expect some of the 'differences'. They always travelled to and from shows in limousines. Not in Buenos Aires, where the answer was a fleet of old Ford Falcons, family-sized sedans that had seen better days.

After the first show, the band and their personal entourage were crammed into these cars, and set off for an official reception in honour of their appearance. The Falcons had to cut a swathe through the thousands of fans, who then raced after the motorcade in enthusiastic pursuit. Pulling free of the crowd, the drivers kept in an orderly line through the city before turning into a gas station. Furious band assistants were informed that the cars needed to fill up with petrol or they would run out very soon! Meanwhile, the pursuing fans had caught up and engulfed the entire gas station, enthusiastically banging on the car bodies. Fred in particular was 'not amused', so this situation was resolved by the fleet of cars being accompanied in by gun-toting police on motorcycles and military armoured vehicles.

IT TAKES TWO TO TANGO

After a small drinks party following the final Buenos Aires show, I was accompanied to the Hotel Principado by a BA Belle (no, not a stewardess from British Airways – that's another story).

There were difficulties getting girls up to our rooms, and keys were never allowed to leave the hotel. So, while some of the crew were occupying the attention of the front-desk staff, I grabbed my key from behind the small reception area.

Having plucked Margarita, my companion, from around the corner, we slipped into the lift and hurriedly ran to my room where I urgently snapped the door shut. Once inside, I proceeded to get us a well-earned drink. Immediately, the phone rang – it was the front desk enquiring about my guest.

I denied all knowledge on the phone, feigned fatigue and, with the parting words of: '*No comprende, senor,*' I hung up.

As I began to build Anglo-Argo relations, there was a staccato knocking at the door. The 'knocker' would not be ignored, so, as the young lady hid in the bathroom, I reluctantly opened up. Despite my protests, the hotel guy insisted I had a girl in the room. Now, I had worked hard to get this far so I was not going to give up easily; besides, accommodating women had not been in abundance in the land of pampas and bolas. And my bolas needed pampering. The guy ignored me and shouted into the room in Spanish. He repeated his words, this time with more urgency, and the girl came into view, opening her handbag as she walked to the door. She then presented the hotel representative with her ID card. I was now getting nervous, as you do when people around you are talking in raised voices, in a language you do not understand and, to top it, in a military Junta!

The hotel clerk was purely a zealous implementer of the house rules and all guests must be registered regardless, and identification shown. I signed some form (anything to get rid of him), which turned out to be an agreement to pay the extra pesos for double occupancy of the room! I would leave that paperwork for our promoter Senor Capalbo to sort out. We were leaving town the next day.

Grateful for the fact that the secret police would not be administering electric therapy treatment, I relaxed. I was also thankful that no extension of the Vatican would be giving me a 'Spanish inquisition' over my liaison with this Catholic girl, who I noticed bore no crucifixes or rosaries. When she knelt down it wasn't to pray, and it was me who was calling for God – in English. I spoke only a few words and short phrases in Spanish, which mostly consisted of the ones required to order alcohol and breakfast, find the lavatory or praise a central midfield footballer.

Margarita: a potent Latin American drink. She was – as was her friend, Christina, who had ended up with another of the crew. We imagined they might be a little tearful as we left Buenos Aires the next morning.

'Don't cry for me Marge and Tina.' Boom-boom!

AWAY VENUES

Queen's next venue in Argentina was Mar del Plata, a coastal resort that, with its genteel elegance and faded European architecture, resembled a Latin version of Brighton. Our hotel, The Provincial, was situated on the sea front and was reminiscent of the grand hotels of the 1930s with sweeping Art Deco staircases that led to a first-floor open area that hosted a string quartet playing in a circular parquet dance floor. People sat at small tables taking tea and coffee under the glass-domed roof. Very pre-war Berlin, very homely. Lots of Schmidts and Vons in the local telephone directory.

By now we were adjusting to the different working conditions and the inexperienced local crews of young guys who helped with the physical loading, unloading and moving of the gear. They would not turn up after the show to load out for two reasons – the first being they had not been paid as promised, and, secondly, some of them only did the work in order to see the show for free.

When Queen left the stage, so did they.

Note in the itinerary: 'For members of the crew wishing to lose weight, consumption of the local water is recommended.'

There was an ever, underlying panic as to when you might get struck down. In the backstage stadium washrooms, somebody did not quite make it and the incident became known the 'Mar del Plata Splatter'.

Next came Rosario, where post-show the curious audience were slow to leave the pitch area, innocently inquisitive of what was happening on the stage as we began breaking down the gear. The military police formed a line the width of the pitch and with snarling Alsatian dogs on leads they moved in a united wave towards the crowd. They left. In a prompt, orderly manner.

This was 1981, the year before the Falklands conflict. After that show in Rosario, I swapped a baseball cap adorned with 'I love New York', which had been thrown on stage during an earlier US tour, for a young soldier's green army cap with brass insignia on the front. He was acting as a security guard as we loaded the truck, and he and I made the exchange over a bottle of Coca-Cola. Inside the cap was the guy's name and address written in blue biro. I have thought about him since. Where was he the following year when the Falklands conflict was happening? Did he survive? If so, how did he feel about the British now?

UP THE AMAZON – WITHOUT A PADDLE

Our 'Boys Own' adventure moved on to Brazil and the exciting prospect of Rio de Janeiro, but still the dates in the itinerary remained TBA: to be advised/arranged or, as it turned out – to be avoided. Our flight from Buenos Aires to Rio was the most frightening I have ever encountered, as we flew into and through a tropical storm that tossed the DC10 (yes, them again!) around as if it was paper. The plane continued to oscillate in altitude and my stomach was somewhere in my throat, then like a tidal wave the aircraft was tossed up again, as a rush burst to the top of my head and squeezed tight. It was pitch black outside and the flashes of lightning that splintered the darkness had me seriously thinking this was it – time was up, we were off to the great gig in the sky.

'*The scheduled aircraft that crashed in the jungle en route from Buenos Aires to Rio de Janeiro is believed to have had several Britons on board,*' the solemn tones of a BBC newsreader echoed in my head.

There was no warning as the storm took hold and shook hard, just to remind you who was in charge. White-knuckle fingers were welded to rosaries and armrests, and spilled hot coffee caused no pain. Signs of the cross were made and personal prayers muttered. I joined in: 'Now listen, I know I've not been to church for a while, but you know how it is, but I did go *regularly* to Sunday School. I even got a book for good attendance – honest – you can ask my mum.'

It must have worked because the storm passed and we landed in Rio safely.

The night bus ride to our hotel meant it was difficult to see the landscape that we had long imagined made up this exotic strip of land between the mountains and the ocean. Despite peering closely through the windows, with one eye cupped to cut the reflection, Rio was not revealing herself. The following morning, however, the Rio stage was open as I pulled back the curtains that followed the curve of our circular hotel. Straight ahead was a lush mountain and with my neck craned I could see the seafront and beach. We were in the Hotel Nacional on Gavea beach, south of the main strip of Copacabana, Ipanema and Le Blond.

Rio immediately had its glamorous edge dulled by the security needs; our hotel keys were issued with no stylish tag or the hotel's name, just a plain key stamped with a coded number and a chain to wear around the neck. Shame, a Rio hotel key tag would have been a great souvenir to attach to the keys of the Ford transit. Strict instructions were given to us: do not take anything, anything at all to the beach. Life was good here (for us) but local life was a cheap commodity, and the further back you travelled from the beach towards the mountains, the poorer it became, to a point at which cars do not stop at traffic lights for fear of attack.

The beaches were great but I never found the elusive and mythical 'girl from Ipanema' – or even any of her mates.

Q. What do a bunch of English and American guys do in one of the most exciting and naturally beautiful cities in the world?

A. They go to an English pub.

Most evenings we would take a taxi ride 'down the pub' in a VW Beetle where the front passenger seat had been removed in order for passengers to climb in the back – and always agreed the fare in advance.

The Lord Jim English pub was run by an ex-pat airline pilot, who, having decided to retire to the sun, brought a few bits with him each trip until he finally built up his collection of horse brasses, dart boards, pint pots, yards of ale, period prints and other pub paraphernalia (I doubt if he got the original red British telephone box on board as hand luggage, though).

Brazil was very welcome after expensive Argentina ($10 for a beer in 1981). In fact, it was relatively cheap and we could enjoy spending our cash despite the galloping inflation – there were prices in shops for the morning and different ones for the afternoon.

The more imaginative of the crew, who had not blown every cent of their per diem, would look for souvenirs that were indigenous to the area and hopefully an investment. Basically, we were on the lookout for items that were cheaper than at home. We had picked up a variety on our travels. In Japan: antique kimonos and prints, pearls and electronic goods. In Australia: opals and … boomerangs. Spain was great for leather goods, France and Italy for 'going out' clothes, South Africa – diamonds, and the USA was tops for Levi jeans, American-Indian turquoise jewellery and cowboy hats. One appealing commodity Brazil offered was precious stones, but jewels were of no real interest for tour manager Gerry Stickells, who was in search of some shrunken heads! Apart from being disgusting, these 'souvenirs' of probably murdered Indians (I don't think many died of natural causes) were highly illegal. Gerry didn't succeed in buying any, but I'm sure they would have looked charming in his suburban Californian home, alongside the war memorabilia, his parrot and Jimi Hendrix gold records.

JUMPING FOR JOY

The shows in Belo Horizonte had been pulled for 'reasons', but São Paulo was definitely on. This was to be our first Brazilian show as, meanwhile, the authorities and promoters were still debating whether to allow the Maracana in Rio to be used for a rock concert. This stadium, with the biggest capacity in the world, is home to what is on par with religion in Brazil – football. The proper game of football – known as soccer in some parts.

The concern was potential damage to the hallowed playing surface; the only other major non-football activities to have taken place being a Frank Sinatra show and a gig by His Holiness the Pope. If Queen were to play, the pitch was to be completely covered to protect it, as had every surface in Argentina, with rolls of artificial grass.

The Brazilian authorities were not convinced, so a small area of the Maracana pitch was cordoned off and a protective covering laid, where several energetic young people were hired to jump up and down on this section continually for two hours. After this simulation of alleged rock-concert behaviour, the pitch was inspected. It was then decreed that Maracana was to remain solely for the use of football.

During this period of 'resting' the crew were invited to play football against a team of Brazilians made up from people connected to the promoter. As Brazil has a reputation for being the best team on the planet, I didn't rate our chances. We were assured it was a 'bonding' exercise and just a 'kick-about'. Nevertheless we decided to take it seriously and packed our side with 'choppers' and 'stoppers' from the sizeable Americans in the crew more used to Grid-Iron American football. Our US cousins mocked our game of 'soccer' as being no match for their tough sport (where they wear heavy padding and helmets). In response, I pointed out that their national sport of baseball was called 'rounders' in England – and played by girls...

After enjoying the splendid sights, sounds and tastes of Rio (at about $20 a gram), we took the shuttle flight to São Paulo on a plane that had curious rows of small symmetric holes down the centre of the cabin roof lining. It was explained that until recently there were straps hanging there and late passengers would stand in the aisle, as on the London Underground, and hold on during the one-hour internal flight! Health and safety? Never heard of it...

The Morumbi stadium in São Paulo was vast, its open arena holding court to a total of 251,000 fans over Queen's two shows, making the event the biggest-ever paying audience in the world for a rock band. It was a truly awesome atmosphere as the band emerged from the dressing rooms via a tunnel that took them on to the pitch and to the bottom of the stairs to the stage. This route was normally taken by the football players to keep out of range of objects thrown by the supporters. Apart from the band's own security, they had local help from the self-named Doctor Death and his associates. The good doctor claimed to have personally 'taken out' dozens of people and been rewarded for it by 'the authorities' and he proudly waved his powerful automatic hand gun around the dressing-room area, posing for pictures with it. He had no problem asking any of Queen for autographs.

Despite the success of the shows, the next day or two were fraught, as we now had to get the gear safely out of the country. Brazil had many exports – coffee, fruit and other domestic products – but these were mainly dispatched by sea and, as we were still in uncharted territory, it was decided it would be safer in the circumstances to quickly fly the gear out. The problem was finding an available cargo plane big enough to handle it. Pan Am's cargo division heard of our situation and offered a high price, confident we had no other choice. However, the Flying Tigers came to our rescue again. Tigers had a shipment of industrial weaving machines arriving from Zurich, and as yet no return cargo. The 747 Jumbo was perfect and a good deal was negotiated to fly to New York. The entire show including the staging, scaffolding and sound system that had been sent to Argentina by sea could be accommodated, and rental time and costs reduced – perfect. Or was it? The Tigers' 747 needed the gear to be loaded onto special pallets that could be fitted in the tracking rails in the hold. Guess who had the only available suitable pallets? Varig, Brazil's national airline had some – but not enough. Pan Am – who were not amused at being undercut by Tigers, had the other suitable pallets. I believe money changed hands during the protracted negotiations to procure the necessary pallets from both airlines. In cash.

Meanwhile, the crew heads of department were tired and very pissed off. We managed slices of sleep on top of the hard flight cases and, when the call eventually came in the breaking dawn, we set about loading pallets aided by local coffee which at its mildest can induce palpitations. The 40 tons of gear loaded, we returned to the shabby Hotel Jaragua in the late-morning. I was a little disappointed I had been denied travel to New York on the chartered cargo plane. Regulations only allowed extra passengers who were US citizens. Flying on the upper deck of our own 747 with whatever we wanted could have been a fantastic experience – 'Let me have a go at driving please, pilot?'

SOUTH AMERICA AGAIN – NO MORE MAÑANAS

Despite the headaches and nightmares, buoyed by the ground-breaking euphoria of the first tour, within six months we were on a second trip to Latin America. First to New Orleans, its Latin Quarter and rehearsals in the Civic Auditorium, before travelling on to Venezuela. Time for a Queen party on one of the wrought-iron, period balconies that overlooked Bourbon Street.

The next day, everybody had to undergo a medical and be pronounced fit and healthy for our visas to enter Venezuela. Most of us were bleary, some still jet lagged and all wondering what condition we were actually in as we did not often see the medical profession voluntarily. A local doctor set up his battered black bag in a faded, nicotine-stained dressing room, and one by one a check-up of the entire crew was done. The doctor reported that we were basically a sound bunch of young men; however, two conditions were generally consistent: slightly raised heart rate (due to sampling South American goods prior to actual arrival?) and dirty, waxy ears (due to the body's natural resistance in blocking out loud nasty noises?).

Oil-rich Caracas was an odd, unsettling experience, a

modern concrete city high up in the mountains and the first place I had seen a dead body lying in the street. The venue Queen were to play was civilised – a contemporary indoor sports arena, The Poliedro. After educating the local promoter that the crew as well as Queen needed to eat and drink at the shows, things went surprisingly well.

The hotel we were billeted in was the Anauco Hilton, a vast tower of a construction where we shared duplex apartments. The South American curse on our digestive systems had not been lifted and the bathroom in our lodgings became known as the Mud Slide. Apart from ingesting the contents of the tiny sealed plastic tubes that had come over the border from neighbouring Colombia, there was not a great deal to do. With all this spare testosterone kicking about, the wildest we managed to get was tearing all the pages from the phone books and making paper planes to launch across the multi-lane highway towards Queen's hotel, the Caracas Hilton. From hardened rock 'n' roll party animals to litterbugs!

Adjacent to the Caracas Hilton was a small park, where, while out strolling with Jobby, I took some photos of the old building at the entrance gates. The two of us wandered into the park and, as we saw little of interest, soon made our way back to the entrance. Blocking our path was a mob of screaming bearded, student types, carrying sticks, clubs and tree branches. I was very confused and very, very concerned, so we ran to the bottom of the park but found that the exit was blocked by more of these people – with dogs. We turned back up the slope with nowhere now to go. I was terrified as these very angry men came storming at us, convinced that we were about to be beaten senseless or possibly to death.

Something logical in my mind was stirring amidst the terror: 'Why so many of them, just to rob us?'

From sheer instinct I put my hands up in a surrender mode and tried to say: 'I don't understand – *no comprende* – *no comprende*.'

The mob slowed, and, realising from my dreadful pronunciation and accent that I was not local, looked quizzically at us – pointing at my camera.

I held my hands out and tried again: 'No – please – *musica, musica, Grupo Queen* – yes?'

A few heads nodded and the weapons were lowered.

'*Me turisto – si?*'

With this comment, I pointed at the hotel and my camera, then Jobby and I began shuffling along the line of the bedraggled bunch towards the exit, as some began laughing – making us feel very humble. Without altercation, we were allowed to pass and leave the park. I believe they thought I was some kind of journalist and possibly working for the security forces or some kind of unwelcome outside political interest. It was one of the most frightening experiences of my life, from just strolling in a park one minute to the possibility of suffering a brutal death the next.

Due to a death, the Venezuelan shows were cut short. The demise of the former president, Romulo Betancourt, in hospital in the USA. Considered the father of modern democracy in Venezuela, the authorities decreed that no music, dancing or entertainment was to take place, and the entire country virtually shut down to allow a respectful period of mourning which could last up to a week, possible more, we were told. While discussions were in place as to whether Queen could finish the series of shows, all we could do was sit around in limbo as the prospect of getting out on schedule diminished.

The powers in Caracas were making no firm decisions as to when Queen could play again, so an escape route was set and we took off for Dallas, Texas, via Miami.

BANDIT COUNTRY

The amount of time in Dallas was undetermined as the final Mexican tour arrangements were still somewhat nebulous – TBA, as we were becoming accustomed to. More problems arose getting into Mexico – a paradox as the usual problem was stopping people from Mexico getting into the USA. We were informed that we were now officially 'assisting Mexican technicians' and the entire crew was transferred to Laredo on the Texas/Mexico border, where we filled in the longest and most complex visa applications ever. The questions, apart from the obvious, asked for your religion, mother's maiden name, whether you can read and write, what other languages you speak, the shape of your face and nose and your general build. We were then subjected to fingerprinting and mug shots – full face and profile.

Even after all this bureaucracy, we were told we would not all be allowed to cross the border as they only issued three of this type of group visa per day. Gerry Stickells was becoming more and more stressed, as we all checked into a Laredo hotel. This dead time was occupied by drinking or reading the Ken Follett novels that had become popular among the crew. These spy stories were fiction but the situation we were in was not.

The next day, we boarded 'El Tigre' the bus to take us into Pancho Villa territory, where at the border the useless promoter had again not arranged things. Time was tight. Time for bribery. The Mexican customs and immigration office was like a stereotypical scene from a Spaghetti Western movie with its dirty, greasy floor, peeling walls and ceiling fans that whirred uncomfortably. People with large battered straw hats holding chickens and grubby children sat forlornly, while behind a counter lines of officials with stained, ill-fitting beige uniforms and twisted peaked caps passed paper around. The temperature was hot, humid and very uncomfortable.

I passed my visa form and passport, with a $100 bill slipped inside the first page to a fat customs official; a filthy handkerchief nestled under one of his many chins, which he pulled out from time to time to dab his puffy red face before replacing it into the void of his fleshy neck rolls. A grunt, a stamp in the passport and a furtive palming of the money and I was now allowed to enter Mexico. So I did.

To relieve the boredom of waiting, Jim and I casually wandered unchallenged out of the gate of the secure area into Mexico. Having quenched ourselves with a drink and an ice cream we walked back – again unchallenged – into the 'secure' customs area. With all passports stamped and the whole crew onboard, we set off down the dusty road to Monterey where half an hour into the journey was another checkpoint, and money once again changed hands. The planned multiple shows in Monterey were reduced to a single one because, despite huge demand, the supermarkets, who were selling the desired tickets, had not printed enough in time!

The show in the Estadio Universitario soccer stadium went off well except for the unexpected arrival of a support act, which surprised us, as there was no support act for any Queen South American show. However, here, waiting at the bottom of the stairs to the stage in full national costume with trumpets and drums, was a Mexican Mariachi band. They were denied access, but protested that they had paid a lot of money to play at the show. But to whom?

There were many other incidents of people paying other 'people' for exclusive interviews, photo and film rights. Somebody was taking the piss, and the pesos. The promoters were elusive and the overall promoter who resided in the USA would greet any challenge to him over the many problems incurred with wide-eyed incredulity and claims that you had insulted his mother, before theatrically storming off to sulk.

After the Monterey show, the satisfied crowd swarmed quickly off the field and over the moat that separated the pitch and the fans at football matches. The ramp that had been constructed collapsed and there was a nasty accident as people fell into the dry concrete canal. Fortunately, the worst injury suffered was a broken leg, but US lawyers are not the only predators to swoop on an injury compensation case. The authorities locked the stadium gates and refused to let Queen or any crew depart.

Eventually, after promises had been made, agreements signed and doubtless money had again changed hands, the band were given leave to return to the hotel, but none of the gear or trucks were allowed to depart and the armed guards positioned at the gates ensured it. This stalling tactic was no doubt to get further money to exchange hands and 'sorry, no pesos' – only good old US greenback dollar bills, preferably in large denominations. By now we had become cynical and mistrusting of the people we were dealing with and also the validity of this exercise. When we eventually left for Mexico City, a serious siege mentality had been established: us against the rest, in this land of Latin lunacy.

On arriving in Mexico City, there was no transport to take the crew on a two-hour journey from the airport to our 'resort' hotel in Pueblo. Our hotel, The Hotel Los Sauces, became the Hotel Lost Causes. It had been built for the influx during the 1968 Olympic Games that were held in Mexico and hardly used since. The swimming-pool water was ink black with a translucent scum atop. Each day the staff added barrels of chemicals until it eventually cleared, and was declared by them to be 'perfect for bathing'. The crew spent a 'tequila evening' prior to this and our mounting frustrations were expelled by light scrapping and the throwing of bodies into this dip. The plumbing arrangements in the bathroom had the diversionary planning of when the toilet was flushed it bubbled back up through the floor of the shower before making its way to the coast.

We still had 'tummy trouble' from the water or from eating the 'chihuahua' burgers containing unidentified small bones in the hotel restaurant.

A young American lighting guy had met a very attractive Mexican girl: 'I woood liike to-go tooo Amerrr-eeeca.'

(I bet you would, love – along with most of your country.)

He took her. Green card heaven. He was young, he was romantic, his brains were below his belt.

ZAPATERIA

Theft was always a constant worry in Latin America, so we had 24-hour security for the stage and dressing-room areas. Despite this, overnight the guitar trunks were locked and chained to a lighting pod which was hoisted in the air, the chain motor then disconnected and the hand control unit taken back to the hotel in our hired vehicle – which was unique. The VW minibus had only three gears and no reverse, and was also fitted with a disabling device, this being a 1/4-inch jack plug which I was used to plugging into guitars. However, this plug had to be inserted behind the steering column in order to start the motor and unplugged to turn it off. If the key was turned to start the engine and you had forgotten to fit the plug, you received a nasty electric shock!

The Pueblo shows were truly shocking – a touring experience never to be repeated. On the first day, enormous pressure built up from the huge crowd that had been queuing for hours and eventually broke down the stadium gates. Along with genuine ticket holders, many thousands of others charged into a space where the capacity was dangerously exceeded. There was clearly a lot of tequila consumed as the punters were in very high spirits. When the show started, all Queen's musical and theatrical efforts were received well, as the audience was awash with cassette players held aloft. Starved of live rock music, it appeared everybody was intent on recording the show.

Then for no apparent reason things turned ugly as objects started to be thrown on stage, not gifts but shoes, a gesture of appreciation? Never a pair, only single shoes. At the end of the show, the owners were making a huge fuss at the front of the stage, and asking for their shoes back! However, when a few bottles rained on stage, it became a concern and, once the hundreds of cassette players had drained their batteries, these were taken out and also aimed at the stage. Fred had started shouting to the band as he sang to 'keep moving' as he dodged the missiles.

At some point in the show, while crouched in my usual position by the piano, I heard a dull thud on the stage carpet to my immediate right and felt something hit my arm. This turned out to be an old metal bolt that was about six inches long and looked like it had been pulled from a railway sleeper – nice! The band escaped unscathed but, in the dressing room afterwards, all hell broke loose. They were enraged, refusing to play any more shows and were off home. Gerry, as always in his role as 'Senor Vaselino', had to grease the wheels of diplomacy, so pointed out that we had a show the next day and then time off before more shows here in Pueblo. If Queen did not play the following night, then it could be very difficult to leave the country and the equipment most definitely would not, plus the possibility of the audience rioting.

Queen agreed to do one more show but demanded reassurances on their safety. Measures were put in place that the audience would be allowed in much earlier and at a slow pace, every single person entering would be searched for potential missiles and all cassette players would have the batteries confiscated as well as any alcohol. This seemed a reasonable compromise, so, on the final chord of the show, the crew would start breaking down and get out and away ASAP. This was despite everybody being weak from various digestive disorders and no edible food being supplied for us at the stadium anyway. It would all be done on adrenaline as everybody was 'desperado' to leave. The battery police did their job in relieving the punters' cassette players of power and projectiles but, upon entering the stadium, other police were seen selling the same batteries back at high prices!

After going through the protracted motions of a second show, the gear finally made it out, accompanied by our armed guards in the trucks, and I took a flight to Los Angeles with John Deacon. He wanted a break there and I had to sit tight, before sorting out the gear to be split between LA and the required studio pieces to be sent to Munich. While sitting around a Beverly Hills rooftop pool with George Harrison, John recounted the horror stories of our Mexican trip. George responded thoughtfully with the Beatles' experiences in the Philippines where they literally feared for their lives as they were physically assaulted trying to leave the country.

When I got word that the gear had crossed safely back into the USA, I flew to Dallas to arrange shipping, and then on to Frankfurt. I drove to Munich, cleared the gear, got it delivered to Musicland and waited for the band, who arrived a few days later. When Queen returned to Munich to carry on recording *Hot Space*, the mood was mixed. It was a great relief to get out of Mexico and fortunately all the gear was safe and sound, but this experience had cost a phenomenal amount of money – a seven-figure sum. Why did it go wrong? And who was to blame?

The excuses were slippery and culprits elusive. Queen had not conquered the entire continent as planned and poignant reminders were dotted around the studio walls in the form of pictures of items equal to the amount of money lost: jet aeroplanes, large country mansions, ocean-going yachts, top football players, etc., all featured, along with handwritten notes about the loss. Queen could easily afford it, but understandably didn't like it.

RIO'S GRAND

Our third trip to South America was for the Rock In Rio festival. Since Queen had paved the way in Latin America, it had now opened up for other acts and was no longer the risk bands and management once feared. The festival in January 1985 was spread over a week buffered by two weekends, when Queen would headline. They were still the biggest-drawing act in Brazil.

We left a grey England that had just caught a fierce onslaught of winter weather and heavy snow for the promise of sunshine in Rio. It wasn't a bad job at times…

Our Varig night flight arrived next morning in a bright and warm Rio de Janeiro, and we exited the airport surrounded by bustling photographers, journalists and news crews. Queen themselves had not yet arrived in Rio, so I had no idea what these people wanted, until I saw myself on the cover of the national *Jornal Do Brasil* newspaper the next day. They thought I was John Deacon. John Deacon, major rock star arriving for a mammoth concert was seen pushing his own baggage trolley, then loading it into a VW van? There was a photo of me on the cover and another inside in a 'Rock In Rio' section that said the bassist looked very calm as he collected his baggage and passed through the multitude...

The Brazilians' organisation of rock shows had improved dramatically since we had first visited, and the venue was a permanent outdoor site to the south of the city.

The stage area was vast, and needed to be in order to accommodate the huge amount of equipment from the many major rock bands playing the festival. All manner of people with backstage passes were wandering around and it was difficult securing Queen's area when they were playing. People in the wings shuffled closer to the action – and had to be pushed back. I got tired of this intrusion into my stage-right space and challenged a middle-aged man.

'Sorry mate – Queen crew only – get back.'

I waved my hands to communicate and was met with a cold stare.

'Listen – move – do you understand English?'

The middle-aged man did understand – he was Ronnie Biggs – 'Great Train Robber' exiled in Brazil!

The Queen show, as expected, was greeted with wild enthusiasm by the warm and expressive Brazilians. I was all set for some relaxation before the next show when Gerry asked me if I would help out with a problem.

'Mmmmmmm, what kind of problem?'

It transpired that the guitar roadie for George Benson had left, been sacked, shot or something, and would I look after things guitar oriented on stage for the two shows George was performing? Money was mentioned: US dollars in reasonably large denominations. OK then. It was not too demanding as there was little gear and it was quite refreshing after the deafening show I was used to. George's shows ran very smoothly and there was none of the tension and angst I felt during a Queen performance, only a broken guitar string to deal with. I did turn down the kind invitation to go to the backstage meeting George held after the show, as the 'meeting' was a Jehovah's Witness gathering! Each to his own, but why oh why do these people always knock on your door *very* early on a Sunday morning? When I'm having a lie-in or suffering a hangover?

Following the second Queen show, I was asked another favour. Would I stay behind for a few days and wait for the tapes and video of the two Queen shows that had been recorded, and personally courier them back to London? Yes.

This seemed a reasonable favour; sunny Rio and a move to the Sheraton Hotel, with its private beach, a couple of days extra per diem and cheap charlie, versus cold miserable grey London. The only snag being I would have to spend the milestone of my 30th birthday in Rio. Well, it could always be used to drop into the conversation at dinner parties in the future. Later, back at the hotel bar after my birthday dinner at a beach restaurant, I tried picking up some Argentine girls but drew a blank. I couldn't understand it, had I lost my touch as I hit 30? Was it too soon after the Falklands?

I compensated by having a couple of the powerful local caipirinha cocktails, with my mate Robert 'Plug' Usher, roadie to Angus Young, the vertically challenged guitarist of AC/DC.

Brazil – where the nuts come from.

CHAPTER FOURTEEN

SUN CITY

(BLIK END WHAAT)

After groundbreaking adventures in South America, what record-buying territory was next in line for the marauding, all-conquering Queen touring machine? Russia was occasionally mooted in huddled conversations, but these were the early 1980s and still Iron Curtain days. The Iron Lady herself was at her peak in the UK as apartheid kept its grip in South Africa and Nelson Mandela still languished behind iron bars in Robben Island prison.

'Guaranteed sell out! Cast iron certainty!'

We went to South Africa.

The year was 1984: Big Brother was watching. And he's a committee member of the Musicians Union.

Mineral-rich South Africa regularly presented Queen a huge cache of award discs in precious metals indigenous to the country; so, after some practical, political and brief moral discussion, a slot was booked to do eleven shows in the 'mixed audience' Sun City Super Bowl Arena. All sold out immediately and could have been doubled, which pleased the band very much. Being big and popular always pleased Queen. Didn't please everybody though.

THAT'S NOT IN THE BROCHURE

After a successful European tour culminating in heavy partying in Vienna, I find myself with the other heads of department in the dim, dank, stark cargo area of Frankfurt airport. I've hardly slept for two days, I'm sweaty and dirty and I ache. My jeans badly need a laundrette.

And so do I, a wash and spin cycle at 60 degrees. Then drip dry. I certainly feel like I've been hung out to dry.

The glamour of rock 'n' roll is given a jolt of contrasting reality when you spend countless hours in cold and miserable airport hangars, surrounded by ton after ton of heavy equipment and mountains of other goods bound for all corners of the earth. International? Yes. Exotic and exciting? No. There is nothing to eat or drink, except disgusting tea or coffee from a vending machine 15 minutes' walk away. Smoking is banned, and any attempt to doze while you wait for the wheels of bureaucracy to turn has to be grabbed on top of the dirty, hard and uneven flight cases; but the combined stale smell, fumes and drone of the airport thwarted any attempt at rest.

When the go-ahead from customs was given, a forced surge of adrenaline gave to fast frenetic activity to load the gear on to palettes as fast as possible, check everything is secure – and get the hell out of there. During these moments in my music business career I often considered other forms of employment. These laborious and depressingly horrible times were not in the rock 'n' roll lifestyle brochure I'd seen.

Did Fred have any idea what I went through during these times? No. As a perfectionist, he simply expected professionalism from everybody involved, and that the known comfort of a 60x40-feet stage universe would appear wherever Queen did. Whether by magic or blood, sweat and tears.

Queen were very successful – and their confidence and belief permeated down through the crew. It bred a strong ethos as we toured and overcame whatever problems we encountered together. Being close to a band that are riding high, with number one singles and albums is a potent panacea.

Loading complete, we managed a quick bite of airport fodder, a fond farewell stein of German beer, then flew out on the next Lufthansa plane to Johannesburg.

I awoke from that altered state of sleeping on aeroplanes where you discover your neck has shrunk, your mouth is afraid to open and your hair aches to gaze out of the window I was hunched against. I saw we were on the ground – this must be Nairobi? Refuelling? My first view of Africa is bare and bland – no lions, rhinos or giraffes, and nothing like the enticing upmarket holiday brochure.

After landing in Johannesburg later that morning, we walked down the aircraft steps on to the burning black tarmac of Jan Smuts airport to be greeted by searing temperature and, through the heat haze in the distance, armoured cars and a heavy military presence. Oh dear! Had they heard about Queen, our parties and general hedonistic behaviour? I've heard they're a bit hard-line down here – are we in for a spot of bother?

As we approached the terminal building of Jan Smuts, I was tired, a bit lagged and thought that Jan Smuts must be the name of some local rude girl. In the arrivals hall I saw signs printed with the word 'Slag' and got very confused – what was going on? Afrikaans was not a language I was familiar with, but where did these girls hang out? More importantly, did they want passes to the show?

After being processed by the delightful South African immigration people, we were met by a promoter's aide and taken to an airport hotel to wait for our call back to customs to clear our gear from the charter plane.

As usual, the call didn't come until the middle of the night, when we were asleep in bed. That ain't in the brochure either.

Having satisfied the customs officer in his smart crisp white shorts and shirt, emblazoned with gold insignia of rank, that everything was in order – and by the way, did he have any friends or family who would like to see the show? We commenced loading the gear into 40-foot sea containers mounted on flat-bed trucks.

I was assigned a team of loaders by a stocky guy from the transport company who had left the East Midlands of England for the 'good life' in South Africa – complete with swimming pool, barbecue, personal handgun and electrified razor wire security fence. He clearly revelled in his new wealth and power and told me how the blacks who made up my loading team were 'as fit as a fiddle, with not an ounce of fat on them'.

I wasn't quite sure what to make of this, but when the

bigot pointed towards me as he shouted at the loaders: 'You do whatever the boss tells you,' I was truly stunned. Tentatively rallying these guys, we started to get the flight cases into the container by forklift. The loading team were very wary of me, but, when they saw me clamber inside the container with my shirt off and getting sweaty and grubby, they looked totally bemused. Why would the white man do the physical, menial, dirty work?

I called out from the back of the container to the guys below, telling them which cases I wanted and in what order. I then went inside to start stacking and rolling them into position.

We got to the row of Brian's Vox AC30 amplifiers, ready for the second stack to be put on top. I told the guy who was with me what we were going to do, so he took one side of the case, me the other and I nodded to him to 'go'. As I lifted my side up and over, he didn't lift his side correctly and the heavy case came crashing down on to the wooden floor as I jumped nimbly out of the way. This was not unusual and I was used to it. When you are loading a truck every night with different loaders who speak different languages, the adrenaline is flowing and you are under pressure to get it packed ASAP, misunderstandings did occur.

This black guy leapt back, pressing himself against the wall of the container and looking at me wide-eyed, with horror on his face. I assumed he thought that he would be given a mouthful of abuse or even physically punished for his mistake.

It was a very unnerving incident, so I assured him everything was OK, not to worry and just carry on loading.

With a bit of patience, we got it all done, and relaxing briefly at the back of the full container I offered the loaders a round of my duty-free Bensons to smoke, which they took with nervous gratitude.

This very obvious two-tier system was a new and sharply unpleasant experience for me and I felt very uncomfortable being seen as some kind of 'master' among these people, who had the misfortune to have been born into a disgraceful regime.

I was not at all politically motivated or even very interested, as I lived my entire life in the insular unreal world of rock 'n' roll. But there was something very disturbing about my South African experiences, that I never forgot.

When all the containers were loaded we were driven, as dawn broke, over the stunning scenery of the Transvaal to Sun City and a welcome bed.

When you have had little sleep, are exhausted and have just done a long European tour, you are entitled to get a little light-headed and allow your mind to play a few tricks, but was it a mirage or reality as we pulled into Sun City after the three-hour drive north? Sun City entertainment centre is in the independent state of Bophuthatswana in the republic of Southern Africa. There are no borders, just a small wooden sign on the roadside informing you are 'now entering' – just like crossing from county to county.

This Las Vegas in the bush was a bizarre place to stumble on and I expected to see signs billing Tom Jones or Liberace strung across the armed security-guarded entrance. This was the dramatic land of Rorkes Drift where the battle of 1879 took place and inspired the film *Zulu*, which made a star of the young Michael Caine. The true battle took place on 23 January, which happens to be my birthday.

Not a lot of people know that!

Would the conquering British rock band have any bother with the locals some 105 years later? Well, all the bother had started long before – back home.

Not black Zulus but blacklisted. When Queen announced their upcoming Sun City plans to the press, they were roundly condemned. And because of the apartheid system in operation in South Africa, it was deemed to be supporting the regime to go and play in the country at all, even if Sun City was supposedly a 'mixed audience' venue. There was also a perverse counter theory thrown into the ring that playing in Sun City was not *really* playing in South Africa, so what was all the fuss about? Sounds like a lawyer to me?

Queen were never a political band and always strived to give people a good product, be it a recording, video or live show. They were constantly looking to new and challenging territories to play and conquer. An imperialist Queen?

Making money was never the primary issue with these tours and the show was never sacrificed just to make a quick buck. As always with Queen, quality came first. Along with being the biggest.

Because they made no secret of their plans, Queen became a scapegoat for many other well-known British and American acts who had played Sun City while keeping a low profile, gone in through the back door and taken the large pot of money just the same. Paradoxically, this included major black acts.

South Africa for me? I really fancied seeing wild animals:

lions, elephants, rhinos and crocs. Go on safari – just like in the brochure.

VOICE WORKS

The Sun City *Works* shows were all planned carefully around weekends so as to maximise the captive audience travelling from the faraway South African cities, and who were buying the concert tickets, to also stay in the hotel, eat in the restaurants, drink in the bars, gamble in the casinos and buy all the merchandise and souvenirs, etc. As the show was so well rehearsed and fresh from the European tour, it was autopilot for band and crew, with Queen's performance and the overall spectacle getting rave reviews. I personally believe that this *Works* tour had the best stage set, lighting rig and sound of all Queen tours. The crew was one of the best and tightest ever, plus the band had put together a great combination of songs for the set, which they were playing particularly well.

Fred's battle cry before the tour was to: 'Give them the works'. Actually it was 'Give them the FUCKING works'. But you never quite knew what you would get with the Freddie Mercury glossy brochure. It kept you on your toes. And him.

All was running smoothly until a couple of shows in when Fred was struggling badly with his voice from the very first song. He looked in great pain and the hot drinks of honey and lemon I gave him every night would be useless with the severity of the strain. After a few songs, he looked over at me, shook his head, mouthed: 'No, no I can't go on,' and paced stridently towards the stage right exit.

The rest of the band stopped playing and were ushered off as the audience started to become, understandably, a little disgruntled.

Gradually, the house lights came up, and a nervous promoter addressed the humming crowd, explaining that regrettably Freddie was in considerable pain and unable to carry on. A further announcement would be made on radio and in the press, and all tickets should be retained as they would be honoured for any rescheduled shows. This explanation was followed by a few boos, whistles and moans but everybody took it reasonably well and left in an orderly manner.

A medical specialist had been immediately summoned from Johannesburg and was on his way by private jet. Fred had never needed that before and there was great concern.

After being eventually allowed into the dressing room to see the patient, there he was in his robe, bouncing around, drinking and chattering away! Fred was enthusing that Queen must make amends by playing a huge show at the national Ellis Park outdoor stadium in Johannesburg. What? This seemed like the normal Fred, upbeat after a good show and a couple of vodkas. Incorrect prognosis; the doctor had administered some type of powerful cortisone injection which gave immediate, but temporary, relief. The steroid took away the pain and inflammation but the inherent problem was bad. Total rest and special climatic conditions in his suite plus further treatment were needed before Fred could sing again.

Voice problems were not new, but this time the problem was extreme and severely aggravated locally by the dust that blew off the desert and bush. It affects most singers, we were told later. Fred's good friend Elton John as well.

That wasn't in the brochure we got, and after Fred received the information I couldn't print the language he used in any brochure. While recuperating in his suite, which was filled with humidifiers and climatic control devices to aid recovery of his voice, Fred invited me over for a drink. He was spending some of his convalescence listening to music and was raving about Prince and the recently released *Purple Rain* album. He loved the image Prince had created and thought he was as commercial as Michael Jackson, but with the sexy and edgy appeal of Jimi Hendrix.

He likened some of Prince's lyrics to Hendrix, citing the song 'When Doves Cry'. '"Dig if you will the picture" – God, I wish I'd written that line – it's fucking great!'

Watch the voice, Fred...

Due to his strong resolve, Fred recovered well and was able to complete the remaining shows. He rarely took direct advice from any people: a doctor telling him to cut down on his drinking? Little chance. A doctor who advised on the future of his wonderful gift of singing? Yes.

The enforced break was very handy for the rest of Queen to fly by private Lear jet to enjoy the lush Indian Ocean island of Mauritius.

During the final show, we had a brief 'pie fight' on stage, utilising whipped cream, other dairy products and Spike, Queen's hired back-up musician. Spike was a keyboard player who also played rhythm guitar on 'Hammer To Fall', and was described by somebody in the audience as 'Who's that fat roadie who comes on stage and plays guitar?'

An insult to roadies if you ask me.

In the black-out before the encore, one of the band assistants came up to me screaming: 'Get all that cream and shit cleaned off the stage – Fred is going mad, he keeps slipping and is panicking he will do his knee in again.'

Fred's voice was fixed but the Mercurial knee ligaments, damaged during some horseplay in a club in Munich before the tour, were still a subject for concern.

Didn't stop him playing tennis at Sun City though. He was good at that as well. Freddie Mercury was good at pretty much everything he decided to do.

DRINKING WORKS

There were several bars in the Sun City complex, and we drank heavily and for free at the bar in the exclusive Club Prive where the high rollers gambled. All drinks and food in here were gratis and, though we were not gambling, our temporary status of being interesting by association allowed us access. We struck up a good rapport with all the barmen and gave them passes for the shows. But it was access denied on an Access All Areas pass if you were a black barman. Come to think of it, I don't remember seeing many black people in the audience. Were there any at all, I wonder?

We drank heavily each and every night and would stagger back to our rooms; scaling a wire mesh fence to halve the journey. Occasionally, we were accompanied by some female companions from Birmingham working as croupiers and dealers in the casino. The girls were blessed with conical hairdos that took an entire can of spray to keep them vertical and, combined with strong make-up, their work-issue shiny casino gowns and metallic accessories, it gave them the look of characters from a 1970s *Star Trek* episode. This was compounded by thick Brummie accents, an extremely alien tongue in warp factor seven.

Seeing them trying to scale the wire fence in their tight evening dresses was hilarious – and impossible. They simply discarded them and clambered over in their underwear and high heels. The sight of an attractive young woman in an indignant pose as she straddles a mesh fence in a skimpy G-string and bra as the blood-red African sun is breaking over the hill was a moving and poetic moment.

To relieve some of the tedium on days off, we took to having early-evening ten-pin bowling sessions with the exception of wardrobe master Tony Williams. Welsh Tony who liked a drink would turn into Mr Hyde, who conveniently forgot what had happened the night before. It was Mr Hyde, not Tony Williams, who was attempting to bowl at an alley in a hotel in Holland some weeks before, and, when his attempt at a strike went directly into the gutter at the side of the lane, Tony, not happy with his effort, punched the neighbouring wall – breaking his hand. After surgery and pinning, he was forced to drink and work with his other hand, so the crew had to thread needles for Shirley, as Fred called Tony, when doing his wardrobe maintenance.

THE DEADLY BUSH

Spending an overnight safari in the game park that surrounded Sun City was great fun, Collie and me setting up the British camp among the fixed site by borrowing Fred's stage Union Jack flag from the wardrobe case to flutter above our tent.

I woke in the middle of the night to hear all the squeaks, coos, squawks and scary noises you heard in Tarzan movies. But Collie *certainly* didn't look like Jane – his leopard skin underpants excepted, and even by the romantic light from the oil lamp.

Now there are many dangerous things lurking out in the bush but the most lethal of all, and a proven killer according to our guide, was a stationary threat: rhino shit!

Apparently, the rhinos like to relieve themselves on the tracks running through the bush and this considerable deposit turns rock hard very quickly under the baking-hot African sun. Safari jeeps come hurtling down these tracks, hit the deadly camouflaged piles, causing vehicles to turn over. That ain't in the insurance policy, even in the disclaimer small print: 'Loss of life, limb or eye due to rhino shit'.

Our guide took us into pens of cats – small lions, followed by big cheetah that had all been given research code numbers except for one who was called Nigel! I kept at a good distance, as they were a bit frisky those rascals, I can tell you!

There were other forms of healthy, sporting entertainment on offer: several swimming pools, tennis courts and a golf course. The Americans in the crew were always keen and some would take their clubs around on tour, stashed in the equipment cases. The golf course itself had a major handicap: snakes! There were many types slithering around the rough and bunkers and in particular spitting cobras.

These tricky reptiles were infamous around Sun City and had claimed several victims. So bearing the warnings in mind, Joe Trovato, Queen's American lighting designer, set off with some of his fellow countrymen to play a round. Unfortunately, Joe had been up most of the previous evening getting hammered in the bar and was feeling very, very delicate indeed.

The Queen Crew Open arrived at the first tee, where by now Joe was greener than the surrounding fairway. Taking a club from his black caddy, he stepped up to tee off. Swinging the club high he brought it forward with great effort and this physiological reaction caused his imbalanced, depleted body to immediately throw up and shit itself simultaneously. Joe had now turned from sickly green, to as white as a sheet and bright red with embarrassment – the correct national colours for somebody of Italian descent. He was wrapped in a towel and escorted back to his room.

None of Queen played golf, neither did us Brits in the crew, so Collie and I escaped from Sun City to have a look around the local area. John Deacon let us borrow the car allocated for him to be driven the few yards from his villa to the stage door of the Super Bowl arena. We set off southward in this top-of-the-range BMW for Rustenberg, the nearest town on the road to Jo'burg.

Though we were probably in no real danger in Rustenberg, the vibe was not right and we cut short our excursion, driving back to the white sanctity of Fort Sun City. But I was no longer white – I was turning lobster red from under-estimating the African sun. And topped off by streaks of blond, blue and red hair colour (fashionable at the time) I began to resemble a parrot. I knew every string gauge of every guitar and the serial numbers of equipment by heart, so

my job was something I could do virtually parrot fashion –
for a handful of seeds tossed in my feed bowl.

MONEY AND DIAMOND WORKS

Thankfully, none of us were serious gamblers as there were
many ways to lose your handful of seeds in the Sun City
casino or on the avenues of slot machines that promised
'More Rand In Your Hand'. The South African unit of
currency was restricted at the time and not at all easily
exchanged. Deals for Queen shows were almost exclusively
done in US dollars, but the promoters would have to supply
local currency for petty cash expenses. So what to do with all
the spare and almost worthless per diem you had at the end
of our Sun City trip?

Spend it all. But on what? Even the airport duty free
wanted the Yankee dollar, pound sterling or deutschmark.
Gold Krugerrands or diamonds bought from the major
South African jewellers, who had a large presence in Sun
City, were popular choices of trinkets to take home and
keep the girlfriend happy – or put away for a rainy day. The
best deal for diamonds, though, was from the independent
'Mr X' (I just can't remember his name and I'm sure he's
glad about that).

Mr X was a contact of the house crew at Sun City, coming
up to shows from Johannesburg and dealing direct with
visiting bands and crews wanting to buy loose diamonds.
Prior to a show, Mr X arrived and was ushered backstage
into the tuning room. The tuning room was often used for
doing deals with local suppliers, though the rocks Mr X had
were size-for-size far more valuable.

The individual who shuffled in looked most unlike a diamond dealer in his 'train spotter's' anorak, shapeless trousers and slip-on shoes. A dishevelled middle-aged man with a bad case of greasy comb-over, who looked like he would offer sweets to youngsters outside the school gates. Over his shoulder was a cheap imitation-leather airline bag which he unzipped, and pulled out reams of folded tissue paper stuffed with diamonds of all levels of the four Cs: carat, colour, clarity and cut.

He seemed nervous, but we assured him he was perfectly safe as he was on hallowed territory in the tuning room. The deals were done and much more favourably than at the other jewellers, who Mr X did not speak too kindly of. Nor did certain wealthy people when having their purchases valued for insurance back in England...

The tuning room was a special place and only a few select people were invited in. Signs posted outside warned off any posers, liggers, agents, lawyers and such like. You might be important enough to fleetingly get into Queen's dressing room but never into the tuning room, unless invited by one of Queen's personal crew. It was our den and secret hideaway.

'Can you come and check the power in the tuning room?' loosely translated to: 'let's go and have a toot'. Also known as attitude application check.

The tuning room trunk was a small flight case that housed the guitar strobe tuners, compact Fender Champ amp, voltage transformers and an inflatable airbed. The case was fitted with secure allen key locks and was also used to store any valuables during the day or overnight. As it was one of the first things to go into the truck at load out, the trunk was used to transfer currency on occasions when carrying large amounts of cash around or through customs was risky, not strictly allowed or impractical. The airbed was pumped up and laid out for the sole use of John Deacon, who believed strongly in the recuperative powers of rest and sleep at the right time. It was also a calm haven for him, away from the dramas of the dressing room. As I was John's roadie, he let me use the airbed too; providing I gave him details afterwards...

I also used the tuning room to chill out, service and clean John's and Fred's guitars and change their strings. A new set of strings would be stretched in every three or four shows, about the same interval that most of the crew changed their socks. The tuning room was a place I could hide away and hone my own basic guitar skills. A solid electric guitar is a very seductive toy, a powerful icon to hold in your hands. It can make a bigger noise than you can – instantly! The volume control on an electric guitar is the extension of your pent-up expression. Shame I can't really play.

The tuning room was a good place to entertain or smuggle girls into, while we found passes for them. Fortunately, I didn't try to serenade them with my guitar playing or they may have left, backstage pass or not. Queen tour passes and their use of the female form were always a talking point from the *Jazz* tour onwards; with a fat-bottomed naked girl on a bicycle, to the final *Magic* tour with another girl's bottom on a stool, with animated characters of the band dancing underneath, which portrayed the deep message of filling stadiums by 'putting bums on seats'.

Spare laminated passes, and those issued to unknown personnel prior to the tour, were put in the name of John Doe or Jane Doe, the names given by police departments in the US for unidentified dead bodies. *The Works* tour that took in Sun City spawned aluminium passes and luggage tags, the metal in keeping with the industrial feel of the stage set. The passes featured an illustrated rotating spanking machine administering whacks to a young female construction worker, and the inscription on the side instructed: 'use this edge'. I wonder what for? Tour passes had evolved from just having long hair and saying: 'It's OK, mate – I'm with the band' into a high-security operation of varying levels of authorisation.

However, soon I wouldn't need a pass to access my working life any more. Decisions had been made. I'd had a look at another glossy career brochure.

Always read the small print.

CHAPTER FIFTEEN

I THOUGHT IT WAS ALL OVER

(ALMOST)

There are four seasons, four corners of the earth, four horsemen of the apocalypse and four musicians in Queen. I'd been there, seen 'em all and done it – and got several T-shirts.

Musicians will tell you there are four beats in a bar – and I had done plenty of beats in many bars. Maybe too many.

It was time to go, time to move on.

Prior to *The Works* European tour, which had merged into the Sun City trip, I decided I'd had enough of living the rock 'n' roll lifestyle – I wanted a new job.

My decision to leave Queen was formulated over a period of time and there was no particular incident or reason that prompted me to give up a life of rock 'n' roll. Despite having a top job with one of the world's biggest bands, I wanted something else to stimulate and satisfy myself, and that was not to work for another band, irrespective of the generous offers I received.

This was Maggie Thatcher's 1980s when there was supposedly 'loads of money' around, but the financial rewards of working for Queen were certainly no reason to stay on, as they had a reputation within the industry for not paying their people the highest rates. Around the time of *The Works* album in 1984, I knew that I was becoming mentally and physically fried as I was working harder than ever. Loyalty can sometimes become a frailty, and, as there was no real opportunity or desire to further myself within the Queen organisation, I decided the time was right to leave and I would go out while at the top of my profession.

I was also becoming disillusioned with the changing music industry.

For a long time I knew I wanted to become a photographer, it's what I really loved doing, what excited and inspired me. However, I would still be jumping into unknown territory and would have to rely on my limited knowledge of the photography world, a bit of talent, a lot of belief and the experience, professionalism and resilience I had accumulated in the music business.

Being head of the crew for Queen gave me confidence in my abilities and the belief that I could go on to do other things, and succeed. Although it was just a job to me, later on I realised what an important position I held and how good I was at my job. But I also knew my limitations.

My decision to leave Queen was filtered through during tour rehearsals in Munich. I had previously discussed it with the few people I trusted and respected; the others found out by default; most, at a dinner thrown by Fred at his boyfriend Winnie's traditional Bavarian restaurant. Not a great place for vegetarians…

I really wanted to tell Fred personally but surprisingly it was hard. Sometimes, despite our close relationship, Fred was very difficult to approach or to get him alone at the right moment. The situation to do it never quite arose. He was never on his own, in the right mood or in the right place.

'Fred, can I have a word?'

'Later, dear, later.'

I think he was trying to avoid the issue, as, despite being a strong-willed, bold man who would take on any challenge, Fred occasionally dismissed certain things and pushed them aside, hoping they would go away.

'Later, dear, later' never materialised, but it became quite clear he knew I was leaving, and that I knew he knew – but nothing was said. He had asked Gerry Stickells why I wanted to leave and Gerry gave him the simple answer: 'that I now wanted to be a photographer not a roadie'.

Then unexpectedly during a lull in rehearsals Fred said to me quite formally in a clipped voice, 'So, you're leaving then?'

'Yes – I am,' I nodded with sincerity.

'Right.' He nodded and smiled back at me.

No more was said.

He knew I would be as dedicated as I ever was until I left – in fact, during that *Works* tour I took on even more responsibilities and worked harder than on any other Queen tour.

If I had left Queen to work for another band, Fred would

never have forgiven me, but because I was going into the 'arts' I was sure he could understand. And he did.

Roger was quite shocked at my decision to leave, but after we had a chat he also understood my reasons. Before I got the chance to tell Brian, somebody else had and he rushed up to me in the Sugar Shack, quite upset and asking me to stay, promising to 'put things right'. It was too late, I'd made my mind up, and money was no longer an issue. John already knew, as we had talked about it together several times.

He was also in a period of change. In 1984, John grew his hair again into a wild bush. He began smoking cigarettes at the age of 33 and went missing from recording, only telling me where he was going. He confided in me and seemed fed up. John understood why I wanted to leave and I felt he somehow wanted it to be him.

I don't think he was ever quite the same again after that period.

I want to break free.

CHARITY BEGINS...

The terms of my leaving the PAYE payroll of Queen Productions at the start of 1985 were that I agreed to do Rock In Rio, and the final leg of the *Works* tour in New Zealand, Australia and Japan in April and May on a freelance basis, as I was now starting to set up my new photography career. After the end of that Japanese tour in Osaka, that was it – I would never crawl under a piano or inside a dirty truck again! Another erroneous assumption in my career.

No sooner had I got back to my shared rented studio, and

was working hard to get my new career moving, than I got a call that the band were to take part in something called Live Aid, being organised by Bob Geldof and Midge Ure.

Queen had not immediately agreed, but once they decided to take part it was business as usual. As this one-off gig in London would not take a lot of time from the focus of my new career, I agreed to help out. Queen rehearsals were at the Shaw Theatre in London's Euston Road and in true Queen professional manner the key touring personnel were brought in from the USA.

A 'blip' involving Fred's Steinway piano reminded me he could still be a difficult sod when he chose to. I may have officially left Queen, but he still wanted to keep me on my toes. For the next few days Queen worked out the 20-minute set that has become solidly set in rock history. I purchased large white plastic clocks that were placed around the stage so the band could monitor themselves as the countdown started. With so much material for Queen to choose from, I thought that it would be a battle within the band as to which songs would be performed, but it actually fell into place quite quickly, and, though other combinations were tried, the final set was reached unanimously – and without too many tantrums. It included three of Fred's songs, two of Brian's and one of Roger's. John? The guy who wrote their biggest-selling single and several others? John rarely made a fuss – he went with the flow.

I feel that John was underrated as a musician; he was not only a great bass player, but a fantastic rhythm guitar player too – the best in the band. As his song-writing matured, Fred could see John's potential and drew out his talent;

encouraging him to write more. Maybe not the obvious partnership within Queen, but there was a great respect between John and Fred for each other's abilities that is often overlooked.

Live Aid was not a normal Queen show; no huge lighting rig, smoke, pyrotechnics or intro tape for them to open with and wow the audience. The obvious choice for a rock band would be to start with an up-tempo, stamp your feet tune. No.

Queen were introduced by comedians Mel Smith and Griff Rhys Jones at Live Aid, seconds after we had finished checking the gear. As the welcoming applause for the band faded, Fred sat at his piano and played the famous intro to 'Bohemian Rhapsody'.

It was brilliant. The whole audience knew the song, and, after the initial roar of recognition, sang along to the section chosen from Queen's most well-known creation. The crowd who had been there for over seven hours were at the point of needing a lift. Queen gave it to them and were magnificent. They were also the loudest! Sound engineer Trip Khalaf had earlier set the limiters on the Clair Brothers PA system – which he unleashed for Queen's performance. If you can't blind 'em – deafen 'em! Fred then showed the world why he was simply the greatest showman of the time and had the entire audience in his hand. The mood, energy and spirit that day was truly wonderful and it was the first and by far the best of the big charity shows. It captured everything at the right time, and the egos of the many stars present did not clash. Fred even offered the unprecedented act of allowing his piano to be used by another artist – Phil Collins. The directive of only 20-minute sets for every artist had been laid down strongly, as the running schedule to coincide with TV was precise. The revolving circular stage was divided into three equal sections of 'pie', which allowed one band to set up as another broke down their equipment, while the third was performing.

This worked very efficiently, and as our gear was whisked away and sectioned for loading I watched The Who play. In front of centre stage was a traffic-light system, of green, amber and red lamps for the performers to monitor. The first light illuminated, to tell the band that they had five minutes left, the second light signalled two minutes remained, so finish your song ASAP, and the red was 'your time is up get off or we will pull the plug on you'.

As I watched the band who made instrument damage and abuse an art form, I saw the red light was flashing constantly. The stage managers and promoters' people were getting twitchy – it would be a brave man who cut the power on The Who.

Signals had been made to the singer, Mr Roger Daltrey, who responded in his own unique style, by kicking all the lights and smashing them before finishing the song.

I found myself smiling and caught sight of Bob Geldof behind me, doing Pete Townshend-style leaps with 'windmill' arm movements as he played air guitar.

The spirit of rock 'n' roll was truly there that day, and humanity too. It was an unbelievable sight and atmosphere – I feel privileged to have been there, and it remains one of the most memorable days of my life. I often get comments that I was 'spotted' on Queen's part of Live Aid – and more less-flattering comments about my cut-off denim shorts! 'It was a very hot day,' I reply in my defence. And they were 'fashionable' at the time...

Queen, too, were hot and overwhelmed with the day, giving them renewed belief and desire. And suddenly they became fashionable again too. I believe there was a real possibility that the band could have broken up around that time, they had become tired and somewhat jaded; their fall in popularity in America had affected them a lot and they needed something to rekindle that drive and belief in their talent. They didn't need to worry – they were the best band on the day, stole the show and surprised a lot of non-Queen fans too. The band appreciated the contribution by all their crew, who were under a lot of pressure, and as always did their job professionally. We were given framed awards with a photo of the band on stage at Wembley and an etched metal plate underneath:

LIVE AID
July 13th, 1985
Presented to
PETER HINCE
Thank you from
Brian, Freddie, John and Roger
QUEEN

After my minor supporting contribution to rock history, I kept in touch with most of the Queen organisation and did some photographic commissions for the band. Then in the following early spring I was asked by Billy Squier's management if I would help out Billy, who was going to be recording in London.

Mmmm – I dunno? That 'rock stuff' again?

However, as it was not full-time and there was some flexibility that let me carry on trying to establish myself as a photographer, I agreed. My business set-up costs had been high and income was still very low. The regular fee would be welcome and the fact that I got on well with Billy was also very important in my decision.

At around the same time I was asked if I would do the upcoming Queen *Magic* tour and, after some thought and on the advice of friends, I decided against it. This was received with surprise as it had been simply taken for granted by the Queen organisation that I would accept. I explained that I had spent a lot of time building things up for my new business and, although I was not yet reaping the rewards, a break from this would upset the momentum and I could miss out on any important jobs or new clients that came in.

And, most importantly, I was now a photographer and no longer a roadie.

It was a wrench to decline as I had good friends who would be on the tour and the rock lifestyle had been a part of me for over 12 years, and traces still lingered in my bloodstream – I was not out of de-tox just yet.

I went to Fred's house to see him personally and explain. He immediately said, 'It's the money, isn't it? Don't worry, we'll sort it out.'

When I explained it was not about money, he understood but was still disappointed.

'Well, you must come to rehearsals and brief the new people,' he insisted.

In addition to being a very successful rock star, Billy was a cultured American and appreciated the finer things that London had to offer. Billy knew Fred well, but had not yet visited Garden Lodge, the home Fred had worked long to create.

A couple of evenings, running into mornings, were spent at Garden Lodge as Billy played Fred some of his new songs. Fred, being Fred, told Billy what he thought and what could possibly be done. Billy was delighted to get Fred's input and, though he insisted, 'They're your songs, dear – not mine,' it was arranged for Fred to come to Sarm Studios, where Queen had recorded so much early work, and sing on two tracks that he particularly liked: 'Love Is The Hero' and 'Heart Of Mine', which Fred changed the title of to 'Lady With A Tenor Sax'. Billy was excited, as he held the greatest respect for Fred. I was now seeing Fred and the people around him quite often, and poignantly got the nod that he was far from comfortable that I would not be on the upcoming *Magic* tour. There were also rumours that for personal reasons he was not going to do the tour at all.

After trying to distance myself from my old life, which of course included Fred, I was being drawn close to him again. I was also not convinced that the arrangements made to cover for my departure would work to the satisfaction of Fred and John.

I had a dilemma.

I spoke to Billy about it and he was very supportive. I did

not want to let him down by going off in the middle of his recording project and I still wanted to separate myself from the past somewhat and get on with my new life and career. Billy said that I should do the tour as he knew how close the bond had been between Fred and me.

After the final recording session, we all went to Al Khayam, Billy's favourite Indian restaurant in Westbourne Grove. Fred loved Indian food but only went to places he was known and felt comfortable in. This was not one of them. We had booked a table away from the main busy part of the restaurant, but people still recognised Fred. However, he was totally cool about it as this was Billy's choice. When Billy and Terry, who was Fred's driver and minder, had left the table to go to the toilet (or something) leaving Fred and me alone, I said to him, 'Okay, Fred – I'll do your tour for you.' He was sincere in his thanks and told Terry the news as soon as he returned.

We all returned to Garden Lodge and stayed up the rest of the night, during which he thanked me again several times, saying: 'You can have anything you want, you know?'

I now felt truly appreciated by Fred, and couldn't change my mind again. I somehow knew I had to do this tour for him – and history tells why.

Billy wanted to thank Fred for his contribution on the two songs, so we went shopping in Chelsea, and bought him a gift that would be in keeping with the Mercury style – an original signed Art Deco bronze statue of a fox, set on a marble base. Billy went off on a short vacation, so I showed up at Fred's house to find Fred very excited. He always loved gifts despite it being wrapped in newspaper inside an old cardboard box. He adored the piece and fussed around to find the right spot for the fox to sit.

I had now convinced myself I had done the right thing; the overheads and responsibility of a shared studio would be covered by the tour money, and I should still have enough to keep me going for a while afterwards.

I struck a deal with Gerry Stickells, which took about ten seconds – $100 a week more than the Australia/Japan tour of the previous year. Hardly 'anything I wanted' but that was never the issue or even mentioned.

It was good to see and reunite with old mates at rehearsals, but something was not quite right. The atmosphere was different and the tight family unit and camaraderie was missing. That final tour, *Magic* '86, was a totally different experience to any other Queen tour. Things had quickly changed despite my only being away for about a year. It wasn't specifically the band or crew that I knew, but the business. The tour was the biggest out that summer and no doubt buoyed by the band's phenomenal performance at Live Aid the previous year.

The Queen extravaganza had grown, but the normally well-oiled machine now spluttered as it had seemingly taken on too much, become overloaded and was no longer as streamlined as it had been. The tour is one I am very happy to have done, considering it was the last ever. However, I did not enjoy it in the same way I had other tours.

The size of the shows, which were predominantly outdoors, obviously meant that more people would be involved, but there seemed to be far too many. It had now become a game as to how important you could show yourself to be – a case of collecting titles. Politics and bullshit! A ridiculous circus.

On every previous Queen tour, you knew who the owner of virtually every laminated backstage pass was, now they were tossed around like confetti – and many of them to tossers.

The situation became so absurd that for the second half of the tour, new passes with a large number 2 printed on were issued to avoid breaches of security.

Queen were big, and the timing was right, but the band had been big for many years, and all the extra hype and spin just creates a false environment which alienates and divides.

We had all moved on a little, and, though I was back doing the same job I had done for years and still had the confidence and ability to do it, it was different. I was still loyal and professional, but this was not my 'real' job now.

The era was gone, and so had the special feeling created on so many tours. The show was good, but the lighting rig which Queen were renowned for was poor. Despite having a huge budget, it looked like a giant Christmas tree. It was just big, and didn't really do anything dynamic like the previous rigs.

At Knebworth, the final ever Queen live show, I somehow felt it was going to be the last for all of us. I had no idea as to Fred's health condition but I just saw it as being the last show for me and for them. John was also in a strange mood and for no apparent reason threw his bass guitar hard into his speaker cabinets after the last song of the set. Before the encore I had fixed and retuned it without any problem. John apologised to me, but was seemingly not enjoying things.

The hard business side of rock 'n' roll had really taken over and a new corporate era had begun. I am so glad I chose to get out when I did. It is important to remember that nobody I know, musician or roadie, entered the business just for money.

After that final tour, I got back to my studio and tried to pick up where I had left off some 12 weeks before. Shortly afterwards, I went to the grand event of Fred's 40th birthday party. It was a 'crazy hat' party held in the grounds of his house and I wore the same hat with clapping hands on that he had chased me around the stage for wearing in Japan.

When later that autumn Fred recorded his 'Great Pretender' single, he commissioned me to shoot the cover in my studio and later the video stills. The irreverent humour was still there on set, as Crystal and I re-wrote the opening line Fred sang, to: 'Oh yes I'm the great... big bender!' But despite this irreverent and ribald reminder of the past, I felt I was finally off the road. The old saying of 'I'm with the band' was no longer true – I was on my own.

Nobody can ever take away from me what I experienced or achieved, but we have to live in the present not the past. More photo shoots for Fred and Queen followed and invites to Fred's lavish parties too – including private jets and club-class air tickets and plush hotels. This was all generously paid for by Mr Mercury. I received dinner invites to Garden Lodge and Queen Christmas and other parties still included me on the guest list. It was comforting that I had been remembered and everybody understood why I had left Queen to work in photography.

The world will always remember those immortal words in 1966 at Wembley Stadium: 'Some people are on the pitch –

they think it's all over...' and at Knebworth Park a few weeks after Wembley in 1986 – it most certainly was.

The last time I saw or spoke to Freddie Mercury in person was at the 20-year anniversary party for Queen at the exclusive Groucho Club in London's Soho. He was sitting at a large table upstairs in the private back room and I was sitting at a table in the opposite corner with my girlfriend, Julie, John Deacon and his wife Veronica. I caught Fred's eye and he beckoned me over, rising from the table to greet me as I walked towards him. He gave me a light hug and a peck on the cheek and said, 'Thanks for coming, I appreciate it.'

That was it; that was the last time I saw him. I had no idea.

Looking back, I am grateful to have had such a great working life with Queen, and I would like to thank them. No doubt they would thank me, too. I owe a great deal to the band and to Fred especially – and I miss him considerably.

POSTSCRIPT

What is Queen's, and more poignantly, Freddie's legacy? Quite simply – the music. Original, bold, intricate, some might say pompous and pretentious. And whether you liked it or not, the somewhat pretentious at the time 'Bohemian Rhapsody' is easily recognised by an enormous number of people all over the world.

But not everybody.

This story is absolutely true. A few years ago at a charity event I'd been invited to, somebody mentioned to a small group of people attending that they had just seen me being interviewed on a Queen TV special.

A posh middle-aged woman's interest was immediately pricked, and she approached me with a voice that sounded like a horse neighing after eating cut-glass plums...

'Queen! Yes I remember – "This Town Ain't Big Enough

For The Both Of Us".'

'That was Sparks...'

'Oh? Now I remember – "Rhapsody In Blue"!'

'No, it was "*Bohemian* Rhapsody".'

'Oh? Anyway, I used to have those small things with their music on – you know?'

'CDs?'

'No, no – before those.'

'Cassettes?'

'Not tapes – the little round things.'

'Do you mean vinyl? Singles?'

'Yes, yes those are the ones – 45s I think they called them?'

As I finish writing this revised edition of *Queen Unseen* it is 2015, 40 years since 'Bohemian Rhapsody' was first released, and I'm sure Fred would have found the story about his legendary creation as hilarious in its absurdity as I did.